Methods of Treatment
in Analytical Psychology

Ed. Ian F. Baker

VII. International Congress of the
International Association for Analytical Psychology

METHODS OF TREATMENT IN ANALYTICAL PSYCHOLOGY

Ed. Ian F. Baker

VII. International Congress of the
International Association for Analytical Psychology

Spring Publications
P. O. BOX 222069
DALLAS, TEXAS 75222

VERLAG ADOLF BONZ GMBH, D-FELLBACH

CIP-Kurztitelaufnahme der Deutschen Bibliothek

Methods of Treatment in Analytical Psychology
/ ed. Ian F. Baker. – Fellbach: Bonz, 1980.
  ISBN 3-87089-197-1
NE: Baker, Ian F. (Hrsg.)

INDEX

INTRODUCTION

Our last Congress in London of 1974 had as its title "The Role of Analytical Psychology in a Changing Civilisation". This theme was apparently not all too popular and consequently only relatively few speakers spoke to the subject of the congress.

All the more you will be pleased that the subject of our present congress is apparently so much more practicable and tangible. I am looking forward to the discussion of this subject which is so near our daily work, concern and responsibility. I am particularly glad to have seen from the resumés of the various papers that we shall have a lively discussion on account of their often very differing views.

It is these different views which I find so important and constructive. We must not forget what Jung has said that "every psychology . . . has the character of a subjective confession," and that "our way of looking at things is conditioned by what we are". Erikson has expressed the same problem pointedly when he said that an analyst "can really only learn a method which is comparable with his own identity . . . so it is not just a question of which method is best for the patient but also of which method the therapist feels most at home with and creative in".

There is, however, one problem in these statements which poses a special question for us Jungians. If you believe in a certain method with clearly defined contours it may be relatively easy to define your own position. I suppose that the followers of Freud may find it relatively easy to call themselves Freudians. But what about us who pride ourselves of the very openness of Jung's teaching and implicitly reject the idea of a fixed Jungian method? Our whole emphasis is so much on our identity as individuals, culminating in the idea of individuation, that we find ourselves in a crucial dilemma. How can we combine this accent on individuality with the existence of a Jungian school or movement? Is there a central point, a focus of fundamental interest which has determined our selection of analytical psychology, our adherence to a Jungian school? Would we be here without a feeling of common concern, of a basic principle, which unites us and gives us the possibility to call ourselves "Jungians"? I think we all agree that such common point does exist. So we have to ask ourselves what is this focus, this basic common interest, which binds us together as Jungians?

If I try to give my own answer, undoubtedly individually conditioned, I would put it into a single word: "the numinosum". Jung himself has stated this very succinctly in a letter of 1945 where he says: "The main interest of my work is not concerned with the treatment of neuroses but rather with the approach to the numinous. But the fact is that the approach to the numinous is the real therapy and inasmuch as you attain to the numinous experiences you are released from the curse of pathology." The emphasis on the numinous does, of course, not mean that we do not have to work very hard and conscientiously through complexes, resistances, defences, or what have you before we reach the motive power behind the screen of neurosis. St. Paul's words apply here: "Per visibilia ad invisibilia."

At any rate, the immediate manifestation of the numinous in human life, such as the need for finding the sense and meaning of one's existence, the intuition of transcendence, man's realisation and relationship to art and beauty, the erotization of sexuality, the power of creativity, to mention only a few most obvious themes, will always shine through from behind the smokescreen of pathology. Is life not a single entity and unity of natural, social, and spiritual conditions? Is it not indivisible, and if so could illness not be explained as the disturbance of this unity?

I have always regarded what I call Jung's metapsychology as his most important contribution. I believe that these metapsychological considerations – so often misnamed "occult" – may become much more important than "curing" symptoms which may have to be left more and more to techniques like physiological feedback or even to chemotherapy. In contrast our psychological approach can from its deepest experiences lead to a new understanding of the world and man's role in it.

Here we may find access to quite new modes and levels of consciousness. If I may define my own position as it has developed over 45 years of analytical practice I would say that the enigma of the psyche has more and more occupied my mind and therapeutic work. Time and again I found myself confronted with situations and happenings which I could not explain by or deal with by any technique or method, events which left me with the deep impression that the psyche is a miracle to which the only approach is respect, wonder and awe. I have gone through a long period of profound doubt when I felt that perhaps I was not sufficiently aware of, not adequately analysing transference, countertransference, childhood and the whole lot. It has been only after strenuous and permanent self-searching that I have regained my courage and confidence to accept what I have felt and perceived to be the truth of my experience and let myself be fully involved in it. I have come more and more to realize that a higher consciousness was working behind the scene, being the true motive power of the human soul, waiting to be released, needing ordinary human understanding and acceptance so much more than technique, demanding eros so much more than method, imagination so much more than models. From my deepest experiences in my work I have come to suspect if not to believe, that what we call the paranormal now may be the normal of the future, perhaps a future not too far distant. Many signs point in that direction.

However that may be, we have to be very careful not to be caught up in the net of techniques and methods. They change so much all the time, that we have to ask ourselves if there is not anything permanent in our daily work. I believe that we can give one positive answer; not in hypotheses, models or theories do we find permanence, but we do find it in the attitude of the analyst himself.

Here again we may quote Jung: "One would do well not to speak of 'methods' at all. The thing that really matters is the personal commitment, the serious purpose. the devotion, indeed the self-sacrifice of those who give treatment." And Paracelsus, several centuries before, said: "The highest degree of medication is love. It is love which teaches the art, and outside love no physician is born . . ." Just in parenthesis it makes one doubt if our highly technicalized way of training analysts is really the best, or at least the only way of producing psychotherapists, true therapists of the psyche.

If we now are going to devote our congress proceedings to the very problem of technique and method we do well to keep Jung's as well as Paracelsus's words in mind. With all our methods and technical knowledge we shall have to keep our sense of proportion and not to lose our humility and reverence in the face of the mystery of the psyche.
Let me close with a few lines from Sophocles:

> What can be learned, I learn,
> What can be achieved I attempt,
> For what one has to pray
> I implore the Gods.

Gerhard Adler, London

ACTIVITY OF THE EGO AND THE IMAGE
Observations on a Theme taken from "Sand Play"

Paolo Aite, Rome

I would like to present some observations made when Sand Play is applied to adult therapy. As you've already seen from Dora Kalff's contribution, this method of activating the imagination consists in putting a scene together in a small field containing sand. The patient constructs his own version by using natural materials or objects representing certain aspects of life such as men, animals, houses, and trees.

The enclosure is evenly distributed with sand and is the site of the patient's concentration. When facing that empty space, the patient experiences a situation completely void of any guiding idea. At that moment his imagination begins to take over. He reacts to the feeling of isolation and unlimited subjective chance confronting him. The way the patient goes about setting up the scene gives the observer certain indications of what is happening at that moment. There is a quick, haphazard way of giving form to the game. In that case, it seems as if the imagination works in fleeting impressions. The patient doesn't concentrate, but quickly puts something together. In other instances, imagination designates a specific goal to be reached. In that way a relationship is formed on the ego and sensitivity level which assumes the characteristics of true involvement with the materials. Many writers define this type of relationship with an image as "imaginative activity." I agree that it must be distinguished from "active imagination" as was defined today in the main report. It is the quality itself of the relationship between ego and image that marks the difference in the two experiences. In fact, in the active image it is the same ego of our everyday selves which, with all its surprising independence, enters into relationship with the perceived image. The awareness of the value of what is happening dominates the conscious which is the expression of this relationship.

Jung made the following assertion: The light of the conscious has many degrees of intensity and the whole of the ego has several levels of accentuation. Jung gives us a dynamic picture of the conscious when he compares it to an archipelago of islands emerging from the sea which gradually stretch forth until they become part of a continent.

I have found that this way of seeing the conscious in transformation, moving from a fragmentary state to unity, matches Sand Play observations. In fact, also in this experience of the imagination, the relationship between the ego and the image, which through the game enters into the conscious, is transformed and develops gradually.

In my opinion, the observations I bring to your attention, taken from clinical experience, are signs of this gradual development. I believe that initially the patient actively relates to each individual part of the play rather than to the entire setting. His working pace, pauses and comments such as memories which may surface spontaneously, vary depending on the aspect of the setting. The form and distribution of space of the entire setting escapes the patient and is experienced in a subjective way as pure chance. In other words, at that moment the conscious seems divided. It relates to single elements but not to the overall structure of the composition. Let me give you an example. The scene was set up by a 23-year-old patient during his sixth session of analysis.

The field is divided into two parts.

On the right side where yellow predominates, representing sunlight to the patient, there are two horsemen attempting to reach the peak which stands at the back of the field. An obstacle lies in their way represented by the little red sticks planted in the sand and by the groove which the patient described "as a bleeding wound." I remember that the groove absorbed all of the patient's attention. When it was over, he himself wondered why that was so. His conscious reason for seeking therapy was a conflict which arose from his doubts about having a small penis. He had never had sexual relations with a woman and in public he felt compelled to look at the genital area of other men. He was considered a good student, but always lacking something to make him outstanding. Where girls and friends were concerned, he was considered a reliable type, but would become embarrassed at the slightest emotional involvement.

The fact that the horsemen are hindered in achieving their goal is indicative of the patient's state of being and the difficulties he encounters in everyday life. On the left, there is a prehistoric animal headed towards the woman standing next to the tree at the back. Another prehistoric animal, a black one, is standing in his way.

The meeting of the two suggests destruction. This aspect of the scene was the result of a childhood memory. For the first time the patient told us that as a 7 year old he had been afraid of the dark. Before going to sleep he found comfort in imagining that he alone was befriended by a prehistoric animal which protected him while terrorizing others. This memory which came out as a comment on the scene, allowed me for the first time to grasp the patient's deepest problem.

The patient approached that play rather nonchalantly. Only twice did he show a different attitude, which I would describe as emotional involvement: once when he turned his attention on the groove to the right and then when his childhood memory emerged represented in the conflict between the two dinosaurs. Both of these instances confirm that the patient was still only partially involved with the scene. Only later during analysis did I realize the relevance of what he had expressed in the play with his own personal situation. We can say that his conscious participation in that moment was not yet complete, being involved only with single elements and not with the scene as a whole.

I would like to point out once again that the form of the game seems to attract the player's attention in an unconscious way. If one were to examine this form, it would open the way to extensive discussion. The objects which the patient placed on the right side are clearly related to this way of facing reality and those on the left, to his deepest and most firmly-rooted conflicts. This is one aspect of the form which we constantly find in first plays. I would like to stress another characteristic concerning the distribution of space which I believe to be closely linked to the transference dynamic which emerged during analysis. If I were to give a concise report of everything that happened between me and my patient over a three year period, I would most definitely have to include the battle between the dinosaurs and the part of the scene involving the horsemen. It was a very important moment during analysis when the patient, remaining in control of himself, was able to express a destructive, critical force which put our relationship under considerable strain. During those tension-ridden moments, there was a struggle going on within him which finds concrete expression in the dinosaur conflict. At times I too felt overcome by that violence; a feeling not easily controlled.

In taking other patients and comparing their first Sand plays with what came out later during analysis, I realized that the patient positions certain objects close to himself. These are objects which best express what he wants to project in transference. They are objects which represent images still hidden in the patient's experiences and are forceful agents in the analytic relationship. According to my hypothesis, the order expressed in "near" or "far away from" the patient in the playing fields corresponds to what the patient is trying to project or recognize as belonging to his private world. We can say that the first plays are similar to the characteristics of first dreams.

There are many aspects which will only come out later during analysis. In the scene we have observed, there is a canal which divides the scene into what appears to be two very different worlds. In this canal there is a fish and a boat coming towards the patient. Like the little sticks and the wound, both the boat and the fish are colored red. Examining this aspect we could say that from the beginning the fish and boat were the symbolic expression of something which did develop later. The messages obtained via the imagination overcome the defense mechanisms present when the patient puts his dreams into words; these mechanisms often influence the patient's very way of telling about his dreams. The analyst's understanding is enriched and the play is completed by that which is observed at the dream and transference levels.

Precisely the way in which the patient uses the space in the field of play opens up a possibility for comprehension and research. After the initial phase, imaginative play often becomes a means of resistance. The desire to maintain the analytic rapport free from the deeper tensions tends to prevail. The aesthetic approach to the game or the rationalization of that which is represented in it are recognizable to me, but only in their most exteme manifestations. I have found it is helpful to compare what has appeared in the game with the perspective offered by dream analysis and by transference in progress. The line followed by dreams is seemingly independent of themes expressed in sand play.

The patient is less conscious of his own oneiric activity, while this activity is itself often indicative of what is really happening. The communication of the analytic rapport apparently proceeds smoothly. Many images which quicken the interest of the analysist are created. The patient is capable of representing himself in the scenes, but as an "imaginary ego" that has incredible adventures. If one takes a closer look, the play tends to hide all types of conflict. For me they may be compared to the resistance expressing itself in verbalization when the patient, wishing to avoid the menace of silence in analysis, talks at length.

Quite different from the situation just illustrated is the one in which patients become interested in the play game only at particular times. After initial contact with the imaginative force, there is frequently the tendency to stay away from the play for awhile. I believe that in many cases this latency has a precise meaning. I am of the opinion that the possibility of the psychological employment of the imaginative force has its roots in the personal history of each individual, in the acquisition of certain fundamental securities by the individual in his infancy.

The analytic work of reconstructing that security takes place in this period. It consists in breaking down or reducing complex situations into their original components, components connected to the personal history reappearing in the analytic rapport. Through his confidence in the analytic relationship, the patient can slowly build up the possibility of finding himself alone in front of the field of play and of using his own imagination in that situation. Upon taking up the play once more, the preliminary situation would seem to be characterized by a difference in potential between the conscious and the unconscious that cannot be resolved by dream analysis or the realization of the transference. The patient reapproaches the experience as a possible way, if an unpleasant one, of establishing contact with what has happened in analysis. I should like to dwell on certain signs that, in my opinion, are the expression of a transformation in the patient's rapport with his own imaginative force. They are signs that indicate a variation in conscious participation, from a yet partial and fragmentary level to one at which the patient has an increasing subjective awareness that "something else," something unknown, is happening in that play.

One can make an initial observation regarding the way the material is confronted. The patient now tends to use the sand to achieve a certain plasticity, a three-dimensional effect, and not as a simple prop for a scene. More clearly delineated forms are increasingly evident, forms that emerge from the background. His rapport with the game, expressed through emotive participation or spontaneous comment, is no longer limited to single aspects of the scene but rather tends to grasp it in its totality. It is as if the scene, given its formal characters, might be expressing a new capacity for perceiving the image with respect to a given setting, in a more definite and unified way.

A second sign is the change in the patient's verbalization. I remember the case of a woman who continually complained about the stupidity of the play and the inadequate material I was offering her, while at the same time evidencing an intense involvement with what she was constructing. Moreover, she wanted me to conserve the created scene from one session to the next, thus demonstrating a profound relationship with what she had constructed. It was a process that was really quite important to her. I have noted that not only the emotional tone of verbalization is enriched in such cases but also that the verbalization can unblock, becoming more open, during the execution of the play. Or it may alternate with long moments of silence.

The convergence of what happens at the imaginative, oneiric, and transference levels is another significant observation for me. There are three points of view that reciprocally integrate, like a single commentary on a single fact. Dreams diminish and acquire clarity and incisiveness, appearing in relation to the situation that reveals itself in the game as well. These are phases, observed in analysis, in which a release of energy occurs and is accompanied by concrete changes at the level of reality.

I remember the case of a young woman who had created something in the scene that she described as "beautiful;" it was a place in which she would have liked to live. In an emotional clash with a person meaningful to her, she had the spontaneous fantasy that precisely that world, the world in the sand, was suddenly submerged. By means of these experiences, patients begin to be aware of a tie between those scenes and

Fig. 1

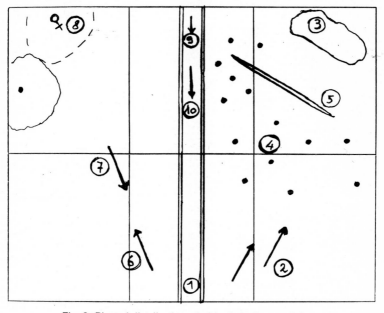

Fig. 2: Plan of distribution of objects in the sandplay

1. dividing canal
2. the horsemen
3. the peaks
4. the small red sticks
5. the groove
6. the dinosaur
7. the black dinosaur
8. the woman
9. the fish
10. the boat

what is unknowingly taking place within themselves. The fact they can carry over the spontaneous fantasies connected with the play into analysis indicates an important step taken in their conscious behaviour towards their own imagination.

Carried away by enthusiasm, I have sometimes made the mistake of having the patient see those scenes again, without my having asked him to do so. Often it involved a brief sequence of photographs which to me were significant and clearly connected with a spontaneous fantasy. I was aware of the force of the images. Not only did the patient fail to assimilate what to me was evident, he further had a sudden regression, revealing through his dreams the existence of a menacing situation.

Thus I have learned to control my desire to interpret. Quite a while may elapse before a patient talks about a given scene. I have asked myself how I might intervene to enable the patient to participate in what was happening. My contribution consists solely in proposing the recall of a certain scene, or of one of its elements that seems to me to be perfectly adaptable to what is taking place in a given moment of analysis. It can change the structure, in other words, of the verbal rapport between analyst and patient. At times it takes on the characteristics of symbolic jargon. An element which appeared in a preceding scene becomes the best and most comprehensive word to describe what is happening in a given situation. The analyst plays the role of a memory that in an opportune moment brings to light something already experienced unknowingly.

It is possible, moreover, that the patient will be surprised at what he has expressed in the play. It is another moment in which one sees a change in the relationship between Ego and image.

In my experience few patients indeed have asked to have another look at the photographs of their sand play – even if they did receive a transformative impulse through the use of the imagination. In the wish to examine the play once again, a successive phase in the encounter with the image is expressed.

Jung observes: There is a conscious in which the unconscious predominates and there is a conscious in which consciousness does the same. Between these two extreme levels of conscious participation in the image there is a graduated movement which occurs in successive stages. From the initial phase of rapport with sand play to those which follow, one can say that a gradual transformation takes place, from a fragmentary conscious, in which the unconscious predominates, into a conscious expressing rapport between a better integrated Ego and the image.

Using the unified conscious employed for daily reality, those patients wishing to re-examine the photographic reproductions of their plays have once again covered the stages of a journey previously illuminated only intermittently by the experience that "something else" was present in the play. And this is the moment in which the patient may be surprised–as he realizes the genuine autonomy of what has taken place in himself. This experience, that is the surprise of one's own imagination, is one of the more transforming moments at which I have been present at the sand play. The possibility of an ethical confrontation with one's own imagination is thus open.

In the play described, the experience of surprise is connected with the recognition of the otherness of what has previously taken place, while in "active imagination" it is present at the same moment in which the image itself is encountered. For this reason also, I feel it is useful for the purposes of clarity to distinguish between these two ways of rapport with the image.

I have wished to emphasize how the use of imagination in therapy always opens up a new point of view for the analyst. It is a point of view which has been integrated through dream analysis and transference, because only in this way do I believe I have begun to distinguish a transformative use of the imagination from a defensive one. And this distinction is a fundamental one, often difficult to achieve, requiring observations far more profound than those I have been able to share with you today.

Only by clarifying this point little by little can one avoid the risk of over-evaluating the imagination or of disparaging it totally.

I feel that careful consideration of the potential and the limits inherent in the use of imagination in analysis at the various levels of conscious participation is necessary.

This is a preliminary step in arriving at a comprehension of specifically which factors influence and determine the movement from a conscious, fragmented attitude, dominated by the unconscious, to an integrated one of rapport with the image, one which finds in the "active imagination" its most evident expression.

Original Italian version to be found in "Oggi Jung" La Rivista di psicologia analitica 17/7 pp 97–106.

CHILDREN'S DRAWINGS DURING FIRST INTERVIEWS AND THEIR UNCONSCIOUS RELATIONSHIP TO THE INVESTIGATOR.

R. Blomeyer, Berlin

1. *Preliminary Remarks.*

The following investigation is based on drawings by children and adolescents from initial interviews undertaken by training candidates at the Institute for Psychotherapy in Berlin, independently of this test which at that time had not yet been planned. I have designated the training candidates with coded first names. They conducted the interviews at various testing places—each at three places. I thank the training candidates as well as the co-workers at the places where the tests were made for their friendly support in this work.

I have compiled data from twenty investigators. Each training candidate had as a rule performed fifteen interviews, in two cases there were twenty. Drawings were not done in all interviews, but in most. On the average, there were about three drawings per interview. Altogether I have seen some 1000 drawings from about 300 interviews. I will only show a small part of these here.

My concern was to test the question whether certain candidates unconsciously constellated similar elements in content and structure in different children or adolescents. If this were so, different children would have made similar drawings with the same candidate.

In other words: correspondences in content or form would have to be found in the drawings which had been completed by different children under the same investigator. This is what I looked for.

At first I found—or thought I had found—more or less clear correspondences in drawings handed in by nine out of the twenty investigators. I then kept on eliminating uncertain findings. In the end there remained two series of drawings–the one produced under Anke and the other under Gert–which clearly showed stylistic correspondences and which also partly corresponded in content; in addition, there are three typical pictures drawn under Elly. Both these series and the three pictures, I show as "evidence". For comparison I show a series produced under Ditta with considerably fewer correspondences and three further pictures from other series (Heinz and Ida).

I was able to examine data from twenty interviews performed by Anke. Correspondences were found in the drawings of ten subjects, five boys and five girls. Gert presented fifteen interviews. Correspondences were found in the drawings of nine subjects, in this case seven boys and two girls. From Ditta, I show pictures from eight different subjects, six boys and two girls. The average age in all three cases was estimated at 10 years.

3. Main Part.

Psychoanalysis may be described as the teaching of the interplay between conscious and unconscious forces, between motivations and fulfilments in the inner-psychic sphere and between interpersonal relationships. An important assertion regarding the unconscious in interpersonal relationships is: When two people, A and B, are talking together about an absent third person, C, then they invariably speak unconsciously of themselves as well. To put it more generally: almost every remark concerning anything outside A and B can unconsciously be related to A and B and be correspondingly brought forth by A and B. To put it more specifically: almost every remark uttered by an analysand concerning matters outside of analysis may at the same time be unconsciously related to the analyst and may go back through the analyst upon an unconscious provocation. The analyst should on his part–if he takes the matter seriously–relate every remark from the analysand concerning "other things" tentatively to himself. He would then behave as if he had a sensitive (analytical) delusion of relatedness.

A special case in analysis is the diagnostic interview. Here the following is also valid: each remark uttered by the patient during an interview may, even if it has nothing to do consciously with the analyst, relate to him unconsciously, and it may have been constellated through him equally unconsciously. It may be a question of verbal or non-verbal utterances. Non-verbal utterances are for example drawings as made by children and adolescents during the interview while the analyst talks to their relatives, after having talked to the children. These drawings have moreover mostly been consciously "constellated" through the analyst. He challenges the children or adolescents to draw something according to e.g. Buck (1), Gräser (5), Koch (8), among other things (a) a person, (b) a tree, (c) the so-called "animal family" (of the patient)and (d) just "anything you like," a so-called "free drawing". That which is drawn in detail within the frame of this outline and the manner in which it is drawn should then, according to what many analysts still think, be interpreted independently from the analyst and as a testimony regarding the patient and his relatives. The following is still valid, however: it may contain an unconscious statement about the analyst which may have been constellated by the analyst with regard to content as well as style.

In this assertion a new concept appears: "style". It relates to the "manner in which the drawing is being made". This also seems to be unconsciously influenced by the investigator. This is more difficult to imagine than an influence in content, but equally possible (see below). First I shall deal with the contents.

It seems obvious to anyone with a little analytical knowledge that when the "animal family" (of the patient) is being drawn in an interview, the investigator might well be included in the drawing. With a colleague, Elly, three children out of fifteen had drawn giraffes (Fig. 1). Giraffes appeared now and then in the well over 1000 drawings I have looked at, but not like with Elly, in families, (Fig. 1 above and below right). With another investigator I would probably have left the result without paying much attention to it. Here it struck me, because it somehow "suited" Elly. When I later referred to the results, she said, amused, "Oh!" and made an involuntary movement with her head and throat which immediately explained the "giraffes".

Under Gert, five out of fifteen children had drawn ships as free drawing: forceful, "martial ships" very in much action (Fig. 2). Gert, as I later asked, had definitely not said they should draw ships. Being asked, he commented that he had also been struck by the "many ships". Gert does not strike one particularly as being an "old salt," and he held the interviews in three different rooms in public buildings where there were no pictures of ships on the walls and where no ships were drawn in interviews by other investigators. Thus the ships which had been drawn under him had not simply been "copied".

The giraffes seem to be a relatively superficial portrayal of a characteristic feature. With the ships it may also be the portrayal of a characteristic feature, but on a deeper level. The difference, the peculiarity about this result, becomes more evident when we describe it more accurately and compare it with other results.

a) In none of the cases which had been investigated had there been so many ships drawn as here. However, Gert may, statistically speaking, just have had "luck": he may have had a series of boys who particularly liked drawing ships. We might add: boys really like drawing ships! That is correct, but it is not so easy to generalize in this way. A very experienced senior colleague said, when I talked the results over with him: "with me they always draw aeroplanes!" Boys may like to draw ships under certain circumstances, but not under all.

b) There were not only many ships, but they had all been drawn in a special manner: ships in action, forceful, "martial" (Fig. 3). In comparison I show the two only ships which were produced under Heinz (Fig. 4): they appear meager and empty, miserable somehow, as opposed to the pictures with Gert. In addition, a ship drawn under Ida (Fig. 5), a gondola; soft, round and dainty. – There are ships and ships. Under particular circumstances particular ships arise.

c) If we place the drawings made under Gert next to each other in the "right" order (Fig. 2), we find something striking: children, who haven't drawn any ships, have partly drawn ship-like things, i.e. pictures which remind one of ships: a house with a fence and a "booth" in front, giving the impression of a ship structure (Fig. 2, upper right), a street of houses with many windows (Fig. 2, below, middle) and cross roads with traffic lights (Fig. 2, below right).

I show the three latter pictures without the ships once more enlarged, adding a fourth one (Fig. 6). Here the pictures have been placed in a somewhat different order. Without the "real" ships they no longer appear particularly as ships, because the immediate association is lacking.

All in all I have compiled pictures from nine out of fifteen children who painted under Gert. The common feature in these drawings is: the pictures are quite lively. The space at disposal has been made full use of. The pictures could partly have been continued to the right and to the left, but they do not seem cut off, as is later the case with Anke. Nothing is "missing". Typical is the horizontal format which is stressed by diagonal lines with inserted rectangles or squares or circles. What they have in common lies not in the ships, but in the structure of the pictures into which the ships fit.

It is no longer simply a question of content, but of the above-mentioned style, of structure and dynamics, of the "manner in which it is being drawn". The implication was that this could also be influenced by the investigator.

That the style plays a part which can hardly be underestimated in the psychic sphere belongs to one of the fundamental postulations of analytical psychology (JUNG, 7). This is in connection with the theory of archetypes which distinguishes between the formal structure of the archetype and its content–the image. Furrer, from whom I have learnt a great deal, has demonstrated something very important in this respect: when a patient and he put down on paper the most "senseless" abstract scribbles possible, without the one knowing what the other was doing, pictures arose which were so similar in formal structure, that the simultaneously drawn pictures could be picked out correctly by a third person and put in right order after having been mixed with other pictures. An unconscious communication must have existed between the two people drawing. The correspondences in the formal structure could not be explained any other way. The other way around, one could demonstrate unconscious communication objectively with this method which Furrer calls "inductive drawing". Furrer explains in brief: "In inductive drawing it is not the contents which . . . are unconsciously perceived but the basic formal psychic structures behind such concrete structures" (4) which in their turn find expression in the formal elements in the scribblings.

With respect to the present investigation, I assume that certain investigators unconsciously "shade" the testing situation so strongly in

Figure 1. Elly 3 × giraffes. Michael (14); Horst (9); Helmut (10).

Figure 2. Gert. Survey. Guido (12), Carsten (11), Arndt (7); Miro (12), Daniel (10), Annick (8); Andreas (14), Annick (8), Heiko (5).

Figure 3. Gert. 4 ships from figure 2. Daniel (10), Guido (12); Carsten (11), Miro (12).

Figure 4. Heinz. 2 ships. Rafael (10); Ulrich (13).

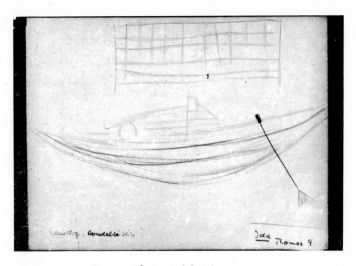

Figure 5. Ida. 1 gondola. Thomas (9).

Figure 6. Gert. 3 drawings from figure 2 and a supplementary one. Annick (8), Heiko (5); Barbara 8, Arndt (7).

Figure 7. Ditta. Trees and people. 6 boys, 2 girls. Ilona (15), Boris (10), Ilona (15), Jochen (12); Detlev (15), Marc (8), Ralf (9), Cordula (7); Claes (5), Marc (8), Detlev (15).

Figure 8. Anke. Survey. 4 girls, 3 boys. Anne (10), Christian (10), Petra (10); Anja (8), Robert (9), Klaus (11); Michael (14), Christian (10), Anne (10).

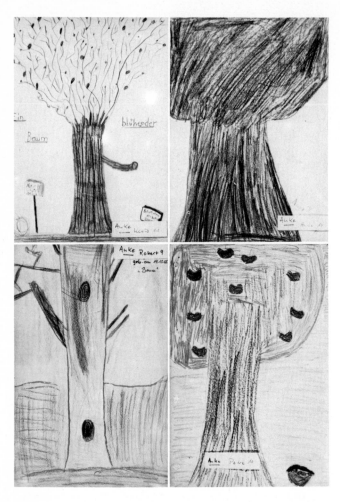

Figure 9. Anke. 4 trees from figure 8. Klaus (11), Anne (10); Robert (9), Petra (10).

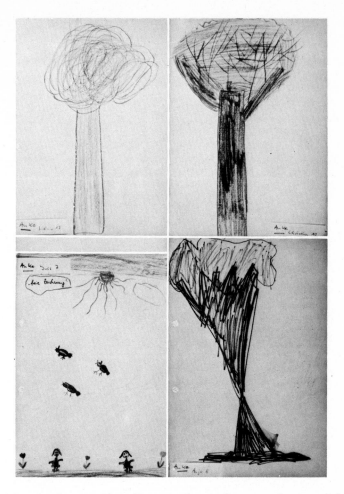

Figure 10. Anke. 1 tree from figure 8 and 3 supplementary drawings. Sylvia (17), Christian (10); Iris (7), Anja (8).

Figure 11. Anke. 3 people from figure 8 and a supplementary drawing. Robert (9), Anne (10); Anja (8), Michael (14).

Figure 12. Anke. 1 girl from figure 8 and 3 supplementary drawings. Klaus (11), Christian (10); Iris (7), Sylvia (17).

Figure 13. Anke. 1 clown. Jörg (6).

a manner particular to them that this shade becomes unconsciously absorbed by different children and finds expression in formal elements in their pictures through some kind of "inductive drawing".

That formal elements or elements of style can at all express a specific experience and behaviour, is not quite so obvious to the doctors among analysts, who inquire more after the contents of the expressions, as to the psychologists. The latter are more used to consider the formal elements of expression, as in the above-mentioned test and as also in graphology, where Robert HUSS, for example, has described the process of writing as a process of movement, space, and form. He sees "... in the image of movement ... the immediate and spontaneous modes of behaviour ... in the image of space, how he deals with it, how he organizes it, swamps it, etc. In the formally structured picture ... the really shaping behaviour, which for instance leans on given forms, transforms them, destroys, expands or limits ..." (6).

The drawing tests, like the graphology tests, belong to the so-called procedures of projective, psychological/diagnostic testing and investigation. I am saying nothing new by stating that their results may be particularly influenced by the investigator. In this respect, Horst and Ingrid VOGEL have recently stressed: "Since projective procedures deal with open stimuli and exercises, specific testing conditions, like the occasion, the institution and the person of the investigator, all become part of the supply of stimuli and gain for themselves stimulus qualities in a broader sense. That is to say, that the investigator must be aware of the fact that in a test involving projective procedure he is himself much more involved–whether he likes it or not–than in investigations with so-called objective tests." (9)

Thus in my work it is not just a question of generally confirming that "such things just happen" and always have to be considered. That would be a superflous repetition of what we know. Here it is much more a question of the particular emphasis on the results, which as such are already known: that they *really* do exist; and particulary that the investigator often "contributes far more–whether he likes it or not"– than he is conscious of.

Psychologically speaking, our analytical-diagnostic interviews are altogether to be classified as projective tests. What I say here about drawing is in general also valid for interviews. For the latter it should be even especially true. In fact, in this investigation, I took as starting point a general question concerning the interviews. It is well-known—and this has been specially studied at the Central Institute for Psychogenic Diseases in Berlin—that different investigators wear different glasses during interviews. The same results are judged differently based on the different make-up of the investigator. I was then struck by the fact that not only do different investigators wear different glasses (the same thing seen differently), but that they indeed see a "totally different patient" while investigating the same patient, i.e. they come to see another basically different aspect of the patient. Not only do they see the same thing differently, but they do actually see something objectively different. This difference they must somehow have provoked, constellated, or brought into resonance through their manner, in other words, somehow called it forth. One step further: different investigators will not only evoke different traits in general, but they will more or less often constellate answers which are specific for them.

After a while this thought was obvious to me with regard to other investigators; with regard to myself, however, it was unpleasant and therefore not at all obvious; in fact it hardly seemed plausible. In order to keep the matter somewhat at a distance from myself, I have—as a safety measure—checked it with the results of others.

A problem soon arose: when I read their accounts of analytical first interviews—during the past year about 400 apart from this investigation—I certainly met with results and interpretations which seemed typical of groups of investigators and of individual investigators. However, with regard to verbatim reference of statements by patients, I was no longer certain whether those were the patients' true statements, or whether they had already been reformulated into the investigator's own language. To this I might add that in my own records the patients talk as it were with my own very words.

In search of objective data, i.e. statements, which, true, at first had been unconsciously constellated by the investigator, but which could not have been falsified by him during reproduction, I came across the children's drawings. At first I looked for correspondences in content and was surprised when I found in the cases of Gert and Anke a style which, in spite of everything, gave the impression of having been drawn by one "painter" with a "handwriting" peculiar to him, and not by several children.

This phenomenon was most pronounced with Anke. In order to show what is typical more clearly, I again compare with other pictures. In addition I show a series which originated under Ditta: four trees and seven people (Fig. 7).

Here it is above all a question of proportions. In the middle row there are two trees to the left and one girl to the right, which almost fill out the paper at disposal. They have turned out a bit big. The third tree in the middle row is still relatively big. The fourth tree in the survey, in the upper row to the left, is–like all the drawings in the upper row–displaced somewhat towards the left. The tree-top is a bit small in contrast to the trunk, but as a whole it is not too big. The people that appear with Ditta, are both small and large. So much for the proportions, which here vary in an average way.

One more peculiarity: two of the trees–the one to the upper left and the other in the middle row below, somewhat to the right–seem, through the actual drawing, smooth and the tree top in particular is sharply contrasted against the background; "phallic" one might say (the upper left one is drawn by a 15-year old girl, the one to the right below by an 8-year old boy. The two have, moreover, also drawn similar people: the boy with the ball in the middle below, and diagonally above the second picture from the right). With Anke (Fig. 8) not only are the tree-trunks and in part the tree-tops "smooth," meticulously coloured and sharply contoured against the background, but this style of drawing is also noticeable in the people, and the drawings have–as with individual cases under Ditta and many other investigators–not only on occasion "turned out a bit big" but they are remarkably often large or too large, so that the space available is not sufficient, with something lacking at the top at the bottom, making the drawing seem "cut off". Unusually often, the proportions within the drawing (figures) do not fit and occasionally something "too small" is facing something "too big". The characteristic "as if cut off" can be noticed fairly often: cut off branches, lacking ears, missing hands, no hair; in addition there is sometimes a peculiar rigidity.

Fig. 9 shows four typically coloured trees which have not enough space; Fig. 10 shows three relatively big trees, two with the characteristic small top, then as contrast below to the left a picture where everything has turned out too small. The small people are the same size as the flowers amongst which they stand. Fig. 11 shows four people, three of which are "as if cut off". Fig. 12: Once more four people, where the vertical accent is noticeable in three of them (through the row of buttons). In contrast to Gert, the vertical accent seems to have been more stressed in the drawings under Anke. And finally Fig. 13: a clown with a big head, small legs, no arms. This is, by the way, the third clown in the row. It may be typical but doesn't necessarily have to be so.

Ten out of twenty children or adolescents have drawn this way with Anke. What is really characteristic cannot even be conclusively described from the individual factors; it is only evident, as with Gert, after gaining an all-round impression by letting the pictures work on one for a while.

Occasionally when I have shown and discussed my results with others, I have met with a peculiar phenomenon: in discussions it would be said on the one hand that, brought into the open, the matter was hardly new; in other words, it was uninteresting. On the other hand, it would be said in the same breath that the whole thing seemed unbelievable. The results were insufficiently founded statistically. One would require to have seen much more extensive material and to place it in correct order. Such as it was now, there wasn't much to be done. In other words, on the one hand it was seen as old, well-known material which had been confirmed long ago; on the other hand, it could not be accepted in the present state.

The results brought about equally contradictory reactions in me as well. The reason, however, in my opinion, rests not with the fact that they are too "thin" or inadequate. On the contrary, they are too "fat". It simply should not be true that nine out of fifteen of Gert's children and ten out of twenty of Anke's have made drawings with the very same characteristic manner and that this may be traced back to the specific "shadings" emanating from the investigator. Perhaps, it is suggested, we are dealing with a special, rare and coincidental constellation which has taken place, and which has caused these results. In other constellations and in the majority of cases they would not be found like this.

The objection is not completely unjustified. A special constellation has certainly taken place, but not a rare one. Something which distinguished the situation from the normal interview situation was that the training candidate was making an investigation at the same time as the children were drawing. If we so assume that unconscious shadings are expressed when the emotional tension is stronger and more intense and when the sensitivity towards such tension is most heightened then we must say:

a) Training candidates, who are under pressure to demonstrate their capabilities, are probably under a stronger emotional stress during the test than trained analysts who undertake such tests as a matter of routine.

b) Children may be more sensitive than grown-ups when confronted with stress situations.

The results shown here might then more easily appear in children's interviews performed by training candidates than in interviews with grown-ups performed by trained analysts as a matter of routine. That is possible, but it wouldn't alter anything with respect to the fundamental importance of the results.

Finally, one might assume that I had drawn a "full house" twice. This cannot be ruled out. However, that would not clear the problem out of the way. Chance would merely have confirmed the results which were expected according to theory and experience, i.e. that the investigator influences the test results through an unconscious communication with the person being tested.

When Freud spoke of a "difficulty in psychoanalysis" and "the resistances against psychoanalysis," he declared that "psychoanalytical opinion of the relationship between the conscious ego and the overwhelming unconscious"–"that the ego is not master in his own house"–"is a serious insult towards human self-love." "No wonder, then, that the ego doesn't turn favourably towards psychoanalysis and stubbornly refuses to believe in it" (2, 3). The insult, I think, could be overcome. In fact, however, the whole thing is uncanny. We are less insulted than hit by the reality and effectiveness of the unconscious processes.

Original German version to be found in Zeitschrift für Analytische Psychologie, Vol. 9, 1978, pp. 213–232.

4. Summary

Projective procedures, to which the analytical diagnostic interview belongs, are strongly influenced unconsciously by the investigator. This relation can be demonstrated with children's drawings which originated in analytical first interviews: different children drew in a similar manner under the same investigator. There were particular stylistic corresponces to be found, like similar handwritings or like results which Furrer has stressed (4). Moreover, correspondences in content (not indicated consciously) attracted our attention. Well over 1000 drawings were investigated, deriving from about 300 interviews, which had been performed by about 20 investigators, all carried out before this investigation was even planned.

REFERENCES

(1) Buck, J. N.: The H-T-P Technique. A Qualitative and Quantitative Scoring Manual. J. Clin. Psychol. Monogr., Suppl. 5, (1948)
(2) Freud, S.: Eine Schwierigkeit der Psychoanalyse. GW XII, p. 11
(3) Freud, S.: Die Widerstände gegen die Psychoanalyse. GW XIV, p. 109
(4) Furrer, W. L.: Neue Wege zum Unbewußten. p. 102 (Huber, Bern 1970)
(5) Gräser, L.: Familie in Tieren (München, Basel 1959)
(6) Heiss, R.: Die Deutung der Handschrift, 3rd ed., p. 22 (Hamburg 1966)
(7) Jung, C. G.: Theoretische Überlegungen zum Wesen des Psychischen. GW 8, pp. 233 f., 244 (Rascher, Zürich 1967)
(8) Koch, K.: Der Baumtest, 6th ed. (Bern, Stuttgart, 1972)
(9) Vogel, H. u. I.: Projektive Verfahren und ihre Anwendung, in: Die Psychologie des 20. Jahrhunderts, vol. V. p. 461 (Kindler, Zürich 1977)

PRACTICE OF ANALYTICAL PSYCHOLOGY
AND ITS RELATIONSHIP
TO PSYCHOLOGICAL TYPE OF ANALYST (1)

Katherine Bradway and Joseph Wheelwright, San Francisco

It was six years ago this week that the nucleus of this study was given life and none of us knew into what shape or size it would grow. At the banquet of the 1971 Congress in London, several of us–I especially recall Jo and Jane Wheelwright–commented on the fact that the papers of that Congress represented more varieties in methods of analytic practice than previously. We had known that California was a kind of hot-bed for new therapeutic methods and revival of old ones, but what we had observed in California seemed to be going on in other areas. We then started to speculate as to the psychological type of the analyst that would tend to use each method. It seemed obvious to us, for example, that extraverts would use group therapy more than introverts would. But exclusively? Or only to a small degree more? Dr. Wheelwright and I felt, based on our extraverted experience, that in a tight spot, or "up against a blank wall," we would look at what was going on in the analytical relationship and that introverts would be more likely to look at dreams. But when we asked a few other analysts of both types, this hypothesis didn't hold up.

It was out of such nebulous inquiries that this study came to life. Some preliminary diggings were made by doing a California study in which some more-or-less expected things were turned up and some totally unexpected ones, (BRADWAY and DETLOFF, 1975, 1976).

(1) This study was funded by a grant from the Ernst and Eleanor van Loben Sels Scholarship Fund of San Francisco.

Then we enlarged our area of exploration, or excavation if you will, and at the 1974 Congress Dr. Wheelwright arranged for the distribution of Personality Type test blanks along with questionnaires related to such matters as one's own self-typing, the typing of one's current and divorced spouses, one's preference in typology of patients, kinds of problems one worked best with, and use of adjunct methods to the vis-a-vis verbal dialogue. We were not too optimistic as to what percentage of return we would get. I know I loathe filling out questionnaires. But the percent returned was sufficiently large to permit the valid application of statistical methods. We want to thank the many of you for your generous participation.

Modern methods of data processing seem to me like throwing a multitude of units of matter into a huge cauldron and waiting for a transformation to take place which, after a series of distillings, leaves a tiny essence of meaningful matter. And it's that small essence that we are going to report this morning. We prepared five tables to supplement what will be orally presented. The tables are in English. Unfortunately, translations into the other three official languages of the Congress were not made. But an understanding of them is in no way necessary for an understanding of this paper. They are for those of you who wish to see more complete data than are contained in the essences to be reported.

The study consists of three principal parts: one, an investigation of incidence of psychological types among Jungian analysts in five geographical locations; two, a study of several variables in the practice of these analysts; and three, the relationship between typology of analyst and practice. The findings will be presented in this order.

When I made a study of psychological types of California analysts in 1961, I used both the Myers-Briggs Type Indicator and the Gray-WHEELWRIGHTs Jungian Type Survey, in addition to the analysts' typing of themselves, as indices of psychological type (BRADWAY, 1964). Since the Gray-WHEELWRIGHTs showed a slightly closer concordance than the Myers-Briggs with self-typing, as well as being much less time consuming to fill out and to score, it was selected as the test of choice in the current study.

Participating in the current study were 172 analysts and candidates from San Francisco, Los Angeles, New York, London and the European Continent. The exact figures for each geographical group are contained in the heading of table 2. In this oral presentation, we are going to try and limit our statistical references to round numbers. Furthermore, differentiation between analysts and candidates will not be made. San Francisco was the largest group with about 60 participants. Both Los Angeles and London are represented by about 30 each, and New York and the Continent by about 25 each. It should be noted that in the New York group are included the few Interregional analysts who were members of neither the California groups nor the New York group. The majority of the Continent participants were from Germany or Switzerland. Many of these participants used the forms of the questionnaires that had been translated into German, the only language other than English that was used for the questionnaires. The total number of analysts participating, then, was about 170.

One of the first items on the questionnaire that the participants filled out was to indicate their own psychological type by checking introvert or extravert, thinking or feeling, and sensation or intuition, and by double checking their primary function. The results of this self-typing were compared with participants' scores on the Gray-WHEELWRIGHTs Jungian Type Survey which is comprised of 81 double-choice items such as "Do you prefer to: (a) read about a thing or (b) hear about a thing?" and, another item: "Is your impulse to be (a) leisurely or (b) punctual?"

A high agreement was found between self-typing and the Gray-Wheelwrights or G-W typing, as has been true for other studies relating the two. Since our attempts to establish which of the first two functions was primary on the G-W by reference to self-typing were not successful, we abandoned using the G-W scores as indices differentiating primary from secondary functions; we combined, for example, all extraverted persons with intuition scores above sensation scores and feeling scores above thinking scores together, regardless of the comparative absolute values of the intuition and feeling scores. Comparable grouping for the other function scores gives us eight basic types on the G-W rather than the 16 basic types which differentation between primary and secondary function provides. The agreement for the eight basic types is about 60 percent. That is, for 60 percent of the participants their self-typing without differentiation between primary and secondary function is identical with their G-W typing. The highest agreement between self-typing and G-W scores is for introversion-extraversion,

about 90 percent; that is, about 90 percent of those who typed themselves as extraverted obtained extraverted G-W scores; and about 90
percent of those who typed themselves as introverted obtained introverted G-W scores. Even the two function dichotomies, feeling versus
thinking (that is, the judging or rational functions) and sensation versus
intuition (the perceiving or irrational functions) have nearly 80 percent
identical indices.

Incidence of Psychological Types

We shall now consider the incidence of psychological types among
Jungian analysts. As will surprise no one here, the overwhelming
majority of analysts in all five geographical locations, regardless of
whether typed by their own self-typing or by the G-W are introverted
rather than extraverted in attitude, and more at home with intuition
than with sensation. Feeling and thinking are more evenly distributed
for all geographical locations, with a nearly 50–50 split for San Francisco and the Continent, and a slight preponderance of feeling types
over thinking types for Los Angeles, London and New York. That is,
in Los Angeles, London and New York feeling slightly predominates
over thinking. In San Francisco and the Continent, neither is predominant.

But how does this sample of analysts compare with a non-analytic
population? How different are analysts from their non-analytic
brethren? The only extensive data for a non-analytic population available to us is for an American group to whom the G-W was administered
during its development, (GRAY and WHEELWRIGHT, 1946). Comparison with this group shows the most difference in the incidence of intuition over sensation: more than twice as many analysts as non-ana-
lysts show a predominance of intuition. Likewise, there is a greater incidence of introversion among analysts: 75 percent are introverted as
compared with 55 percent of the non-analytic population. There is not
so much difference in the predominance of feeling over thinking.

A replication of the study of Dr. A. PLAUT (1972) regarding confidence in typing of oneself yielded nearly identical findings for a nearly
identical number of subjects. In both studies about 3/4ths of the ana-

lysts indicate confidence in typing themselves. These findings are re-flected in the high agreement between self-typing and G-W test scores reported earlier in this paper.

The data on what an analyst believes is his or her inferior function are interesting. The same proportion of approximately 3/4ths that felt confident in typing themselves responded to this question. Half of the respondents indicated sensation as their inferior function. This is a higher proportion than would be expected from the proportion indicating intuition as their primary function. This led to our looking at whether respondents always indicated their inferior function as the op-posite of the function they indicated as their primary function, which would be required by Jung's typology theory. Most did; but a sizeable number did not. Nearly 1 in 4 indicated an inferior function that was not the opposite of their self-typed primary function. The most frequent departure from theory was found in typing self as having primary feel-ing but as having inferior sensation. The next most frequent discrepan-cy was typing self as having primary sensation but as having inferior feeling. So sensation and feeling are often experienced as opposite ends of the hierarchy of availability of functions. I have heard analysts argue as to whether this is possible in personality structure. Some insist that it is not, whereas others insist that whether or not it is consistent with theory, it *is* consistent with their reality.

I think this is the time to briefly refer to three sub-studies which were made, one having to do with psychological type of current and divorced spouses, one with preference in psychological type of patient, and the other with Zodiac signs.

Our only index of typology of spouses is the typing of them by the analysts to whom they are, or were, married. Two essential criteria obtain in such data: the Jungian sophistication of the typer and the familiarity of the typer with the typee. However, in the absence of validating data, we would be safer to speak of perception of typology of spouse rather than actual typology of spouse. With this fully acknow-ledged, and not completely lost in the unconscious, we shall proceed to speak of "type" of spouse rather than of "perception of type".

Nearly 3/4ths of the participants filled in data regarding the typology of their current spouses. Of these spouses, 65 percent are introverted, which is less than the 75 percent of analysts who are introverted, but not to a statistically significant degree. A statistically significant differ-ence *was* found for both the judging and perceiving functions. The per-centage in which feeling predominates over thinking is 70 percent for current spouses as compared with 60 percent for analysts, so there are more feeling types among spouses than among analysts. The percentage in which intuition predominates over sensation is 55 percent for current spouses as compared with 75 percent for analysts, so there are more intuitive types among analysts than among spouses. Despite the signifi-cant differences in percentages, it will be noted that all three compari-sons indicate that analysts and current spouses deviate in the same direction from a 50–50, or half and half, distribution of the opposing dichotomized typologies. The modal typology for both analysts and current spouses is introverted with feeling and intuition predominating over thinking and sensation. We must admit that the data do not sup-port the contention that both Dr. Wheelwright and I have held that one tends to marry one's typological opposite. It was true for each of us in our marriages, but apparently it is not true for the majority of ana-lysts (at least, as they perceive their spouses).

Comparison of the spouses from whom analysts have become di-vorced with spouses to whom analysts are currently married shows a greater incidence of extraversion, thinking and sensation among di-vorced spouses than among current spouses. The data have to be looked on as suggestive rather than conclusive, however, because of the relati-vely low number of divorced spouses for whom we have data, only 35.

A somewhat related area to spouse selection is patient selection. What psychological type do analysts prefer? Analysts in all five geo-graphical locations prefer introverts overwhelmingly over extraverts, feelers over thinkers, and intuitives overwhelmingly over sensates. Thus the patients preferred by most analysts are introverted, intuitive and feeling, just as the majority of analysts are and as the majority of cur-rent spouses are.

A third sub-study related to type rather than to practice of analysis is incidence of Zodiac signs among the participating analysts. Neither Dr. Wheelwright nor I are among the analysts who pay attention to Zodiac sign in the practice of analysis, but we think the obtained data merit being included in this report. In the pilot study of San Francisco analysts, Taurus and Virgo outnumbered the other signs. When these were combined with Capricorn under the element heading of earth signs and compared with fire, water and air signs, a greater than chance incidence of earth signs obtained. A similar preponderance of earth signs was found for the Los Angeles group. The total incidence of earth signs among California analysts was greater than chance expectancy to a statistically significant degree.

And how is it for New York and Europe? The predominating element sign among analysts in both London and on the Continent is water: Scorpio, Pisces and Cancer. New York does not conform with either California or Europe in this regard. Its slightly predominant element sign is fire, which we will recall is also the element category in which Jung's sign of Leo falls. Applying tests of statistical significance to these data shows a statistically significant difference at the level of .03 between California as one group and the other three locations grouped together as one group, with earth predominating in the California group and water in the outside-California group. Moreover, a statistically significant difference at the level of .02 was found between United States as one group and Europe as one group, with earth predominating in United States and water in Europe. So regardless of which grouping is used, a valid difference obtains, with California predominating in earth signs and Europe in water signs. The level of .02 indicates that the difference would occur by chance fewer than two times in one hundred comparable samples. It deserves noting that both earth and water are associated with the *feminine* principle.

Analytic Practice

We shall now look at the data on analytic practice of analysts. The first of the three lists of aspects of practice to be considered differentiates between kinds of patients one thinks one works well with and those one tries not to accept into one's practice. The eight categories of patients listed in the questionnaire were: children, adolescents, persons past 70 years of age, psychotics, alcoholics, character disorders, terminally ill, and hospitalized. Fewer than half of the respondents indicated they thought they worked well with any of these eight categories of patients. There were three categories which more than half of the respondents indicated they actually tried not to accept: children, alcoholics and hospitalized. The list was selective and did not include adult neurotics, probably the bulk of the practice of nearly all analysts.

The next section, considered the most significant of the threepart questionnaire, consists of 20 items such as the use of dreams, sandplay, active imagination, typology, comforting by touch, role playing. The respondent is asked to check each item according to whether he or she uses it with more than 50 percent of patients, or with 5 to 50 percent of patients, or with less than 5 percent of patients. For example, 90 percent of the analysts checked that they use dreams with more than half of their patients. This means, of course, that 10 percent of the analysts use dreams with fewer than half of their patients. Dream interpretation was the most universally used item on the list. The only other items used by the majority of analysts with more than half of their patients are making connections with reference to transference and making connections with reference to process (as opposed to content). Moreover, it is rare that an analyst does not refer to transference or does not refer to process in making connections or interpretations with at least some patients. So most analysts focus on transference and process, in addition to dreams of their patients. Sandplay, role playing and astrological signs are the least frequently used of the items listed.

The data for number of visits per week that patients are seen are of interest. One visit per week is the usual practice. Only 1 in 4 analysts sees more than half of their patients oftener than once per week, and only 1 in 10 sees the majority of their patients oftener than twice per week. These items are significantly related to geographical location of analyst; more than half of the London group see the majority of their patients oftener than twice per week. Frequency of visit is relatively high on the Continent. Frequency of visit is lowest for New York and Los Angeles.

Other statistically significant relationships between geographical location and practice of analyst are found for (1) typology, with highest use of typology in San Francisco and lowest in London; (2) self-revelation to patient by analyst which is highest for California and lowest for London and the Continent; (3) intense relationship with patient which is highest in San Francisco and lowest on the Continent; and use of body language in making interpretations which is highest in London and lowest in Los Angeles.

The third and final section of the questionnaire also has to do with kinds of practice but uses a different format—not as successful a one, I must admit. We were trying to study not only whether the analyst actually performs an item, as in the previous section, but what his or her experience is with the value of the item for patients. The list includes some items which might reflect adoption of, or new attitudes toward, different kinds of therapy which are today being used both exclusively and as adjuncts to the traditional one-to-one dialogue. The list of 16 items includes, for example, group therapy, family therapy, meditation, horoscopes, I Ching, body involvement techniques, psychiatric drug medication, sex therapy. The instructions are to check an item under the column labelled "self" if the respondent has performed the item for or with one or more patients; under "refer" if the respondent has referred one or more patients to someone else for it; and under "other" if neither "self" nor "refer" applies but the item has been found valuable for one or more patients. It can be seen that the criterion for checking was lenient: even if the item applied to just one of the analyst's patients, the appropriate checking could be made. Even so, more than half of the items remained unchecked by the majority of analysts. The three items checked the most frequently with approximately two-thirds of the analysts indicating they performed the item themselves or referred the patient out for the item were family therapy, group therapy, and psychiatric drug medication. And about half of the analysts checked self-performance or refer-to-others for psychological testing and I Ching.

Some significant relationships with geographical location of analyst were found for this section of items. Psychiatric drug medication, including by referral, is significantly more frequent in San Francisco than in the other groups. The practice of meditation is significantly more often used in connection with analysis in Los Angeles and on the Continent than in the other groups. The use of horoscopes and I Ching is significantly more frequent among analysts in Los Angeles and New York. We looked for patterns of similarities between the groups, such as are Los Angeles and San Francisco generally alike, or Los Angeles and New York, etcetera, but found no significant consistencies in these kinds of comparisons.

The next area of consideration, and the area in which we were initially the most interested, is the relationship between kind of practice and psychological type. Do extraverts do more group therapy and introverts more meditation in their practice? Do intuitive types focus on different aspects than do sensation types in analysis? Are feeling types and thinking types different from one another in their practice of analysis? Or isn't psychological type a significant variable in practice?

The methodology of analyzing the data for this part of the study was the most challenging, and we are indebted to Dr. Wayne DETLOFF of San Francisco for most of the planning for it.

Despite the fallibility of our indices, self-typing and Gray-Wheelwrights scores on the one hand and the checklists on the other, the data yielded some statistically significant measures of relationship between the two sets of variables: typology and analytic practice. Our focus will be limited to statistically significant results or especially relevant tendencies that approach statistical significance. Because of the large number of chi squares, some would be significant "by chance". We have allowed for this in evaluating the results by inspection for whether the statistics make sense in terms of consistency with other findings. I could go into this in more detail, but it makes for dull listening, so I am going to largely dispense with statistics and report the relationships descriptively. Perhaps it should be noted that the typology index we gave most credence to was where there was agreement between self-typing and G-W score. And the chi square probability we set for statistical significance was one of .05 or better, meaning that the indicated relationship would occur by chance fewer than 5 times in a hundred comparable samples.

There is considerable evidence that extraverts use more adjuncts to the analytic dialogue than do introverts. Extraverts more than introverts: (1) use verbal art forms and diaries, (2) enter into intense relationships with patients, (3) comfort by touching the patient, (4) use typology in making connections or interpretations. Although astrology is infrequently used by analysts, those who do use it are much more likely to be extraverted than introverted. In our study of California analysts we found that extraverts showed a higher regard for family therapy and group therapy than did introverts, but this relationship did not reach a statistically significant level in the international data. Two adjuncts which are more important to introverts than to extraverts are chirology or hand analysis, and graphology or hand-writing analysis. Neither of these is used by many analysts, but all 12 analysts who do use chirology themselves or have referred patients to others for it scored introvert on the G-W. And all 16 who do graphology themselves or have referred patients to others for it scored introvert on the G-W. No other significant relationships were found between attitude type and analytic practice.

Turning to the intuitive-sensation differentiation, we find that analysts with higher sensation like to work with character disorders more than do intuitives. The intuitive, on the other hand, likes to work with adolescents more than do sensates.

As it is for extraverts, it is the intuitives who use more adjuncts in their practice than do their counterparts. Intuitives as compared with sensates make more frequent use of (1) nonverbal art forms, (2) family therapy, (3) group therapy, (4) body involvement techniques, and (5) marathon therapy.

No statistically significant relationships between the feeling-thinking dichotomy and analytic practice were found.

So it is the extraverts and the intuitives as compared with introverts and sensates who are branching out and making use of more of the innovations that have been introduced into therapy in the last several years. Sensation dominated analysts work more with character disorders. Introverted analysts have a higher regard for chirology and graphology. Thinking and feeling are not significantly related to the items which we included in our questionnaire.

The Five Treatment Methods on Congress Program

As a final step we will summarize the findings of our study that are particularly relevant to the five treatment methods focused on at this congress. Use of dream analysis is nearly universal among the participating Jungian analysts; only ten percent do not use it with the majority of their patients, and only one analyst indicated using dream analysis rarely or not at all. No significant relationship between use of dream analysis and either geographical location or typology was demonstrated. Unfortunately, we have no data on the question arising so frequently at the first session of this congress: How many analysts specifically ask for dreams and if so, how many at the first meeting with the patient?

Active imagination was broken down in this study into sandplay, verbal art forms such as poetry, nonverbal art forms such as painting, and other forms of active imagination not included in those three. This last category showed the highest frequency of use, but none of the frequencies of use was high. Eighty-five percent of the participants use sandplay rarely or not at all. The enthusiastic response to Dr. AITE's paper suggests that use of sandplay may be increasing. Nearly half of the participants use verbal art forms rarely or not at all. About 25 percent of the analysts use nonverbal art forms rarely or not at all. And about 25 percent use "other" active imagination not included in the above rarely or not at all. As regards geographical location: Nonverbal art forms such as painting are used the most by New York, the home of Dr. Wallace, who presented the paper on art therapy. It is used the least by London. Verbal art forms are used the most by New York and the least by San Francisco and the Continent. Other forms of active imagination, including the kind discussed by Dr. von Franz, are used the most by New York and Los Angeles and least by London. As regards psychological type: Verbal art forms are used more by extraverts than by introverts; nonverbal art forms are used more by intuitives than by sensates.

The third subtopic of this Congress, alchemical themes, was not included in this study. However, the overall use of archetypes in making interpretations is a prevailing practice. Nearly one half of the participating analysts make use of archetypes with the majority of their patients. And only 10 percent make only rare use of archetypes in making interpretations. No significant relationships between use of archetypes and geographical location or typology were found.

Apparently child therapy is not a prevalent practice among the participating analysts. The majority of participants indicated they try not to accept children into their practice, and only about one fourth indicated they work well with children. The greatest interest in working with children was shown by Los Angeles and London, and the least by San Francisco and the Continent. No relationship with typology was found.

The fifth subtopic of this Congress is treatment of psychotics. More of the participants indicated interest in treating psychotics than in treating children. About one third believe they work well with psychotics. However, 40 percent indicate they try not to accept psychotics into their practice. No relationship with either geographical location or with typology was found.

These essences we have reported are to some extent isolated bits. Do they have an over-all significance? We think they do. We think they mirror that there are generally more differences in analytic practice within each geographical area than there are differences between the geographical areas, and that differences in typology, although sometimes important, are not the only differentiating personality factors. Furthermore, the results seem to be consistent with what has come out so frequently in this Congress: Jungian analysts generally respect the development of a variety of methods of analytic practice without losing sight of an over-riding confidence in what we might call a central or ongoing process which is unique for each individual and which is related to what Dr. Adler referred to in the opening of this Congress: the numinosum.

REFERENCES

Bradway, K. Jung's psychological types: classification by test versus classification by self. *Journal of Analytical Psychology*, 1964, 9, 129–135.

Bradway, K .and Detloff, W. K. Psychological types and their relationship to the practice of analytical psychology. *Professional Reports, Joint Annual Conference, March 1975*, 29–53. C. G. Jung Institute of San Francisco.

Bradway, K. and Detloff, W. K. Psychological types and their relationship to Jungian analysts classified by self and by test. *Journal of Analytical Psychology*, 1976, 21, 134–146.

Gray, H. and Wheelwright, J. B. Jung's psychological types, their frequency of occurrence. *Journal of General Psychology*, 1946, 34, 3–17.

Plaut, A. Analytical psychologists and psychological types: comments to a survey. *Journal of Analytical Psychology*, 1972, 17, 137–151.

Table 1

Percentages for Sixteen Basic Self-Types of 163 Analysts
(9 persons not completing the self-typing are not included)

I = Introvert, U = Intuitive

| IUF 18 | IUT 14 | EUF 7 | EUT 4 | IFS 5 | IST 7 | ETS 1 | ESF 3 |
| IFU 17 | ITU 10 | EFU 4 | ETU 2 | ISF 4 | ITS 1 | EST 1 | EFS 1 |

Totals

| 35 % | 24 % | 11 % | 6 % | 9 % | 8 % | 2 % | 4 % |

Table 2

Percentages for Kinds of Patients Analysts Work Well With
(172 Analysts: SF 63, LA 29, NY 25, London 30, Continent 25)

Instructions were: "Check to show kinds of patients with whom you think you work well, and those whom you try not to accept into your practice."

Work well with	I try not to accept	
22 %	59 %	Children
49 %	27 %	Adolescents
23 %	29 %	Past 70 years
35 %	40 %	Psychotic
12 %	63 %	Alcoholic
36 %	37 %	Character Disorders
26 %	24 %	Terminally ill
13 %	57 %	Hospitalized

Table 3
Percentages for Analysts Using Various Items in Their Practice

Instructions were: "Check each of the following according to the percentage of individual patients with whom you use each."

Used with more than 50 % of patients

    ↓   Used with less than 5 % of patients

91 %	1 %	Dreams
11 %	23 %	Expression in nonverbal art form (such as painting)
4 %	44 %	Expression in verbal art form (such as poetry)
2 %	86 %	Sand play
15 %	28 %	Active imagination (not included in above items)
15 %	37 %	Diaries or other written reports
3 %	73 %	Role playing
9 %	57 %	Comforting by touch
22 %	29 %	Self revelation to patient (such as dreams and feelings)
25 %	32 %	Intense relationship with patient
23 %	26 %	More than one visit per week
12 %	73 %	More than two visits per week

Interpretations or making connections in terms of:

46 %	11 %	Archetypes
60 %	5 %	Transference
23 %	37 %	Body language
12 %	54 %	Synchronicity
28 %	26 %	Typology
3 %	83 %	Astrological signs
55 %	10 %	Reference to process (as opposed to content)

Table 4
Percentages for Usefulness of Therapies or Therapy Adjuncts

Instructions were: "Check those items in the following list that you have found useful to one more of your patients:

under Self if you have performed the item for or with the patient,
under Refer if you have referred a patient to someone else for it,
under Other if neither Self nor Refer applies, but you have found a patient's experience with the item helpful to him/her."

Self or Refer	None*	
60 %	25 %	Family therapy
63 %	16 %	Group therapy
28 %	57 %	Confrontation therapy
14 %	66 %	Marathon therapy
32 %	56 %	Sex therapy or treatment of sexual dysfunctions
21 %	67 %	Behavior therapy
34 %	40 %	Body involvement therapy or techniques
9 %	79 %	Biofeedback
63 %	27 %	Drugs (Specific for psychiatric conditions)
18 %	73 %	Hypnosis
27 %	39 %	Meditation
51 %	42 %	Psychological testing
24 %	58 %	Horoscopes
7 %	81 %	Chirology (hand analysis or "palmistry")
9 %	79 %	Graphology (hand writing analysis)
50 %	29 %	I Ching
11 %	66 %	Tarot cards

* Indicates that none of the three choices was checked.

Table 5
Summary of Relationships Between Psychological Types
and Aspects of Analytical Practice

	I	E	U	S	F	T
Works better with						
Character Disorders				X		
Adolescent			X			
More frequently used						
Verbal Art Forms		X				
Diaries		/				
Role Playing			X			
Comforting by touch		/				
Intense Relationship		X				
Interpret: Typology		X				
Astrology		/				
Nonverbal Art Forms			X			
Higher Regard for						
Family Therapy			X			
Group Therapy			X			
Body Involvement Techniques			X			
Chirology	/					
Graphology	/					
Marathon Therapy			X			

I = Introvert; U = Intuitive
X = statistically significant at .05 level or better
/ = strong tendency

ON THE METHODOLOGY OF DREAM INTERPRETATION

Hans Dieckmann, Berlin

The literature on dreams has always been fascinated by the fact that our dream world is so different from that of conscious experience. Thus, in the literature too, emphasis is made of the fact that the ego complex dissolves in dreams, that a dissociation occurs, that ego boundaries no longer exist, or that the ego no longer commands the corresponding ability to co-ordinate the individual psychic components. KOHN-STAMM 1927 (1) writes for example: "The monarchistic rule of the collective psychic processes is eliminated and with it the conscious composition of our physical and psychic being which comprises the unity of the ego."

Freud was the first to consider dreams as a state similar to psychosis, and reference is constantly being made to the confused and seemingly senseless and abstruse dream world which it is so difficult for us to place within our waking consciousness. If one, however, follows a large number of human dreams over a very long period of time doubts appear as to this interpretation, and for some time I have been concerned with the question as to whether, as a result of the appearance of new qualities of experience and combinations of fantasy, we do not often overestimate the difference of dreams as opposed to our waking experience. It is quite certain that new and different qualities of experience which do not correspond to reality may appear in the dream ego. One need only think of dreams about the ability to fly which occur with great frequency during puberty, or of dreams about a meeting with a double, or of the splitting of the ego into two persons, one observing and one acting. Here we are clearly particularly fascinated by the extreme forms and metamorphoses of the ego. There is scarcely a dream book today which does not quote the famous dream of the Chinese philosopher Chuang Tzu in which he dreams that he was a butterfly, then adding the philosophical comment as to whether he was a man who had dreamed that he was a butterfly or a butterfly who dreamed he was a man. This is of course a most striking dream and it cannot be denied that there are such dreams. Nobody has, however, as yet, written about how frequent such dreams are, and in which people or related to which symptoms they occur. From my material of more than 50,000 patients' dreams, from knowledge of my own dreams and from questioning other colleagues I have established that such dreams are extremely rare. Throughout the period during which I have worked as an analyst I have met with only two such dreams, once in the case of a female addict who dreamed for example that she was a flower which could walk, and on the other occasion in the case of a female psychotic who dreamed she was a vase. Both of the cases which I observed also displayed in their waking experience severe dissociational disturbances in the ego complex, and it seems probable to me that such dreams only occur in serious psychic pathological states or, if we wish to believe the dream of Chuang Tzu, in personalities of an especially creative disposition who are capable of very unusual identification processes.

The behaviour of patients in their dreams is mostly extremely similar to that of their waking experience. The dream ego employs the same defence formations, experiences the same feelings and emotions as it would have experienced in a similar situation in reality too. Contrary to what is always stated, the ego complex possesses, with certain restrictions, a far greater measure of consistency and stability and is largely concerned to maintain its function even in the dream ego. This does not, however, exclude the fact that very clear relaxing processes are present and that dreams are well suited to conveying repressed or new qualities of experience to the ego complex.

In an earlier paper (c.) I described these very processes of integration in the dream ego. I came to the conclusion at that time that most processes of transformation during analysis pass over the dream ego via which they most easily reach the area of conscious change. In the experiential and behavioural qualities of the dream ego we find at first as a rule a confirmation of neither the wish-fulfulment theory nor of the theory of compensatory function, but in dreams, too, the dream ego attempts to maintain the continuity of the ego complexes. A 14 year old girl dreamed that while she was going upstairs in an institutional home another child caught hold of her and she was involved in a terrible fight with the other child. In reality this girl was liable to have fierce attacks of aggression as soon as she was touched by anyone else. A patient who constantly seeks to escape from his problems will at first do so in dreams too and will not make a heroic stand against his opponents. In a series of dreams which I described in the paper mentioned above a female patient with an extremely strong oral inhibition dreamed at first that she was always in empty shops where she could buy nothing or got nothing because other people had pushed in front of her. It was only during the course of a long analysis that she dreamed of buying what she wanted in a shop at last and getting it too. Promptly after this dream there appeared a corresponding change in behaviour in the patient's waking experience. The dream of the sexually inhibited philistine who, lying in bed beside his unattractive spouse of long-standing, dreams of orgies with other girls does not exist in reality. It is much more likely that in the case of a sexually inhibited person a long analysis and a corresponding relaxation are necessary before dreams appear in which he can experience sex. This would mean: only when the dream ego registers a problem can the problem enter the person's consciousness. (b.)

The continuity which the ego complex maintains in waking experience and in dreams seems to me to bring very considerable advantages in method. For it becomes possible at this level for the patient to talk about the parallels which are mostly clearly evident between his customarily existent schema of experience and reaction and his dream ego. This developing of similarities and parallels leads then on the one hand to the patient's discovering recognizable qualities in dreams which were to him unintelligible. On this basis the first bridge of relationship and understanding can be built to dreams. The ego feeling which very clearly occupies the dream ego facilitates this process. The unusual, curious and strange experiences, motifs and symbols ensure on the other hand that the relaxation processes which we desire in the analysis can begin, permitting the confrontation with suppressed or repressed psychic material or enabling the ego to concern itself with and to integrate the new acquisitions necessary for its situation. Thus the old rule of thumb formerly established by JUNG (3) that the object level is to be interpreted before the subject level gains a validity and meaning which differ from the mere confrontation with personally related people. For if one considers firstly as objects the figures and symbols, with the exception of the dream ego, which appear in dreams at the start of an analytic therapy, concentrates on the dream ego and emphasises the continuity of the ego complex, one gives the patient a greater amount of reassurance to move into the inner world which was up to that point incomprehensible and unknown to him. This is all the more important as we know that practically every patient who comes to us has firstly an ego weakness and the analytic process aims, at the same time, on the one hand at ego strengthening and stabilizing processes, but on the other hand has as its goal the possibility of confronting unconscious material.

It is this missing ego stability which is the reason why we only seldom get really constructive co-operation from the patient as regards his unconscious material and his dreams at the beginning of an analytic therapy. As a rule we meet at first with quite definite defence processes and defence formations which we are constantly having to deal with later during the course of the therapy. I should like to talk first about the most usual and frequent manifestations of this defence. For this I will use the typological model since it best describes, with certain restrictions, the ego functions and defence, and I want to demonstrate besides how the continuity even of this ego function is maintained to include dreaming. In this I will restrict myself to the dealings of the conscious ego complex with the dream material. A typological diagnosis based on the contents of dreams alone still does not exist. I will proceed mainly from the attitudinal types introversion and extraversion and will finally make a few remarks about the functional types.

The dreams of the introvert and his attitude to his dreams may be, in my experience, of two characteristic types. Firstly, as is usually described for this type, it is possible that the introvert may live more in his dream world than in reality. He moves in this world as though in a closed system. Such patients often produce at the beginning of the analysis a variety of extremely lively and colourful dreams and move about in these dreams as if they were at home there. Whenever they produce free ideas or amplifications they do so abundantly but it is noticeable that these ideas have, if at all, only a slight connection with exterior reality. Most characteristic is the introvert to whom, in connection with a dream motif, only another dream occurs and then, about this dream, another. In extreme cases it seems at first as though this type is wrapped up in his dreams as if in a cocoon and one can move about in this cocoon in an extremely interesting, colourful and lively manner–one can absorb the other in a wealth of exciting and inspiring amplifications (especially if the analyst too is an introvert) –, but nothing at all changes, and it seems almost as though a life outside the dream motifs no longer exists (3). If this type of defence is more prominent then the intervention of the analyst intending to refer to objective associations is of no use. How I deal with these patients as a rule is to allow such a process to continue for a while until it is more than clear to both sides and then I interpret it directly in order at the same time to discuss with the patient the extent to which he persists in his real life in such a regressive introversion, the size of the gaps in his perception as regards the environment, and to what extent his pathological symptoms perhaps relate to this problem.

The second form of introverted defence is that dreams and fantasies have no relationship to the ego complex and that the relationship has broken. Most characteristic is the type of day-dreaming in these patients. They have fantasies, and indeed in abundant and superabundant quantity, so that they may lead to considerable disturbances in work and concentration, but they do not really know what sort of fantasies they have. If one mentions the fact to them, and they often seem lost in thought, they return to reality and often have great difficulty in remembering that they had just a fantasy, of which they can as a rule only just grasp the remaining fragments. It seems similar with the dreams of these patients. They often relate that they have had long and detailed dreams and that they can remember having dreamed all night but that they could not remember anything. Only after further questioning does the fact perhaps emerge that quite small fragments are still present, and it is characteristic of these patients that in relating these fragments they insist that these were only quite unimportant parts of the real dreams and that they cannot remember the real dreams. It is quite possible that one will get no dreams at all from these patients over a long period of time. The first task of analytic therapy is then to explain how this break with fantasy has arisen and what fears lie behind it causing this form of defence against the patient's own fantasy world. It is typical of these patients that their defence against fantasies is not simultaneously accompanied by prejudice against them, but they value dreams and fantasy very highly, consider them to be of some worth and are convinced like all introverts that they are really more important than external realities. Thus one also finds in these people clear signs of regret that they cannot remember their dreams and fantasies no matter how hard they try.

The extravert too may react to a corresponding disturbance in the relationship with the unconscious with both mechanisms described, namely with dream superfluity on the one hand and a blockade on the other. But both have a different character in the extravert. The dream flood is more readily found in those patients who have strongly hysterical structural constituents. JUNG (4) indeed described extraversion at first in connection with severe hysteria. The patient can in extreme cases fill whole therapy sessions with dreams which are often exceptionally colourful and lively but mostly divided up into many confusing episodes. These dreams, however, stand as a sort of foreign body beside the ego complex which is concerned with quite different things and has no use for dreams. The abundance of the dreams thus becomes a defence in that it is intended that the analytic consultation be filled up by them so that no time remains to confront the problems contained in them or the attitude to events in the world outside. The extravert blockade between ego complex and dream also seems different from that already described for the introvert. Although patients here too remember only insignificant dream fragments or no dreams at all, it is clear that they were by no means immersed in a fantasy world which ran parallel to consciousness. They do not create the impression of the introverted whose souls have flown away like exotic birds, to speak the language of primitive peoples, but they simply orientate themselves towards the external object. Fantasies or dreams are for them the famous worthless nonsense for which they were taken to be in rationalist circles during the last century. As the extraverts' libido is so exclusively orientated towards the external object they are not able to pay attention to their dreams or to remember them. A large section of the patients who admit during the consultation "I dreamed something but I forgot it again at once" belong to this type. A patient whom I have described in detail elsewhere (5) produced during the first phase of treatment, if at all, only dreams which consisted at most of one sentence, as for example "swam in the water with a lot of women". Only through persistently recording the motifs contained in the dreams and through an analysis of his defence was it possible to remove the dream barrier, and in due course this relatively simple and uneducated patient produced lively and impressive dreams until his symptoms subsided, his behaviour and experience had altered and he was well again. Then he ceased to dream, that is to say to observe his dreams.

It is quite evident that the forms of relationship disorders of the attitudinal types described here clearly correspond to the narcissistic disorders described by KOHUT (6). This is only to be expected since the attitudinal type is always built upon the subject-object relationship, and any deep disturbance of these functions must always come within the range of narcissism. It is also clear that this is respectively either a question of a partial inflation or alienation in EDINGER's (7) sense and that the disorder at the core lies in the region of the ego-self axis (8). This also explains the fact that the disorders between the ego complex on the one hand and the recall, understanding and processing of dreams on the other are by no means easy to remove but often, especially in severely disturbed cases, last throughout a whole analysis. The analyst who loses patience here and tries to correct the situation by means of behaviour directives receives for his pains symptom displacement, strengthened resistance or the breaking-off of the analysis.

Methodologically all these disorders require to be treated differently. As usual in analysis there is no general know-how. Added to this is the factor that these differing forms of disturbed relationships to the unconscious have in each individual case their own individual, causal-genetic background. Although the analysis should not in our opinion be conducted purely regressively in childhood, this background should be known all the same. The analyst must be aware of why and in which phase specifically this defence against the unconscious appeared and why it was the only appropriate defence for the psyche against still greater damage. This insight into the meaning of the resistance allows the analyst to tolerate concentrating on the now and here and not to expose a still weak and unstable ego, which was unable previously to develop its functions, to an influence of the unconscious to which it is not yet equal. This thoroughly conforms to JUNG's (9) explanation in the "Psychology of Transference" that a purpose of resistance consists in protecting the damaged ego functions and that it must therefore be respected.

As far as the functional types are concerned they too react respectively in a specific and characteristic form to the phenomenon of the dream. There is not room here to go into detail on the type-specific characteristics of dreams and on the manner in which the ego complex deals with dreams when certain typologies dominate. I will then restrict myself to an accentuated description of the typical and prominent feature in each case.

The thinking type is notable for the fact that, apart from his being annoyed and irritated by the "senseless" and illogical structure of his dreams, he omits the emotions. One gets from him as a rule a description of the events in the dream from which elements which are often unclear or irrational or do not fit into the action are left out. These, as well as the accompanying feelings, may be ascertained only through corresponding questioning during the course of the session.

The feeling type too often suppresses the unclear and irrational dream elements which do not fit the context. His descriptions of dreams are notable for their abundant and varied narration of feelings and sensations. In an extreme case I had experience of a female patient who described in constantly varying hues taking up two A4 pages a state of feeling connected with a meeting with another person in the dream.

In the case of the intuitive type it is the fascination with the unusual or indeterminate which is conspicuous. It makes no difference whether he has more fantasy dreams or more everyday dreams; he is impressed by what seems to him new, unknown or outside the compass of the normal, this making it difficult however to process them with him. In the next dream something new is bound to appear again and if it turns out not to be new, but the same problem in different symbols, he answers mostly by withdrawing his interest. In contrast to the more rational types one seldom hears from these patients, at least in the early phases of treatment, the complaint that the analytic process is too disconnected, that too many different themes appear in the dreams and that no problem is properly dreamed to a conclusion or processed.

The sensation type portrays the factual material of his dreams true to type. Typical for the extravert sensation type is, according to my observations, an accumulation of dreams which report external daily events quite or wholly realistically just as they really took place. One can make use of this only if one can make the patient think why is unconscious selected just these events and not others. The more introverted he is, however, the more magical, mythological or ludicrous his dreams may become, although here too value is attached to the detailed description of objects, persons or symbols. One may for example learn from him exactly what clothing a certain person was wearing but hardly how he affected the dream ego.

It goes without saying that all these descriptions only ever occur in pure form in extreme cases. As in reality, all four functions are involved in every dream experience and the auxiliary functions are especially involved in the description of dreams in the analytic situation. The typological picture only results from a certain accentuation and is especially clear as long as the other functions have not already been developed alongside the main function in the analytic process.

The ego complex must apparently be regarded as one of the most stable points in dreams. This is necessarily so, since the alien experience must be recorded by something or opposed to a supporting ego for it to be registered or processed at all. As long as anything at all is experienced the bearer of the experience is always the identical ego (10). Within the analytical process a direct relaxation of the ego structures now takes place under the protection of the transference and countertransference situation. The ego can give up its defence mechanisms and, especially in neurosis, broadly develop damaged and restricted functions, relinquish controls and organisation structures, give up ego boundaries and admit new experiental contents. Correspondingly, according to de SANCTIS (11), dream consciousness develops parallel to ego consciousness and consciousness and ego are combined in the closest possible way.

Thus, with restrictions, emerges the methodological demand for greater accentuation of the dream ego in dream interpretation and dream processing and the need to place the dream ego in the centre of the development and maturation process of individuation. What the ego cannot do in dreams it cannot do in reality either, and so long as it has to seek to escape from certain experiences there, too much is demanded of the patient if we except him to integrate them. A female patient, severely disturbed in the formation of hetero-sexual relationships, dreamed during the first phase of analysis almost exclusively of men who dominated, persecuted and raped her and against whom she was powerless, which corresponded to the beginning of the breach by the patriarchal uroborus of the dual mother-daughter union according to NEUMANN (12). Only when dreams occured in which these male figures were less brutal, supporting and assisting figures were present and she was able to confront her pursuers in the dreams was she able to relate to men in reality and to her unconscious. Up to this point she had built up between herself and men a wall of defence which could not be breached.

The same is true of the integration of new feelings. A 40 year old businessman, who has leading the life of a totally overstressed and harassed manager, dreamed: "I am in Liv Ulmann's house (Scenes from a Marriage). I have a very warm, tender relationship with her. She takes me into her bedroom. I ask her where her husband, in the dream Hans Albers, is. She says he has gone out and is angry at not having obtained any theatre tickets. In such cases he usually got drunk. I was worried that he might come back and did not allow our activity to develop any further. I persuaded her to leave the house and to look for a quiet undisturbed place."

The women in his earlier dreams were always purely sexually seductive and anonymous figures with whom he went to bed without much ado. In this dream he encountered for the first time an anima figure who represents for him inner confrontation and individuation. On the other hand, his shadow, which had previously exerted a strong inflationary force on him, is the impulsive and primitively sentimental actor Hans Albers, who is separate from his dream ego and whom he tries to avoid. He is also able to, and this is for him a completely new acquisition, set aside a sexual impulse in an ego syntonic decision and look for a quiet place. From this dream on it became possible to talk to him about these things and he was able to reduce his frenzied activity and to develop more feeling in isolated peaceful oases at first.

It is of course a prerequisite for the processing of such transformations in the ego complex that the dream series be observed (13), which in a current analysis with a busy analyst is not easy. It would be too much to expect an analyst to remember all the dreams of all his patients. Yet there are, however, certain signals enabling one not to overlook such dreams as show clear definite changes in experience and behaviour. Firstly the dreamer realizes it himself and he experiences such a dream as important, lively, lasting or something similar. There is a different accentuation of meaning without it having to be necessarily a question of direct archetypal material. Secondly one should train oneself to a certain extent to notice these processes. With the appropriate direction of attention one relatively quickly gains insight into the typical patterns of the dream ego, as we retain them for the conscious ego, and we begin to notice even slight changes in these patterns just like a new hair style. It is methodologically helpful to accentuate these points by drawing the patient's attention to them or asking him directly whether he has ever dreamed about himself like that before.

It remains only for me to touch briefly upon the problem of interpretation at the subject level, which is apparently somewhat neglected in such an approach. Gestalt therapy (14) has recently taken up work at the subject level particularly intensively as a method. The patients are requested to imagine the experience of the other figures appearing in their dreams, as for example related persons or animals etc., and thereby to acquire, often most successfully, different possibilities of comprehension and experience. The patients often find this most impressive, to which must be added that many Jungians were doing this long before gestalt therapy. The effect achieved by this is, however, in my experience only transient. Especially in severe neuroses the ego establishes its former boundaries very quickly again, and the method does not spare one the laborious and often lengthy process of working through at all levels the meaning of the dream symbols.

On the other hand, to emphasize the subject level in the methodology of the therapeutic process always seems to be important when, in EDINGER's sense of "psychic life cycles," the phases of "reconnection" with the self and the production of "original wholeness" are concerned. Thus the ego function is strengthened making it possible to abandon defence systems, to give of oneself, to make one's own boundaries more permeable and to experience the relationship to the self. This adds methodologically, with certain restrictions, a new aspect to the interpretation of the subject level and also to the active image forming of dream contents at the subject level, as opposed to the old rule that the subject level is to be used only when the object level has been exhausted as regards interpretation.

NOTES

(a.) Lecture delivered at the 7th International Congress of Analytical Psychology, Rome 1977.

(b.) The ego too is an archetype and the dream ego an image of the archetype. So it is not surprising if it is the dream ego which in many cases forms a bridge via which new material is absorbed into the archetypal energy field of the ego complex.

(c.) Thomas Kirsch: Dreams and psychological types. Lecture delivered at the 7th International Congress, Rome 1977.

REFERENCES

1 Kohnstamm: zit. Siebenthal Die Wissenschaft vom Traum (Springer, Berlin 1953)
2 Dieckmann, H.: Integration process of the ego-complex in dreams, J. analyt. Psychol. 10: No. 1 (1965)
3 Jung, C. G.: Gesammelte Werke, vol. 8 (Rascher, Zürich 1967)
4 Jung, C. G.: Gesammelte Werke, vol. 6 (Rascher, Zürich 1960)
5 Dieckmann, H.: Über einige Beziehungen zwischen Traumserie und Verhaltensänderungen in einer Neurosenbehandlung. Z. psychosom. Med. 1962: Okt.-Dez.
6 Kohut, H.: Narzissmus (Suhrkamp, Frankfurt 1973)
7 Edinger, E. S.: Ego and archetype (Putnam's Sons. New York 1972)
8 Neumann, E.: Ursprungsgeschichte des Bewußtseins (Rascher, Zürich 194?)
9 Jung, C. G.: Gesammelte Werke, vol. 16 (Rascher, Zürich 1958)
10 Jung, C. G.: Gesammelte Werke, vol. 6 (Rascher, Zürich 1960)
11 Sanctis, S. de: E sogni e il sonno nell'isterismo e nella epilessia (Roma 1896)
12 Neumann, E.: Zur Psychologie des Weiblichen; in Umkreisung der Mitte (Rascher, Zürich 1953)
13 Dieckmann, H.: Träume als Sprache der Seele (Bonz, Stuttgart 1972)
14 Perls, F. S.: Gestalttherapie in Aktion (Klett, Stuttgart 1974)

THE ARCHETYPAL SPHERE OF EFFECT
IN THE INITIAL PHASE
AND IN THE EVOLUTION OF THE PROCESS.

Ursula Eschenbach, Stuttgart

In every neurosis the archetypal sphere of effect is set in motion, thereby leading to the acquiring of complexes which build up in layers above it and which are situated in a permanently autonomous area of tension and, as the symptoms emerge, demand integration.

The archetypal sphere of effect manifests itself in the unconscious projections from the field of energy of the entire matriarchal and patriarchal archetypes and of the Self. This enables one to see the internal and external aspects of the patient as a system of relationships. The potential of the individual emerges in the differentation of the separate areas of symbols, as do the neurotic mechanisms that impede individual growth.

From the energic point of view, it is from the archetypal field of effect that the healing motivation emerges, and it acquires its own specific symbolic language through the maze of the neurotically charged complexes.

In the course of a series of comparisons made over a number of years we have observed that there is remarkable similarity in the way that quite specific stages occur in the treatment of children when the therapy is carried out primarily via an understanding of symbols.

"It does not matter that the symbolism was not clear to the consciousness of the child, for the emotional effect of symbols does not depend on conscious understanding." (C. G. Jung, Complete Works, Vol. 4 Freud and Psychoanalysis, p. 215, para. 490)

This raised the following question: is there such a thing as a specific process for the course and healing of neurosis?

These observations were based on the treatment of children and young people, with a particularly close examination of the individual stages in children up to 10 years of age.

This showed that after the early developmental stage of the child, the 10th year seems to be one of the most significant threshold situations in the overall psychic development of the human being. The psyche seems to be particularly vulnerable at this age, so that in therapy we have, whenever possible, proceeded to discourage such sweeping changes as changing house, separation of the parents by divorce or any other similarly traumatic separations.

But even after the 10th year we have been able to observe, with varying degrees of clarity, fragments of these phases of the treatment, often only fleetingly or on close scrutiny of unconscious remarks. The greater the energic distance between the conscious ego and the unconscious sphere of effect the slighter generally is the flexibility of the ego in relation to direct contact, to the dynamics of the transcendent function or to the "abaissement du niveau mental". But it is precisely here that we can find the real bridge to the healing of the neurotic disorders.

The stages of the process

The decisive factor in these stages of the process is the symbolic phenomenology. It can always be recognised when it becomes apparent in its specific content as the statement of one of the stages to be described. In order to bring a certain order into our observations in this multifacted field of treatment, we have dealt with the individual stages of the process under the following headings:

1. The Initial Phase.

The initial phase comprises the early period of the treatment, with the initial events usually being expressed in the form of a "symbol scene". An initial image may be repeated at later stages, usually at the onset of a new phase of development. The therapeutic symbol contact is a decisive indicator here. For even in this primary relationship, the psychic area of reception of new models of behaviour begins, especially through the transference and countertransference situation. When the "right" material is offered, it is immediately seized upon by the child and responded to in the form of dialogue reactions. This material emerges from a recognition of the symbol language.

For symbols are basic impulses of the unconscious and are indicative of a definite direction of the individual development and thus the individuation process. What is of vital importance and essential to the therapy is the effectiveness of the symbols, which can be seen again and again. They trigger off a dynamic mental process the meaning of which can be recognised as a path and an experience.

It is particularly in the initial phase in the child that the whole psychic cosmos can be seen, with its archetypal potential. Yet it is not always easy to judge the undifferentiatedness of the basic potential, especially for an adult, in this case the therapist, whose consciousness is already oriented towards one single facet that is more or less clear. Nevertheless, we were able to observe on many occasions that the child responded with an overwhelming flow of psychic energy to the scope of the creative possibilities made available to him. Finally, it was constantly being manifested that the neurotic symptom receives its real motivation from the archetypal fields of effect, in other words from the probably inexhaustible source of energy of the psyche.

What we understand by initial events is the emergence of the matriarchal and patriarchal spheres of effect, usually involving a form of self symbolism, the symbolic representation of the symptom or the modalities of the fields of disturbance and the first indications of the individual dynamic process of the individual course of treatment.

The initial images have therefore, as their symbolic content, the sum total of the diagnostic-therapeutic indications for the course of the process.

Here is an example from the case history of the treatment of a 9-year old boy with the following symptoms: bed-wetting, problems at school, violent outbursts of anger. Problems at school are the clearest way of warning the parents that something is wrong. They are easy to detect and are a source of shame because they are apparent to others. Violent anger breaks out when a complex is hit upon and it is sure to hit on a complex in the opposite. The symbolism of bed-wetting comprises the great symbolic image of water, for depth, transparency, receptivity, fertility and externally induced dynamics all prevail. Psychodynamically speaking, it can be the border-line situation between conscious and unconscious, between the matriarchal and the patriarchal. The archetypal sphere of effect to be expected could be the parental archetype in its earliest undifferentiated form of the primeval parents. This archetype presents itself as the intact birth shrine so as to transcend the more or less disturbed sphere of parental experience that is always found in such a symptom. This releases the ego consciousness and sets it on its creative path.

In the first session Johannes did nothing except shoot with the guns and make a lot of noise, the expression in his eyes being enigmatic and fearful. He left the session without saying goodbye. This behaviour was already a response to his being allowed to show his fear and to the fact that this fear was not referred to; it also revealed his fear of what the treatment would lead to—his positive development. Johannes soon showed signs of rapid regression and played intensively with water and sand play. The primal model of union and separation thus revealed openly the real sign of the symptom: the personal sphere of parental relationships was lacking in maternal warmth and depth and was also without paternal protection and constructive creativity. The line of defence of the this child's psyche lay in the harsh battlefield of a failed marriage. But from the unconscious field of knowledge it symbolised the embryonic primeval image of wholeness: the child took sand in his right hand, water in his left and put them together, saying: now they can mix.

One so often has the impression that children are the wise men of this century (1).

In another case the following puppet games are described, in which the archetypal spheres of effect and thus the internal plan for the course of treatment are presented:

12th session

The 6-year old boy opens the curtain of the puppet theatre and says: "It's dark, but God can still see everything." Then, very softly, after a pause: "Maybe not, if we make ourselves really tiny?" He storms out of the puppet theatre, runs around wildly and bangs against the door several times.

Interpretation: This spontaneous statement may be translated as follows: only by regressing into being small, in other words with the mother or inside the mother, can one save oneself from the "great father" i.e. the step forward into the conscious patriarchal sphere. At any rate, the main danger lies outside at the door, at the exit. The second game deals expressly with his Oedipal situation; with the Hansel and Gretel fairy tale as a background. This was in the next session.

13th session

The child is playing and tells a story: "The witch is lurking behind a tree. She wants to catch Punch and eat him up . . . like in Hansel and Gretel. Those are wicked parents, leaving their children alone in the forest, and at night, too. But the moon is kind. The witch is stupid, though. She does not notice that the robber is stealing all her nice things, a whole bag full. But the witch has a magic wand in her apron pocket and she puts a spell on the robber and turns him into a little man. He cannot carry the bag now and she catches him. He is a mouse."

Interpretation

It is difficult, well-nigh impossible to break free of the magic powers, i.e. of the magic sphere of the negatively charged matriarchal sphere of effect. Granted, there are great treasures, that is, powers, to be found there and the anima sphere in the symbolic interpretation of the "good moon" promises some development, but the apron strings still have the upper hand. The phallic image of the mouse shows the situation at present of the overcoming, by means of the symbolic background, of the all-sheltering but also devouring Earth-womb as the home of the mouse. The maturing motif of the Hansel and Gretel fairy tale means the overcoming of the oral fixation and thus the dominating fascination, with the aid of the anima figure Gretel.

The third puppet game in the 15th session hints at the broad outline of his inner quest. The child is playing and relates:

"Punch is on a treasure hunt. It's very dangerous. He has no idea where the treasure is. Perhaps it's buried. But there must be wild animals there. Here comes the crocodile. It's a dragon now and he has

64

an awfully long prickly tail. He can catch everyone with it and eat them up. But Punch pokes his eyes out so that he can't see any more. Then Punch is very tired. Blood is pouring out of all his many wounds and he is in great pain. But he has to fight on, for a big lion comes along. He is the King of all the animals and he is very fierce and dangerous and roars loudly. But Punch is a good shot and he shoots at the lion and hits him. But the lion is not dead and he starts talking. He can talk just like a man. Perhaps he is under a spell. Before he dies, he tells Punch where the treasure is. And Punch puts on the lion's skin and goes on his way and everyone is frightened of him."

Interpretation: A threshold situation actually means discriminating and fighting, or being involved in a conflict. Self-discovery can only be achieved by surving a downfall. There has to be fear, need, wounds, aggression and the overcoming of obstacles: for three days and nights Wotan hung on the tree of the World Ash, the tree of knowledge, with his head bowed, till he learnt the secret of the runes, the secret of the word, of the logos.

After the initial phase the second stage begins at about the 20th session.

2. *Latency or testing phase or area of receptivity:*

This phase is usually less remarkable than the often rather dramatic initial phase. The play phenomenology in this phase can be very varied, but usually reveals the modalities that belong more to the psychic field of energy of the personal unconscious. The depth of the initial phase, which is often so startling, with its maximum demands on the whole breadth of the diagnostic-therapeutic field, often shows a levelling-off here leading to the important questions of relating: who are you? what are you like? what is different here? For example, games with partners are often chosen, sometimes there are conversations, the child often reads or occupies himself with similar activities; here it is generally gain and loss that are being tested. The ego seems to be testing itself in the conscious field of contact and testing the therapist to see how much he can take. It is precisely during this period that the sphere of spiritual receptivity in the temenos of the treatment often crops up but it calls for really close scrutiny to detect it, for although the symbols are very specific, they are also at times either fleetingly apparent or disguised. Usually something is hidden in the sand or the cupboard, and it is not to be dug or taken out. For instance, an image may appear that will unconsciously represent the phallic procreator and/or the creative receiver. It can occur in a puppet or Punch and Judy game or in sand play, but also in a dream as with adults. The therapist is often called upon to take part in intensive searches, but under no circumstances must he find what is undoubtedly there. Here particularly it is very important to acknowledge the secret and to keep it; not to interpret it.

Oddly enough, and yet in a very striking way, after about 9 months there often appears a birth image, albeit disguised and only apparent to the perceptive observer. One of the secrets of pregnancy is the non-verbal contact. Silence must reign when the mystery reveals itself.

Here is an example from a case history:

25th session

After a flood in the sandbox which has wiped out a whole town, the 6-year old boy buries a glass marble deep in the sand and says: "That is my treasure. Nobody must find it except me." Then he seizes the pistol and aims directly at the stomach of the lady therapist. He leaves with a laugh, saying: "But that does not hurt . . ."

The psychodynamics of the whole process is autonomously guided in such a way that the psyche's ability to regress seems to have the function of allowing the energic flow of libido to return to the neurotic fixations; then, by gradual overcoming of the inhibitions arising from anxiety mechanisms, it can bring about an activation of the complex fields. It is precisely this anxiety, activated once again by such an inner search, that brings tremendous pressure to bear on the ego, which frequently responds by manifestations of depression. The extent to which the ego is able to overcome the depression and arrive at the threshold of anxiety, (acquiring so much strength through the psychic energy thereby activated that the anxiety threshold can be crossed) corresponds exactly to the extent to which the obstructing complex can be penetrated. Once this breakthrough has been made into the healing sphere of the archetypal sphere of effect, creative energy can then pour into the conscious. This involves dominating the negative aspects of the archetypal spheres of effect. In dealing with aggression, struggles, violent outbursts of anger, destructive feelings and murder, Man's powers of defence against his own darker side are put to the test. In other words, the ego is no longer powerless against the unconscious, and can, in C. G. Jung's words:

"... beget a new and fruitful life in that region of the psyche which has hitherto lain fallow in darkest unconsciousness and under the shadow of death" (C. G. Jung, Complete Works, Vol. 12, p. 437).

The more clearly the aggressive potential can be projected onto the play material and also onto the immediate situation in the therapeutic treatment, the more the ego becomes burdened. Only then are the complex-ridden, dormant, unconscious guilt feelings offered to the ego for integration. The handling of the energy-laden inferiority complexes can transform them with the aid of the newly-discovered potential.

It is true that with an individual range of variation, not only of child neuroses and their victims but also of therapists, the living dynamic of the phrase "as a rule" must apply. (I would remind the reader of the transference and counter-transference, the complex confrontations thereby involved, the ego functions in particular and the spheres of effect of typology). Nevertheless, despite the concept of "as a rule," it has become apparent that the actual process begins at about the 30th hour with the spiral movement of the regression phase–the 3rd phase of negative and positive regression.

It must be pointed out to the beginner that neither in the separate stages nor in the overall process are there such things as linear developments, but that the lines of development proceed from areas or layers of development, as we have termed them. In actual fact, especially with the abundance of material, this gives rise to confusion and lack of clarity. This is why the recognising of symbolic phenomenology is of the greatest assistance. The symbolic phenomenology of the negative regression comprises above all the whole broad field of the struggle, with the variations being chosen from the sphere of development of human history. When this occurs, it often looks at though children become the medium of an archetypal dynamic, with spiritual images being formed as unconsciously as emotions and affects, which are simply acted out in a release of tension and can in no way be registered, let alone considered, as personal experience.

These struggles, which are to be viewed as risking the regression to anxiety-inducing neurotic fixations and the negative aspects of the archetypal spheres of effect; dragons, crocodiles and witches etc. are usually collective, group-oriented, anonymous and murderous. Each side simply kills the other. This can be repeated several times in the course of one session when the dead come alive again. At the beginning there is not even any direction: enemies come from left and right, from all sides, even from above and below. The aggression seems emptied of feeling, with a tremendous amount of anxiety being subdued and restrained. Then the fighting games become more differentiated: groups are formed, then leaders are chosen, there are one-to-one fights, and finally the great arena of death, which devours all indiscriminately, can be abandoned.

It is particularly during this period that there arise formations of images of wholeness or self symbols, which must be studied very closely by the therapist as they are constellations of warning and protecting symbols about extremely dangerous descents into the depths of the unconscious. At this stage, the therapy should concentrate on dealing with the symbol rather than the interpretation.

The change into positive regression manifests itself in a symbolism that transforms itself into a positive one. From the point of view of the dynamic process, it is the dipping into the intact archetypal sphere which is experienced without fear. As a sign of things to come there are indications, for example, of the life-giving or providing matriarchal aspect instead of the devouring and clinging one, or instead of the castrating and destructive dominating figure there is a creative, ordering principle.

Here is a brief example from a case history of the treatment of a 9-year old boy with a difficult problem of aggression. It occurred after several weeks of fighting games:

56th session

After the usual start with the puppet theatre, where all the puppets are thrown out, the child, in a totally different voice, asks the therapist to make some broth and to darken the room. He lights a candle and falls under the spell of the giant shadow figures on the wall, which he calls "the mysterious ghosts". With his hands he changes the ghosts into bears and giants. A hitherto unknown mood of closeness and confidence is created and the therapist has the feeling that something new is starting. The therapist and the boy play with the shadows, allow themselves to be frightened by them and yet at the same time dominate them by controlling the movements. In a whisper Markus asks the therapist to eat out of the same dish with him, then together they go into the puppet theatre to escape from the "wicked mother bear shadow". The she-bear comes along but is appeased with the remains of the broth. The tense atmosphere in the room and the feelings of the therapist, cooped up in a small room with a child bubbling over with life and yet whispering mysteriously, created a sensation of a definite regeneration. The therapist had the impression that it was a turning-point both for the child and for the course of treatment.

In this process the child seems to be immersed in total regression, in a form of relationship in which at the same time his ego appears clearly constellated.

From this point on, the hitherto essentially negative side of the symbolism begins to move over into its positive aspect. Markus allies himself with the therapist against imaginary enemies, and his extremely malicious aggression in the confrontation with the evil powers is now expressed more openly, and the partner is recognised as an opposite.

This phase of the regression comprises a period of 70 to 100 hours, with the negative regression usually reaching its highpoint in about the 50th session.

Regressions that appear after this are always to be regarded as the onset of new stages of development and often serve the purpose of recovery and regeneration, with necessary introversion to the archetypal spheres of effect.

When the positive regression, and thus the attendant progression, begins, it is vitally important to keep an eye on how the parents are cooperating. The child's symptoms were specifically signals to the parents. Thus they generally become "the revealed secret" of the family set-up, creating unconscious and often conscious guilt feelings but also bind energies at the cost of the creativity of the family members. One can be sure that at the time of the final positive regression and progression the family structure will be jolted for all to see. The stereotyped phrases and roles no longer fit, normal procedures crumble and the whole family mechanism is disengaged. Here at the latest the close observer of the whole process must expect a counter-attack intended to prevent the neurotic presentation of the family drama from being turned inside out by the collapse and outburst of the carriers of the neurosis.

Now begins the 4th phase of the development, which we have termed

The Individuation Phase.

This is subordinate to the autonomous development dynamic of the individual child but is also dependent on the severity of the primary elements of the factors causing the neurosis or the constantly prevailing influence of the milieu. It is that stage of the therapy in which the approach of protecting against all the regressive processes is gradually abandoned. Instead there should be increasing confrontation of the conscious ego with its inner potential and the external realisation of this potential. The unconscious is the maternal abode of the symbol and the actual experiences are converted into images by the shaping power as a transcendent function with the creative spiritual libido. The ego consciousness, however, is able to abstract the "sign," which orders and sets limits, and thus links up with the archetypal ordering centre– the Self.

The amount of work to be done on the conscious depends on the data in the unconscious statements, in other words in the symbol signals. The positive or progressive nature of the signal for the ego is elucidated and stressed as confirmation. It is precisely this understanding of the symbol that releases the child from the oft-experienced situation of not being understood.

On the level of transference and counter-transference the overwhelming amount of material dealing with the shadow and its opposite actually marks the preliminary stage of the resolution.

This gives important scope for exercise in the search for identity in that the childish ego can test itself in saying Yes and No to the Self and thus to the partner. The progression from the energy areas of the whole archetype brings autonomous releasing images and thus genuine desire for release on the part of the child.

In the case of a genuine spiritual pregnancy, the separation must be symbolically visible and consciously brought about by the therapist. How gratifying it is when a child can say: "When I need you, I'll come back. But later I'll come back when I don't need you."

THE PRINCIPLES OF ANALYTIC PSYCHOTHERAPY IN CHILDHOOD

Michael Fordham, London

It is with much pleasure that I accepted the invitation by the programme committee to open today's discussion on the analytic psychotherapy of children. I appreciate the honour conferred upon me because this is the first time a planned discussion has been arranged on that subject at our international congress. It represents, I hope, a growing recognition that child analysis has brought about a revolution in our understanding of children.

Before child analysis was practised there were many theories but no children; child psychotherapists have introduced them live and child analysts have found ways of communicating with them directly as in adult analysis.

Theories are needed to organize the wealth of data collected. Jung (Neumann has followed him in this) contributed theoretically and though, as I know from personal discussion, Jung did not hold child analysis in high esteem, he allowed that it had a place. Amongst the many helpful ideas he produced I would like to pick out the child's individuality, the theory of archetypes and indications that he understood the idea of the primary self. All these help us to conceive of a child as sufficiently organized for him to make use of analytic psychotherapy. They furthermore lead to the conception of an infant who is born with an archetypal capacity to adapt himself to his environment, who is, in other words, programmed from the start. That program will work itself out as growth, increasing differentation and individuation so long as the environment is good enough.

It took a long time before such conceptions came to be understood as forming a theoretical basis for introducing child analysis as a practical and useful procedure. For many years it was thought that the innate characteristics of a child were sufficient to ensure his healthy maturation so long as the family was in good enough shape. Therefore child therapy was mostly identified with the treatment of parents.

I do not propose to discuss the merits and demerits of that view. I have done so elsewhere (FORDHAM 1957) and furthermore this symposium is about child analysis which has been accepted: we accept the need of children for help in their own right quite apart from the present or past noxious influence of their parents, recognise their capacity to be positively or negatively motivated for analytic therapy, whose nature can be understood (cf especially WINNICOTT 1977).

I can, I believe, best illustrate my thesis which, as you will have inferred, is about the self in childhood, and which I contend is basic to the practice of child analytic therapy, by outlining development from the time of conception onwards, till an infant has attained what is well called unit status at about the age of two years. If by that time psychic organisation has taken place then it will increase as time goes on.

The fertilised ovum develops from a single cell into a full formed infant ready to be born in about nine months. It is an amazing demonstration of what genetic influence can accomplish and provides the subject matter for a special science—embryology. It all takes place within the mother who must consequently be regarded as the environment of the growing embryo. It is separated from her first by a cellular membrane and later by a skin. Her only direct connection with him being through the umbilical chord. The environment is dark, it soon becomes aquatic and protects the embryo from impingements; it provides, except when the mother has a fever, a constant temperature. From within this immediate environment, sounds will be heard when auditory perception is sufficiently developed; the heart beat and borborigmi amongst them.

As yet very little is known about the psychology of the foetus but information is being collected about what it does when sufficiently developed and what stimuli it responds to: it exercises its skeletal muscles, it swallows amniotic fluid and urinates; it performs breathing exercises; it thumb sucks; it responds to sounds coming from outside as well as from inside his mother's body and it discovers a limit to its activities when it kicks with its legs or hits out with its arms to encounter the mother's abdominal wall. It is often assumed that it is sensitive to this mother's affective states; that seems likely but has not been adequately established. It is known, however, that drugs can effect body growth, sometimes disastrously, so his responses to his mother's affects is quite conceivable on a biochemical basis.

Birth begins when development has proceeded sufficiently and, when completed, the infant's separateness from his mother is made visually apparent. He will soon be ready to start developing a relationship with her. It is a strange kind of relationship having few of the characteristics known to children or adults.

Once a baby is picked up and put in a vertical position he soon initiates approach behaviour made up of movements which, with his mother's help, lead to feeding. At the start of their relationship, therefore, the infant plays his part. He continues to do so in an ever increasing variety of ways and so refutes the idea of him as a passive agent in relation to his mother. That idea has changed through the growth of knowledge of the ways in which an infant can play on his mother's feelings. His cries, his smiles, his cooing noises all have the effect to either compelling her care through playing on her emotions or endearing himself to her. It is the successful operation of these signals that contribute to the infant's feeling that his mother is under his control; they feed his growing sense of omnipotence to which so much attention has rightly been given. It is also contributed to by his precarious perceptual organisation: how much a baby can perceive reality, as we adults know it, is not understood but it is not very great and there is some evidence that sensory experience is not differentiated so that vison, hearing and touch all play into one perceptual pool. It is conceived on good grounds that, whatever the nature of his experience, he only perceives parts of his mother at one time and that these part perceptions are often creations of his own, more like archetypal dream or fantasy images than images of reality. Later on they are represented in fantastic images of parents.

The integrity of the self is important to an infant – it is sustained by his omnipotence. Recognising this, whether consciously or no, a mother allows it and behaves so that she does not impinge upon it. Thus such relatively complex feelings as dependence which could overwhelm her baby if realized too soon, are not aroused.

I contend that it is safe to introduce archetype theory here by conceiving archetypes as parts of the self brought into being by deintegration of the self. Their images sustain the infant's omnipotence and lead on to the state of primary identity, often referred to as fusion, between self and mother objects. A word of caution here; the idea of fusion is liable to be confusing because it is sometimes used to mean that mother and infant feel the same at the same time, whereas fusion is between the real object and the images of it that an infant constructs.

The affective life of an infant during states of primary identity is dominated by the pleasure principle, by the contrast between pleasure and pain related to omnipotence. The next step arises through a failure on the mother's part; she cannot always be there when required and may not at once find out what she is being summoned for. Then the infant's aggression asserts itself and can be very frightening to him. Though such situations result in distress the infant has means of relieving it: he can cry, scream, evacuate his bowels, urinate or break off relations with the distress producing object altogether. He can also overcome the absence of her as a desired object by hallucinating her or later by a thought.

Much attention has been directed towards these affective states of the infant in relation to his mother and it has been shown that there are quite wide variations between one infant and another in his capacity to tolerate and manage them as both ESCALONA (1968) and MAHLER (1975) have shown: thus a baby's individuality is well demonstrated if so it needs to be.

Focusing on the mother-infant relation only too easily makes us overlook that a great deal goes on when an infant is not with his mother: information has been accumulated about the states of mind an infant can achieve by a host of investigators amongst whom Piaget is perhaps the most interesting. Latterly sleep and its development has come under scrutiny together with the distinction between being asleep and being awake. These studies may be important for understanding the infant's development if only because an infant is asleep for longer periods than he is awake and soon dreams, certainly before eight months. We know the importance of dreaming in assimilating day time

75

experiences and organizing them from the study of adult dreaming and it may also be so in early infancy. It is during these periods that the infant is assimilating his waking experiences or recovering from stress situations that have arisen in relation to this mother. Sleep study might well tell us why some infants can tolerate and use stressful situations better than others.

I hope that I have now said enough to suggest how knowledge about infants can throw into relief characteristics on which analytic therapy depends: the infant's individuality and selfhood.

My picture is a sketch so I want to emphasize, without further documentation, that in the first place an infant has an existence apart from his mother and that, when he does come into relation with her, that relationship is largely based on his capacity to make her psychically a part of himself. It is only gradually that he comes to distinguish his real mother from the images he makes of her, then going on to discover objects separate from her. The first attempts at separation from primary identity, the first beginnings of individuation, are conducted at about three months of extrauterine life.

It is during this early period, and in regressions to it by older children, that therapy for an infant will require his mother's special care, attention and management. Most mothers can provide it. This is a positive view of a mother's capacity and I want to draw it to your attention because it is the most frequent. This is not to deny the good evidence that her conflicts can impinge on her baby. It is when she does not realise what has happened that damage can result. There are mothers who need help and too little is given to them when difficulties arise in their early relationships with babies. Studies in this field show that provision of it can be most rewarding.

Before leaving the early period in a person's life, I would like to make one further comment upon it: the capacity of a baby to manage conflict with his mother: it is upon derivatives of this, as well as internal conflict, that the success of child psychotherapy can depend. The capacity can be observed in babies and I have listened, fascinated, to descriptions of it from students in London who are making observations on mothers and their infants during the first two years of life. Time prohibits detailed description, but I cannot refrain from referring to an occasion when an aggressive confrontation between a mother and her baby took place and threatened to become catastrophic. In the midst of his rage and his mother's growing exasperation the baby smiled and patted his mother's face thus converting the crisis into a loving exchange.

The capacity I am referring to operates not only in acute crises but also in the longer term. As an example I would remind you of "Bruce" in Mahler's book on infant observation. There she distinguishes three phases in maturation: there is the phase of relationship with mother within the period of pervading primary identity; this is followed by a first effort at separation during which a baby will start to spend time away from her in exploring his environment: there is then a rapprochement phase during which the baby makes new approaches to his mother as a real person so that the first real love affair begins. Bruce was not well mothered during the first phase. He went on to make his first separation prematurely and then, during the phase of rapprochement, presented himself to his mother in a way that was acceptable to her. She could then go far to make up for her earlier style of infant care. By three years his achievements and overall adaptation was surprisingly good.

An infant, then is endowed with an active psychic existence both in relation to and apart from his mother and, since this continues to increase and become more complex as maturation proceeds, it is understable if quite small children develop states of mind which require psychotherapeutic assistance. This has long been known. Indeed twenty years ago I demonstrated the case of a two year old girl who could be helped to work through magic feelings of having destroyed her mother and baby sister (cf FORDHAM 1957, p. 148). During her treatment she found ways of distinguishing her fantasy from reality and reconstructing, in fantasy, the destroyed couple. This treatment was conducted without the mother present, though she had to be sitting outside the treatment room so that her daughter could reassure herself of her mother's continued existence by taking a look at her when her fantasy became too real.

I hope, that by now you will be thinking: "Well, well, but is he not telling us in elaborate terms, what is obvious?" If that be so I can go on to consider a single interview with a boy "coming up to three" as his mother put it. She joined in as a holding person so that her child could elaborate his conflicts and indicate their origin. Before doing so, however, I will outline the method of interviewing with which I approached the child even though it did not work out as I intended. First then, a note about technique:

One and a half hours is made available because one hour has frequently proved inadequate for exploring sufficiently what the child has to communicate. Two chairs, a table, paper and chalks are provided in my ordinary consulting room. Toys are not displayed but I keep some in a drawer, partly open, in case they are needed.

My object is to set up an ongoing dialectic between the child and myself as follows. After the child has had time to settle in, look around and such like activities, I ask him whether he would like to play a game, without rules, that I know about. In this way he is intrigued and we sit down in the chairs with the table between us. I take a piece of drawing paper and we each choose coloured chalks. I make a scribble and show him how to make this into a picture. Then I make another scribble on another piece of paper and suggest he makes a picture. Having done this he makes a scribble and I make it into a picture. We then proceed alternatively and each talks about the results achieved, if he wants to.

This technique, you will note, is based on interaction and so plays on the earliest and basic feature of a child's life. The technique is derived from the "squiggle game" invented by D. W. Winnicott.

I can now go on to the interview with "Alastair". I knew something about him because his mother had been in analysis with me and has come to see me intermittently when she had a recurrence of symptoms. One interview is usually enough for them to resolve. As a result of her analysis she had married and now had two children of whom Alastair was the first. Alastair who, as his mother said was "coming up to three" years of age, had been waking up at night and coming into his parents' room. He had also become "impossible" during the day so I suggested that his mother bring him along to see me telling her that the interview would take about one and half hours and that I would like to see her at a second interview on her own.

You will realise that I had considerable information about the home background and you may want to know about it first. I shall not present it because the object of the interview I shall describe is to get to know the child at first hand and when I do that I erase from my mind what I know beforehand. With this aim in mind I did not ask Alastair's mother any more about him.

Before the interview mother and child were in the waiting room and I came in. I asked Alastair whether he would like to come and play a game with me. His mother looked mildly surprised when he strode out of the room and followed my instructions about where to go. Magisterially he entered my room, walked straight across it and looked set to take charge of what went on. Only for a moment, however, for having reached his destination his omnipotent feeling collapsed and he quickly secreted himself behind the entrance door, which was still open, peering out at me. He said that he wanted his mother. To sustain his omnipotence I complied with his wish and together we fetched her. She sat in a chair with him on her knee. I sat opposite and started the squiggle game. As you will see this was not followed in the way I have described as standard procedure.

I shall reproduce four squiggle pictures out of twenty, the first, the third, the eight and the fifteenth. I will make notes about the rest so as to give an impression of the speed and the mixture of vigour and timidity in the child's actions.

* *Picture one:* the brown squiggle is mine. When I had finished but before I could turn it into a picture, so as to demonstrate what I wanted of him, he added a faint squiggle down the right side of the paper.

Picture two: Alastair made circular scribbles and I started on making a female figure. Before I had finished he started scribbling out the eyes.

* *Picture three:* His tentative purple scribbling becomes much more active and vigorous.

Picture four: I somewhat provocatively draw a mouth as a hole and a long object coming out. My reason for doing so was not conscious. He took no apparent notice but

Picture five: I drew eyes and mouth both of which he scribbled out with me aiding and abetting by scribbling too. This led him to hit the objects saying "naughty eyes and mouth". I was looking at him. That it was my eyes he was referring to was shown by

Picture six: He wanted me to draw spectacles which I did quickly.

Picture seven: He wanted a hand to be drawn and talked about "fuger" and "fugassests". (Possibly a bit of private language).

* *Picture eight:* a fierce attack on an eye scribbling very hard. There is a change in the use of colours.

Picture nine: He calmed down.

Picture ten: Another fierce attack on an eye drawn somewhat provocatively by me.

Picture eleven: A change in technique: he requested me to draw objects which I did–a bowl, a mouth, a knife, some bread and a bread knife.

Pictures twelve, thirteen and fourteen: All were also drawn at his direction. In fourteen a number of queer shapes and birds were to be made. He added a sun in the sky which was a spider.

* *Picture fifteen:* He started off with very fierce jabs with his pencil.

He asserted that he was making "snack holes". He then said "mother and father can not walk on him" and he wished a river to be drawn with a bridge over it which I did; mother and father were to be on it with he himself on "the other side". Somebody was drowning in the water–I drew that. This appeared to be the end of a development.

Alastair then became restless and directed me to draw trees. He shifted about in his mother's lap. Something new had to happen. So I got out a big drawing pad. On it he made vigorous and very rapid drawings of trees followed by some more made to his requirements by myself. The last one was to be of "dady's trousers in a pot" and of "a door that opened and shut". In all this speed of action was increasing.

By now he was beginning to get out of hand it looked as if he was going to have an outburst of temper. He had been angry with me for pressing him and, in a sense seducing him, with the big sheets of paper. Possibly I had been the person to be drowned i.e. got rid of.

As his mother was getting into difficulties with him I said that there were some toys in the drawer and she then got down on the floor and played with him. They settled to co-operative play till the end of the time.

Fig. 1

I asked Alastair's mother what she thought of all this and she replied that the cessation of scribbling was related to his nightmares.

This interview is complex and it is tempting to enter into a discussion of it in detail. My objective is however limited: to show that by using a simple technique it is possible to obtain a very good picture of the ways in which the child manages a new situation. First he tries to mobilize his omnipotent feelings and then, when these cannot be sustained, he regresses and there are suggestions of fear. It is apparent that eyes and mouths are central objects of fear and he attacks them, uses power words and then goes on to make up a story which shows that he feels isolated from his combined parents. He also seemed to preserve them by a splitting of his father image in as much as I can be got rid of as his real father cannot.

When I saw her again Alastair's mother remarked on how much she had been able to get from all that went on and we talked it over at some length. She thought that she would like to continue in her efforts to help him through his conflicts and fears which she did: a year later, however, she came back. Alastair was easier to manage but she welcomed my suggestion that she take him to a child analyst. Alastair's omnipotence was difficult for his analyst to manage at the start but he has settled in and is getting benefit from it.

The interview technique that I have described is non-interpretative and so not what I would think of as analytic though transference is taken into account. It would have started to become so had I interpreted the primal scene material and Alastair's wish to drown me his therapist-father. The aim of an interview like this one is not to analyse but to create a situation in which the child can reveal the conflict for which he has come to see me. That he did.

Analytic therapy

To conduct analytic therapy with children it is necessary to provide conditions for much more acting out, especially in the form of play, than is the case with adults, but its essential principles are the same: exploring the content of material produced by the child, interpreting it and allowing time for working through conflicts. The place given to the transference and counter-transference is even more important than is the case with adults because there is less time taken up with exploring current conflicts at home and at school etc.

To demonstrate how important it can be to analyse the child's transference and counter-transference just as we do with adults, I will now consider an episode with an older boy whose parents were both unstable, and who both had restricted capacity for parenthood.

John, aged ten years, had been in analysis with me for about two years. At times it had been exceedingly stormy but he had greatly improved. A recurrent theme had been his hostility to this parents' treatment of him, especially over his education. He disliked his school and

Fig. 3

wanted to go to a free school where he could, as he imagined, do as he liked. I could not make much headway over his anger for a long time till one day he sweepingly asserted that his father was a washout, no better than a piece of paper hanging on the wall. Now I knew that his father had manic depressive characteristics, he drank heavily from time to time probably when he was depressed and that he sat, according to John, for long periods in his study doing nothing.

As to his mother John asserted at this time that she was mad. I knew that she was given to animus projections, dignified as intuition, which bewildered him: she would claim that she knew what he was feeling and thinking but got it wrong because of the projection. It was therefore tempting to decide that John's ideas were a good enough statement about reality not to be interfered with—serve them right, I began to reflect, if their son hated them. It was this countertransference feeling that alerted me to John's probable transference. Was it not something that had interfered with the development of his analysis? I had controlled it but could it not be used. So I considered the possibility of my missing something important and so was being a bad analyst parent.

I reflected that I had previously noticed how some of my interpretations had made him look confused and go silent. This gave me a clue and I told him that though his parents had failings, I believed he was talking to me about his mother in that way because he was afraid of telling me that what I said was mad and I gave him examples of the occasions when I thought he had so felt. This led to a better dialectic between us after a furious attack on me for confusing him over his sexual and aggressive fantasies. Similarly I told him that there was another feature of my behaviour which infuriated him and in which I was like his father: it was my passivity, just sitting in a chair and talking from time to time. It had provoked him into trying to force me to be more active in various ways such as going round the room threatening to break ornaments and the mantle shelf, or throwing cushions at me, or wanting me to make love in a cuddly affectionate way. In all these respects I was no better than a piece of paper on the wall and I told him he felt so.

Interpreting in this way made it possible to reach into the unorganised and rejected infant parts of himself in a new way and especially into his fear of being mad himself. He became more tolerant of his

Fig. 8

parents, more specific about his difficulties with them and more able to arrange his life so that they impinged on him less. As a result he became better prepared for going to a boarding school and less likely to make projections onto the schoolmasters as he had been previously at his day school.

This bit of analysis was crucial. I have demonstrated it to show how easy it can be to miss a bit of transference because of knowledge about a child's parents. Using my interpretations he began to modify his omnipotent fantasies so that when the end of his analysis came, his distress and objections could be managed. He became grateful for what I had done and sad at going away. He wrote appreciatively about his new school and kept contact with me with messages and Christmas cards, for the next two years.

Conclusion

In this discussion I have indicated how it is possible to see children as whole persons right from the start of extrauterine life and that because of this they can be motivated for and it is possible to conduct analytic psychotherapy with them from the second year. If, in my presentation, I have left out the noxious influence of parents in inducing child psychopathology, I hope you will understand that I do not underestimate it. Cases for therapy must be carefully chosen so that the therapist start from the position that he is treating what has been organised within the child self.

Having said this I recognize that, in treating a child, parents are also influenced and that they, as well as their child, develop a transference to the child's therapist.

REFERENCES

Escalona, S. K. (1968) *The Roots of Individuality*. London, Tavistock
Fordham, M. (1957) "Child Analysis" in *New Developments in Analytical Psychology*. London, Routledge
Fordham, M. (1957 a) "Observations on the self and ego in childhood."
Mahler, M. S., Pine, F. and Bergman, A. (1975) *The Psychological Birth of the Human Infant*. London, Hutchinson
Winnicott, D. W. (1977) *The Piggle*. New York, International Universities Press

Fig. 15

ON ACTIVE IMAGINATION

M.-L. von Franz, Zürich

In this paper I would like to concentrate on what is specific about our active imagination compared to the many other imaginative techniques which are coming to the fore all over the world. We often meet people today who have already practised some such technique before their Jungian analysis and I find it very difficult to teach them how to proceed towards "real" active imagination. I propose therefore to subdivide active imagination into four different stages.

I. First one must empty one's mind from the trains of thought of the ego. This is already very difficult for some people who cannot stop; what the Zen-Buddhists aptly call the "mad mind". It is easier to do it in painting and still easier in sand play, but the latter only offers already existing images to the mind so that this first phase of "barrenness" is somewhat omitted, which is apt to lead to difficulties later, when the analysand should proceed to "real" active imagination. Most of the Eastern techniques of meditation, such as Zen, Yoga-practises, Tao-ist meditation, etc., confront us with that first step. In Zen, one is not only taught to stop one's ego-ruminating but also to stop all phantasies which well up from the unconscious. One has either to keep them out by concentrating on a ko'an or to let them flow by and ignore them. The outer "sitting"-exercises are only to be understood as a symbolic expression of this immobilizing of all ego activity.

II. Then comes the second step: It is the phase of letting an unconscious phantasy image enter into the field of inner attention. In contrast to all Eastern techniques we welcome this image and do not dispel or ignore it. We focus on it, and here one has to look out for two kinds of mistake: either one focuses too much and thus arrests the image, fixing it literally so to speak, or one focuses too little and then the inner images are apt to change too quickly – a kind of "inner cinema" begins to run. In my experience, it is especially intuitive types who tend to fall into this trap. They write endless phantastic stories with not much point or rather they do not *relate* to what happens. This is the stage of passive imagination the "imaginatio phantastica" in contrast to the "imaginatio vera". Nowadays this is widely practised in Germany as the "Katathyme Bilderleben" of H. LEUNER (2). Leuner took his idea admittedly from Jung and decided to simplify Jung's rather difficult technique, with a very bad result. I find it extremely difficult to teach analysands who have practised this form of imagination. The next step to a real active imagination. W. L. FURRERS *Objektivierung des Unbewußten*, Bern 1969 (and NEUE *Wege zum Unbewußten*, Bern 1970) stops short at the same point. So does the older technique of Le rêve éveillé de René DESOILLE. These techniques also allow an interference of the analyst (3)–a great mistake of which I will speak later.

III. Now comes the third step. This consists in giving the phantasy some form of expression: in writing it down, painting it, sculpting or noting the music which one heard, or in dancing it. In the latter case the body comes into it which is sometimes very necessary, mainly when the emotions and the inferior function are so unconscious that they are practically "buried" in the body (4). It often also helps to perform a small ritual like lighting a candle, walking in a circle etc. because through it *matter* enters the play. Jung once told me that this was more efficient than "ordinary active imagination" but he could not explain why.

In my opinion this also answers a problem which is sometimes raised nowadays, the question of the involvement of the body. Actually the alchemistic work is nothing else than an active imagination according to Jung performed by the mixing, heating etc. of material substances; The Eastern alchemists, mainly Taoistic, usually did this by trying to influence the matter of their own body, but also that of the materials in their retorts. The Western alchemists mostly used matter outside their body, asserting that "our soul imagines great things outside the body" (extra corpus). Paracelsus and his pupil Gerhard Dorn however also tried to experiment with "the inner firmament" within their own bodies

89

with some outer magical performances; these had–per analogy–a synchronistic relationship to the matter in the body. Thus active imagination is actually very much concerned with the body but essentially with its basic chemical components in their symbolic meaning. I have often observed strong physical positive and negative reactions in case of a rightly or wrongly conducted active imagination; one analysand even once suffered a severe but purely psychogenic heart-attack, when he betrayed his feelings within an active imagination (5). A great problem is raised by strong affects and emotions. In his own experiment Jung sometimes used yoga exercises to master them first, before he could, so to speak, extract an image from them to which he could relate in active imagination (6). Certain active imaginations can be done as conversations with inwardly perceived parts of one's body, or hearing them speak. This can be especially helpful in cases of a psychogenic physical symptom. Whenever matter is touched upon, be it inside or outside one's own body, there is a chance that markedly numerous synchronistic events will occur, which shows that this form of active imagination is especially powerful. On the negative side it touches upon the subject of magic and its dangers to which I will return later.

On this level two major mistakes can occur as Jung points out in his paper on the "Transcendent Function" (7): either one gives the phantasy too much aesthetical elaboration, it becomes a "piece of art" and in one's eagerness to cope with the form one overlooks the message or meaning of it. This happens in my experience mostly with painting and writing. Too much form kills the content just as art has in many historical periods "buried the gods in gold and marble," so that one prefers to see a primitive fetish or the clumsy art of the early Christians. Sensations and feeling mainly lead us astray in this respect. One forgets that what one creates is only a replica of an inner reality and that the aim is to relate to the latter, not the replica. The other mistake is the reverse: one sketches the phantasy-content only in a sloppy way and jumps at once to asking after its meaning. This is a danger which mostly threatens intuitive and thinking types and worst: the intellectuals. It shows a lack of love and devotion. One can see it at once when a patient brings a sloppy sketch or a badly written bit of paper with an air of knowing already what it means. This third step which lends the unconscious a mode of self-expression in creative form brings generally already a great release. However, it is not yet "real" active imagination.

IV. The fourth step is the decisive one, the step where most other modern parallel techniques miss out. It is the *ethical confrontation* with whatever one has previously produced. Here Jung warns against a most frequent and fatal mistake: namely that one enters the "inner play" with a ficticious ego and not with one's own true ego (8).

Let me give an example: an analysand dreamt that he found in a desert a hore's hoof, which was highly dangerous. It began to pursue him. It was a sort of Wotanic demon. In active imagination he continued the dream. He ran away on a horse. The horse foot-demon began to become bigger and bigger and came always closer. Then the patient turned and somehow overcame it and stamped it into the ground. When the analysand told me this story, I felt an strange discrepancy between his actual looks and the outcome of the story. He looked deeply worried and anxious. I told him that I did not believe that it happened as in the story but I could not tell why. A week later he confessed that when the horse foot-demon reached him. he became split: only one part of him overcame the demon, the other part "jumped out of the drama" and was only looking on at the scene. So the victory over the demon had been only achieved by a ficticious heroic ego, his real ego just jumped out and secretly thought: "This is only a phantasy." In my experience– when the actual observable emotional state of the analysand's ego does not coincide with that in the story one can see that the drama was only lived through by a fictitious ego. This mistake is very difficult to detect. Another analysand had a long love affair with an anima figure in an active imagination. But he never told her that he was married. When I asked him he said he would never do this in reality. So his ego in the active imagination behaved differently to his every day-ego. The whole thing was obviously not quite real, it was more like writing a novel, but not an actual active imagination. This is most important because the effectiveness of active imagination depends entirely on this point. Very split people and people threatened by a latent psychosis generally cannot do active imagination at all or they do it in this fictitious way and nothing comes of it. As you know Jung warned against letting borderline cases do active imagination altogether. The second example which I gave does not concern a sick analysand but an intellectual. The intellect is a great trickster who can make one quite inadvertently overlook the moral issue and sneaks the semi-unconscious thought into one's head that it is all "phantasy" or "wishful thinking" and thus undoes the whole thing. It needs a certain naiveté to do real active imagination.

Jung once remarked that in psychiatry nowadays, one has generally discovered the proceeding up to the third step but that the fourth is not understood. All the techniques which I mentioned before stop short before this fourth step. Another point that is not yet realized is that in most of the before-mentioned therapeutical creative-phantasy-techniques a certain interference of the analyst is permitted or even called for. Either the analyst suggests a theme as in Carl HAPPICH's technique (9) or in the advanced stages of J. H. SCHULTZ's "autogenic training," or he intervenes when the analysand gets stuck and suggests an issue. Jung on the contrary left the patient stuck, right up against the wall, until he found an issue for himself. He told us once how he had a patient who in life always fell into the same trap. He told her to do an active imagination. She promptly had the phantasy that she came in a field up to a high wall and knew that she should get to the other side, but she did not know how. Jung only said: "What would you do in reality?" She could not think of anything. He left her there. Finally she thought of walking along and looking if the wall ended somewhere. It did not. Then she looked for a door or window. There was none. Again she was stuck for a very long time, but Jung did not help. Finally she thought of fetching a hammer and chisel and making a hole into the wall; this worked and she could get on. The fact that the woman could not imagine such a simple thing mirrors the inner fact that she behaved exactly in the same way in outer reality. It is therefore essential *not to interfere with a helpful suggestion,* which would keep her just as helpless, infantile and passive as before. On the contrary if she learnt the hard way within the active imagination to overcome the obstacle, she would have also learnt something for outer life. Even if a patient was stuck in active imagination over weeks Jung did not give a helpful suggestion but insisted that he or she should continue to struggle with the problem himself and alone.

In controlled drug-taking this fourth step is again missed. The controlling person carries the responsibility instead of the producer of the phantasy. I came across an interesting book by two brothers Terence

and Denis McKENNA: *The Invisible Landscape* (10). These two courage-
ous young men went to Mexico and experimented on themselves with
a hallucinogenic plant. They experienced according to their own report
schizophrenic states of mind, which led to a great widening of consciousness. Unfortunately they could not keep track of the experiences
except that they went to other planets and were often helped by an invisible guide who was sometimes a huge insect. The second part of the
book contains the speculations which they derived from their visions.
*They are not different from any other wildly intuitive modern specula-
tions about mind, matter, synchronicity etc.* In other words they do
not actually convey anything really new or which the two well-read
authors could not have thought out consciously. But what is decisive
is the fact that the book ends with the idea that all life on earth will be
definitely destroyed in an approaching cataclysm and that we must
either find means to escape to another planet or turn inward and escape
into the realm of the cosmic mind. Let me compare this with a dream
which an American student allowed me to use and which is concerned
with the same theme. This student, let me remark, is in no way psychotic and is in a Jungian analysis. He dreamt:

I am walking along what appears to be the Palisades, overlooking
all of New York City. I am walking with an anima figure who is unknown to me personally; we are both being led by a man who is our
guide. NYC is in a rubble–the world in fact has been destroyed as we
know it. All of NYC is just one heap of wreckage, there are fires everywhere, thousands of people are running in every direction frantically,
the Hudson river has over-flowed many areas of the city, smoke is
billowing up everywhere. As far as I can see the land has been leveled.
It was twilight; fireballs were in the sky, heading for the earth. It was
the end of the world, total destruction of everything that man and his
civilization had built up.

The cause of this great destruction was a race of great giants–giants
who had come from outer space–from the far reaches of the universe.
In the middle of the rubble I could see two of them sitting; they were
casually scooping up people by the handful and eating them. All this
was done with the same nonchalance that we have when we sit down at
the table and eat grapes by the handful. The sight was awesome. The
giants were not the same size or quite the same structure. Our guide

explained that the giants were from different planets and live harmoniously and peacefully together. The guide also explained that the giants landed in flying saucers (the fireballs were other landings). In fact the earth as we know it was conceived by this race of giants in the beginning of time as we know it. They cultivated our civilization, like we cultivate vegetables in a hot house. The earth was their hot house, so-to-speak, and now they have returned to reap the fruits they have sown, but there was a special occasion for all this which I wasn't to become aware of till later.

I was saved because I had slightly high blood pressure. If I had normal blood pressure or if my blood pressure was too high I would have been eaten like almost all the others. But because I have slightly high blood pressure (hypertension) I am chosen to go through this ordeal, and if I pass the ordeal I would become like my guide, "a saver of souls". We walked for an extraordinary long time, witnessing all the cataclysmic destruction. Then before me I saw a huge golden throne, it was as brillant as the sun, impossible to view straight on. On the throne sat a King and his Queen of the race of giants. They were the intelligence behind the destruction of our planet as I know it. There was something special or extraordinary about them which I didn't become aware of till later.

The ordeal, in addition to witnessing the world's destruction, or task I had to perform was to climb up this staircase until I was at their level—"face to face" with them. This was probably in stages. I started climbing, it was long and very difficult, my heart was pounding very hard. I felt frightened but knew I had to accomplish this task, the world and humanity was at stake. I woke up from this dream perspiring heavily.

Later I realized that the destruction of the earth by the race of giants was a wedding feast for the newly united King and Queen, this was the special occasion and the extraordinary feeling I had about the King and Queen.

The giants had elongated heads, with humanoid bodies. The back of their heads were elongated and the lower front part was extended. They had no eyes in their sockets, but had a piece of skin where eyes are, through which they had vision as we normally know it, in addition to some special kind of perception process that could project images telepathically into others' image receivers. There was no external ear structure, although there was an internal ear, also no nostrils were protruding and yet there was some kind of internal nose structure. The skin looked taut and in plate-like segments, four sides to each segment that narrowed towards the front of the face. The mouth seemed similar to ours. I don't remember any hair; some kind of one piece suit was worn which looked like a combination of rubber and silicon; it seemed to be unaffected by fire, water, or anything that hit it. (End of dream).

This scene reminds one of the invasion of giants in the book of Enoch, which Jung interpreted as a "premature invasion of the collective unconscious," which caused a general inflation. The angels who generated the giants with mortal women also taught men a lot of scientific knowledge which caused their inflation. It is clear that this dream mirrors our similar modern situation and the book of the McKennas' among others shows clearly how such premature exploiting of visions of the collective unconscious leads into dangerous states of mind.

The great difference between this dream and the drug phantasies of the McKenna brothers lies in the fact that there is a *task* set for the dreamer, namely to reach the King and Queen who are on earth for their wedding. In the McKennas' phantasies there is nothing to be done for the individual, he can only run away, if possible, or succumb. A more constructive aspect of the unconscious is probably only constellated when it has a conscious ego as vis-à-vis. The same holds true for active imagination and this is why controlled drug-taking as well as active imagination in which the analyst participates are not the right thing. The ego remains infantile and will fall into the same traps as it did before, as soon as it is left to itself again.

The apocalyptic view of an end of the world in *The Invisible Landscape* and in our dream are related to all our apprehensions about a third world war. But the difference is striking: instead of an escape into outer space or into the spiritual realm, the dreamer is burdened with the heavy task of reaching the King and Queen. They represent the uniting of the opposites, of Father and Mother, Spirit and Matter. This reminds me that Jung once said, when we asked him about another war to come, that in his opinion another war could only be avoided if enough individuals were standing the tension and holding the opposites together in themselves. The whole task is now put on the shoulders of the individual and one can understand the fears of our dreamer. But the unconscious can only sketch a way out for us *if we are and remain individually conscious.*

One important motif of the dream is the guide who turns up and leads the dreamer. This can only happen when the analyst does not push himself in as a guide. That is why one should not interfere in active imagination; not even a little bit! Hermes, the guide of the alchemists, said that he was "the friend of anybody who was alone" (cuius que segregati–of everyone who is separated from the flock!). One essential effect of active imagination is, according to Jung, that it enables the analysand to become independent of the analyst–so if one interferes, everything is spoilt. (This naturally does not mean that one must not interfere when the analysand does some wrong kind of imagination). When an analysand reads an active imagination he has had to me, I often think silently at certain points: "Oh I would not have done (or said) that." This shows one how individual the ego's reaction to the inner figures is and that this reaction should come completely and only from the analysand is therefore essential. It decides the "turns" which the course of the active imagination takes.

An interesting new (or rather age old) attempt towards active imagination is described in Carlos CASTANEDA's tales about Don Juan's, the Indian sorcerer, method of what he calls "Dreaming". This seems to be based on older Mexican medicine mens' traditions. It is as you know now very much read by the younger generation in America. "Dreaming" is an active imagination which is performed with phenomena, which one encounters in nature. The Indian master Don Juan takes Castaneda for a walk in the completely deserted wild chaparall in the dusk. Suddenly Castaneda sees a dark shape of what he thinks is a dying animal. He gets terrified and wants to run away, but then he looks once more a bit more closely and discovers that it is only a dead branch. Don Juan says afterwards (11): "What you have done is no triumph. You've wasted a beautiful power that blew life into that dry twig . . . That branch was a real animal and it was alive at the moment the power touched it. Since what kept it alive was power, the trick was, like in dreaming, to sustain the sight of it."

What Don Juan calls power is mana, mulungu, in other words the active energy-aspect of the unconscious. By rationalizing his fearful phantasy, Castaneda has chased away this power so he lost his chance to learn how "to stop the world". (This is Don Juan's expression for stopping the ego's train of thought). Don Juan calls this form of "Dreaming" also "controlled folly" which reminds one of Jung calling active imagination a "voluntary psychosis". This doing the active imagination with outer phenomena in nature reminds one of the alchemists who operated with metal, plants and stones, but the difference is that the alchemists always had a *vessel*. This vessel is the "imaginatio vera" or the "theoria," they did not get lost, but had a "comprehension" in the literal sense of the word, a religious philosophy. Don Juan has one too, but he cannot convey it to Castaneda and thus remains the controlling guide.

As I mentioned before, this ritual form of active imagination is especially powerful but also dangerous. It constellates a lot of synchronistic events, which can easily be misunderstood as magic. And psychotic people tend to misinterpret them most dangerously. I remember the case of a man, who in the beginning of an episode attacked his wife. She called for the police and a psychiatrist. When the two arrived and they were all standing in the passage of the flat, the only electric light bulb exploded and they were all plunged in darkness and splinters. The man interpreted it in this way: He was the saviour and just as Sun and Moon were eclipsed when Christ was crucified, so now darkness came when he was unjustly arrested. However the synchronistic event contained on the contrary a healthy message, it warned him that the light of his ego consciousness was exploding–just what it did and he fell into a mental blackout. You see how much one moves here on dangerous ground. Though this incident did not happen in an active imagination but in a state near psychosis, it is apt to illuminate what kind of error can happen in the state of "voluntary psychosis," the excitement over synchronistic happenings blurs one's judgement of what it could mean. That is why Zosimos warns against demons which can interfere with the alchemical opus. Here we touch upon nothing less than the difference between magic especially black magic and active imagination. As you know Jung advised his pupils against doing active imagination with living persons. This is because it can have magical effects upon them and also because magic, even "white magic," *has often a boomerang-effect on the one who exercises it.* It is therefore destructive to oneself in the long run. I remember however one incident where Jung advised me to do it: I had an analysand who was so totally animus possessed that she was no longer accessible and was close to drowning in a psychotic state. Jung advised me to do an active imagination with her animus. It would help, but it would do *me* harm. However it was a last resort, so I should do it only as an exception. It had in fact a salutary effect upon the analysand and Jung then helped me out of the boomerang-effect, but I never dared to do it again. The borderline between active imagination and magic is sometimes very subtle. In magic there is always a *desire* or *wish* of the ego involved, either a "good intention" or an evil destructive wish. I have also seen that strong animus or anima possession generally prevents people from being able to do active imagination. Both destroy the objectivity of the ego which is needed. One should do the latter with the object of getting near the truth and only the truth about oneself. But in practice some desirousness often sneaks in from behind and then one falls into the "imaginatio phantastica" instead of "imaginatio vera". I have noticed a similar danger in casting the I Ching. If one is in a mood of desirousness one misinterprets its oracles. The reverse danger is that one doubts too much what one hears or sees in active imagination, thinking that it is only wishful phantasizing. Generally this is cured by some turn in the active imagination which comes as such a surprise that one gets convinced of not having made it up.

Finally, there is one more step about active imagination namely that one has to apply whatever is said, ordered or asked for in active imagination to ordinary life. I remember a case of a man who promised his anima in an active imagination to speak at least ten minutes with her every day in the immediate future. He then neglected it and fell into a very neurotic state before he realized that it had been caused by his having broken his promise. But this is naturally true for all realizations in analysis.

This is so to speak the opening of the retort in alchemy; something which just naturally follows if one has really understood the former steps. If people don't do it, then they actually have not achieved the fourth step of a real ethical confrontation.

REFERENCES

(1) First published in the "Zeitschrift für Analytische Psychologie und ihre Grenzgebiete". ed. Biller, Diedemann & Meier. Berlin 1977.

(2) H. Leuner, *Katathymes Bilderleben*. Unterstufe. Ein Seminar-Kurs. Thieme, Stuttgart 1970.

(3) Cf. for instance Ilse Henle, "Die Anwendung des Katathymen Bilderlebens bei der Therapie ehelicher Virginität" in *Materialien zur Psychoanalyse und analytisch orientierten Psychotherapie*, ed. Hahn-Herdieckerhoff. Vaudenhoeck, Göttingen-Zürich 1977, III. Serie. 4. Lieferung.

(4) Cf. also Elie G. Humbert, L'imagination active d'après C. G. Jung. Cahiers de Psychologie Jungienne. Paris. and the literature stated here.

(5) See M.-L. von Franz, "Active Imagination in der Psychologie von C. G. Jung" in: *Geist und Psyche*, ed. Bitter. Kindler Taschenbücher (without date).

(6) See *Memories, Dreams, Reflections*, ed. A. Jaffé. Passim.

(7) Collected Works, Vol. 8 (1916–1957). In "Spring 1971" R. F. C. Hull has assembled a bibliography of all texts of Jung on active imagination (p. 115 ff.).

(8) *Mysterium Coniunctionis*, Collected Works Vol. 14, last 3 chapters.

(9) Cf. W. Kretschmer, "Die meditativen Verfahren in der Psychotherapie". Zeitschrift für Psychotherapie und medizinische Psychologie. Bd. I, No. 3, Mai, 1951.

(10) Seabury Press, New York 1975

(11) Carlos Castaneda, *Journey to Ixtlan*, Simon and Schuster, New York 1972, pp. 132–3

ALCHEMY AND ANALYTICAL PSYCHOLOGY

Robert Grinnell, Rome

At the very outset I should perhaps make clear the limits I have set myself in discussing alchemy in analytical psychology. I am not attempting in this short space to give a resumé of Jung's work in alchemy, nor to embark on a study of alchemical literature. Also, although I have chosen a painting by a 5¹/₂ year old schizophrenic boy as an illustrative basis for our discussion, I am not attempting a study either of child psychology of of schizophrenia as such.

Chiefly, I would like to concentrate on the psychology of projection which this painting exhibits, and the autonomous activities of an emotional and intellective order which are present in so notable a way: activities, moreover appearing at a transpersonal, nonpersonified level, which seem to illustrate psychoid process in the young artist's personality.

For Jung, alchemy provided the richest possible model for the psychology of projection. Its antiquity and widespread diffusion gave it the status of an archetypal activity of the psyche. The range of its imagery and the extraordinary richness of its symbolism provided a variety of positions from which the psyche's activity could be viewed: and especially the reactions of consciousness in the face of the unknown. Practically, this appears in the enormous suggestive powers of its images in provoking dreams and fantasies.

The arcane substance of the alchemist and Jung's subjective factor as the animating principle of the psyche show close analogies. In addition, the "chemical" level of symbolism in alchemy–lead, salt, sulphur, mercury, and the rest–permitted certain insights into processes which Jung called "psychoid": that is, processes that cannot with certainty be designated as only "matter," on the other hand, be regarded as purely "spirit" and which, in any event can not be directly experienced.

The alchemical model thus permits us to follow the psyche's symbolic fantasies commenting on events at a pre-personified level, that is, at a neuro-biological level–the unconscious psyche "within the body," or "below the ego". Here, it is a case less of "facts" than the psyche's myth-making projections in regard to facts, conditioned by the archetypes and man's physiological and phylogenetic past.

And on the other hand, the alchemical model also offers us a symbolism of a cosmological and cosmogonic order, likewise conditioned by the archetypes and arising from subliminal intuitions sharing the space-time relativity of the collective unconscious. The vicissitudes of Sol and Luna as cosmic luminaries exhibit the psyche's projective fantasies on the macrocosm, while the qualities attributed to their chemical equivalents, sulphur and salt, elucidate the psyche's fantasies about happenings "within the body". Thus, the polarity between cosmos and body is regulated by the archetypes as subjective correlates to objective facts.

We accordingly have what amount to a physiological mythology juxtaposed with a cosmogonic mythology. In between is the psyche itself–the arcane substance, the subjective factor–which achieves a personified level in the divinities of mythology. It is the psyche's own image-making activity, its self-creation through symbols, that is central to this model. It represents a process of the "psychization of instinct," the transformation of instinctual and biophysical phenomena into psychic experience. These phenomena can then to a certain extent be brought within the range of conscious will and reason. In this process instinct loses some of its primordial autonomy. It is an *opus contra naturam*, so to speak.

Alchemy accordingly gives us a model for the psychology of projection; it points at once "upward" and "downward". It is radically symbolic in its insistence on the "arcanum". And finally, in the obligation it imposed for the careful elaboration of *theoria*, it included the formation of apperceptive concepts and symbols as a fundamental part of the *opus*.

The painting by the little boy appears peculiarly adapted for our purposes in that it reproduces what we could call a primordial mentality; in the coniunctio of Sol and Luna we have the prototype for the union of opposites, male and female, spirit and matter: the central components in an archetype of consciousness.

It also reflects a child's normal openness to the subjective factor–the fantasy activity of the psyche. And finally, because of the nature of the disturbance–schizophrenia–it at once magnifies the subjective factor in the face of the world of subjects, and at the same time reduces it to the essential elements of the mind. The painting is symbolic of a trans-personal psychic world–the world of the collective unconscious. It presents us with a "psychoid" world: non-personal, subjective, neither entirely "matter" nor entirely "spirit".

The painting consists in a central star-like sun, brilliant yellow in colour. This is bisected by a dark purple serpentine, cloud-like figure, which represents the moon. The little boy regarded this figure as *written*. Above is a dark blue sky, and below, a patch of green, the earth. All of these elements are super-imposed on random rays of the sun.

Above on the left, untouched by the sun's rays but touching at one point the lower level of sky, is a dense black, roughly oval figure giving an impression of great inner turbulence, called Darkness. On the right, issuing from the extremity of Luna, is a jagged red-orange crayon scrawl–the artist's "signature". It resembles a flash of lightning or the flickering of a serpent's tongue.

Still farther above on the right border of the paper, after a couple of random crayon strokes, is a small horizontal stroke whith a small rotary motion, done with such intensity as to perforate the paper. This is the one element in the painting that the little boy did not identify. It seems to me that this hole, resulting from a "scintilla" of "red sulphur" struck off from the "signature," symbolizes the boy's ego.

There is thus a central coniunctio of Sol and Luna, giving rise to the red-sulphur signature–the little boy's "identity". But the fact that Luna is "written" suggests that certain autonomous intellective functions are going on his mind, turning Luna into a conceptual symbol, a sort of vaporized cloud-like serpent-nous quite different from the other "natural" symbols in the painting. In other words, an autonomous process is at work leading to the formation of apperceptive symbols of a conceptual order, and so giving rise to a new psychic fact: the logos-signature which constitues the litte boy's archetypal identity as Homo. This is extracted as it were from the Sun-Anthropos and the Luna-Serpent. The strange livid purple colour of Luna suggests some putrifying, corrupting influence. The main orientation is toward a masculine mentality and spirituality. All of these activities are unconscious, impersonal, and archetypal.

We thus have, already, certain basic alchemical themes. We have the coniunctio of Sol and Luna as the transformative manifestation of the self. But we have a Luna that seems more allied to Mercurius–a predominantly masculine and "duplex" form, giving birth to a "signature"–a basic "imprinting" or "character". This "signature" seems to have the qualities of "red sulphur," in the alchemical model: that is to say, it symbolizes the active agency in a crude archetypal consciousness such as appears in the primary perceptions of infancy. It has been extracted or born from the golden solar star and the sad, darkening salinity of Luna. For Luna, in our painting, is already complex. She is the only "mixed" colour in the painting: the redness of passion and the blueness of her heavenly waters have coagulated into this livid putrescent colour. Her form is at once snake-like and cloud-like: a vaporized mercurial serpent–and furthermore, a serpent that has become the quintessence of meaning: the logos-nature which the young artist insisted on so strongly.

The painting exhibits an interesting contrast in tensions. There is a "minor tension" between the Sun-Anthropos and the Homo-signature. This tension is contained within the cosmological context of earth and sky, and its components participate directly in the central Sun. The meaning of these components, with the exception of Luna and the signature, consists in their colour. They have no perimetral form: the Sun is simply a sort of star-explosion, and both sky and earth are horizontal smears that bleed off the paper.

On the other hand, the painting also exhibits a "greater tension". This tension consists in the tension between Blackness–which is the only relatively contoured figure in the painting–and the "ego-hole". These figures are not only totally dissociated from each other, but they are also dissociated from the central Anthropos archetype. Only the reflective continuum of the paper–the undifferentiated psyche–contains them. The paper thus constellates the psyche as a sort of subjective factor of reflection, and as a continuum. This greater tension accordingly consists in a black Rotundum, impinging at one point on sky, and a sort of "solid state" fragment of dissociated red-sulphur consciousness which, in perforating the "psyche," opens on nothingness.

If we take the diagrams in *Aion* as models, the components of the "minor tension" can be located at the "lapis" level, with a central serpentine factor, Luna, which could be considered to allude to the serpent quaternio. Blackness, on the other hand, would represent the level of the Rotundum, set in opposition to an ego-symbol formed in such panic fury as to perforate the psyche.

But, by comparison with the schemes in *Aion*, an interesting shift in tension has occurred. The major tension is no longer constellated by Anthropos and the serpent, and the minor tension no longer consists in the opposition between the lapis and Homo. Instead, it is the black rotundum and the empty ego that represent the central problem, and by implication this casts a shadow not only over the whole ego-world of objects, but also drains off the "ferment" of endosomatic tensions from which a normal ego might arise. It also paralyzes the "leverage" mechanics by which the ego complex relates to the object world–a leverage commemorated in the panic fury with which the little boy perforated the paper.

As far as the psychology of the little boy is concerned, the black rotundum represents, at a psychoid level, a deep source of anxiety having toxic effects. Without directly altering the fundamental functions of Anthropos, but casting a mourning shadow over a Luna which becomes "conceptual," this toxin poisons the psychoid "ferment," aborting the ego, and drains the energy of Anthropos-Homo back into its own dense blackness. The rotundum would thus symbolize a deep psychoid depression, a symbol of totality having toxic effects, and through the purple Luna, producing metabolic disturbances and discolorations.

And if we follow the alchemists and associate Sky with the brain, then the depression would seem to be located in the lower part of the brain, at that point, anatomically, where symbols of totality could be stimulated. In addition, if the Luna pictured here as a sort of vaporized serpent-nous is associated, as the snake was, traditionally, with the

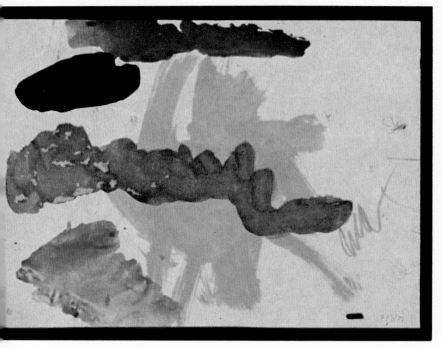

Fig. 1

spinal column, then this aspect too has been "mortified" by the black entity of the depression, disturbing reflex reactions.

The strange composite nature of Luna raises other considerations. She has identified with Mercurius in his serpent form, and has been vaporized: "above the earth" in alchemical language. Hence, a conjunction between Sol, and Mercurius has led to the extraction of the red-sulphur identity of the young painter. But there is also the "duplex" aspect of Mercurius: his dangerous side, and the deadly poison carried in the aqua permanens in this crude, uncooked state. This duplex aspects seems to me to account for Luna's livid colour and also for her logos nature.

For although the coniunctio of Sol and Luna has apparently taken place–the *gamos* or sacred marriage of spirit and matter has apparently been consummated–it seems incomplete, lopsided. The suspicion arises that in the shadow of Luna's mercurial serpent form there is another *gamos* hidden in her darkness. A "black sulphur" and fiery black Typhonian factor is in the background, pointing to a poisonous archaic dragon-like element in her depths. This represents the shadow side of Mercurius–a black fire, dry burning heat, and no glow or light. Mercurius, in his hidden coniunctio with Luna, has become the Logos, the "meaning-as-such," of this infernal black fire. It is as though the Logos of St. John had allied itself with total blackness, and shaken off the role of light of men.

Now, if we take this situation as the psyche's picture of events "within the body," we see that in a manner of speaking a "black star" having characteristics attributed to Saturn or Hades has been constellated. Physiologically speaking, the psyche has pictured the lower brain as having turned black, and a secreting a sort of "radical vinegar" and "hyssop". And so the black rotundum as an image of the self works through the putrescent colour of Luna and the poisonous nature of the Mercurial serpent Logos. A radical bitterness is being secreted, but more, this bitterness has a logos meaning coded into it.

If such is the case, then the toxin in the little boy's personality has two antecedent components at a psychoid level that must appear in his comportment. One would appear as a paralyzing dread, a sort of radical "anxiety as such," inhibiting psychic growth at this "black brain level". But the other component would be worry–an endless obsessive rumination that eats away at the mind in an effort to find meaning.

For anxiety seems fundamentally poetic in character in both negative and positive forms. It arises at moments of crisis in the psyche's aesthetic view of itself and its world. Worry on the other hand seems to arise in moments of crisis in the psyche's intellective view of the world—when conceptual structures are breaking down or in process of transformation. In our painting, these activities are expressed cosmologically. But sighting them through the alchemical model we can see them also as events transpiring at a psychoid level "within the body," at a neurobiological level. The psyche is not only trying to feel itself. It is also trying to understand itself.

Both of these activities—both the poetic and the intellective—could perfectly well be conscious. Yet in our painting they are not: they go on in the unconscious, dissociated from our ego-complex, transpersonal and autonomous, and receive expression through projective symbols having an eros nature and a logos nature. Taken together they presumably form aspects of the psyche's apperceptive functions and lead to the formation of conceptual symbols. Through this activity cognitions become recognitions; *theoria* is elaborated, and *memoria* becomes an autonomous primordial psychic activity. For the alchemist this "redemption of ideas," this extraction of meaning from the opacity of matter, was an essential aspect of the *opus*. Practically, this means a continuing re-examination of unconscious pre-suppositions and apperceptive functions as they emerge symbolically from the *opus*, from our involvement in our encounters with the unconscious.

We have seen that, looked at neurobiologically, our painting gives us the fantasies and the comportmental characteristics coded into them which express anxiety and worry as functional constituents in the toxin. These have been detected in Luna's livid shadow. Yet all of this is unconscious, transpersonal, transpiring without the intervention of an ego-complex.

Somewhat similar characteristics emerge if we look at this painting as reflecting a situation "outside the body". The painting can then be taken as symbolizing transpersonal events in the collective psyche, of which the little boy is merely the unconscious carrier.

Here too we are confronted with the radical Blackness of the unknown, the Rotundum, presented on a cosmic scale. Like the alchemists, we are constrained to develop apperceptive concepts–*theoria*–in the face of a fundamental shift of tensions in the central archetype of our age. This apperceptive concept-forming activity is already present in our painting, as we have seen.

The painting seems to be saying that the traditional oppositions associated with Anthropos and the serpent no longer adequately express the problem. They have become "intelligible," as it were, through Luna and the Homo-signature. Instead, Anthropos, for all his sun-like radiance, is undermined by a rotundum as black and dense and empty as a gravitational hole in the universe, and the ego-symbol reflects this. For the ego-symbol, here, with its "nihil" world, is no longer a relatively constant personification of Homo-Anthropos, but rather, has become the attenuated personification of a self symbolized by the black rotundum.

If confrontation with the archetype is a moral problem of the first order, here this problem is presented on a cosmic scale, and suggests, perhaps, the amoral constellation of a moral archetype in the dense and empty blackness of the rotundum. In other words, the painting seems to be foreshadowing a deep depressive experience in the collective psyche, a death experience without any particular indication of a resurrection, unless, indeed, it is the experience itself which will constitute wholeness and bring a new illumination.

The painting seems to be presenting us, from this point of view, with a world view which shows a fundamental disturbance in the archetype of consciousness as well as in the ego. For if the waking ego consciousness is an imaginal and symbolic reflexion of this archetype, then its ephemeral picture of the world would be supplemented or refer back to an "eternal," millenary world view built into the very stuff and dynamics of the psyche. And consciousness would then appear, in the alchemical model, as growing out of endosomatic tension at the psychoid level which receive symbolic expression in the "chemical" language of alchemy, growing by a mechanics of "fermentation". Such a view of the ego stands in contrast to that of an ego whose origins lie in collisions with an object world, based on a mechanics of "leverage". The "alchemical' 'view of the ego would present it as a symbolic representative of an archetype of consciousness, the product of physiological and phylogenetic world processes, and reflecting the timelessness of such processes.

In this sense, our painting not only gives us a picture of the neuro-biological bases of an ego consciousness which refers back to an archetype. It also looks forward to events incubating in the future of the race. It moves out of the normal world of space,, time, and causality into a world that lives in an "eternal present," a world less of "origins" than of essential relations in the psyche, a world apperceived through subliminal intuitions having a timeless quality, conditioned by the archetype.

The little boy here appears as the carrier of transcendent activities in the collective psyche. The painting is conditioned by the archetypal nature of these activities. And if the archetypes are subjective equivalents of objective facts, they have a cosmic character. The painting shows us at once neurobiological processes and cosmic processes in a state of radical tension.

What is striking is that on both planes there is a resolute refusal to picture a personality or a world centered on an ego complex. The ego refuses absolutely its heroic role: in our painting it appears as a mere hole in the paper. The mentality here pictured would seem to resemble what Neumann called the "nihilist" type of mystic man, characterized by a denial of the world and all its works. Or, following Eliade's view, it would represent the specific denial of the active empirial individual human being. The mentality in our painting refers back to a pre-human world, primordial, *illo tempore*, a world of cosmological happenings. The painting refers to a transpersonal and non-temporal world, a sort of eternal cosmogony, without an active human ego component. The whole nature of collective consciousness appears as profoundly threatened by these developments in the archetype.

There seems to have occurred a general attenuation of faith, a loss of soul, in everything going under the name and habits of an ego-centered consciousness. The ego appears as an "image," but without faith in the reality of "image". It appears as a "son of darkness," but its inner substance is drained back into that darkness. Dread and worry of pathological proportions have petrified its growth and obliterated its control over its identity. It is as though it were forced to renounce its parentage in the species of humankind. This appears both at the neurobiological level and cosmologically. A radical disturbance of instinct, not only biological but psychological, is pictured in our painting. It is as though the whole mental and moral basis of its being had vanished.

Given the depth of this disturbance as it is pictured for us, at this point we must return again to the Sol-Luna coniunctio. It will be remembered that there seemed to have occurred an "inferior," non-manifest conjunction in Luna's darkness which brought into view the serpent-nous, but also the poisonous blackness in the situation. This blackness was intelligible–it personified meaning,–but its inner nature, its "utter dreadfulness" remained unenlightened.

It seems to me that a fundamental split in the anima factor in our painting has occurred: a split between the anima as the animal soul and the anima as psychopomp lies at the root of the disturbance. This means that everything going under the name of life and instinct is disturbed–not only biological but also psychic life. Most deeply of all, the religious instinct to wholeness has been put in crisis.

Sol has allied himself more especially with psyche rather than with the serpent-nous of Luna. This appears from the fact that Sol is the only centered figure in the painting, and the white paper itself we identified with the stable, undifferentiated reflective capacities of the psyche itself. Thus, Sol in allying himself to the psyche, has also allied himself to a "bleaching" or "whitening" principle–the albedo, in alchemical language. The large uncovered areas could therefore be regarded as potential areas of development–spaces for reflection, so to speak. This leads one to conjecture that Sol has entered into a coniunctio with the anima as psychopomp, as a "guide of soul". This constitutes a purely *psychic* coniunctio aiming at a psychization of instinct and the production of a *psychic* body, a "subtle body" in the language of the alchemists. Fundamentally, it is this coniunctio that produces the "signature," the red sulphur identity imprinted in the depths of the little boy's personality. And it is this signature that hints at a rubedo in process of realization. The chaos of the four elements–earth, air, fire, and water–has polarized around the signature, so that the albedo– the psychic dawn-state born from the coniunctio of Sol and Psyche–has also extracted a primitive solar consciousness from Luna's mercurial, serpent-like aspect, and this has become the archetypal *Homo*, the human aspect of our painting. This means that the *psychic* identity, and the *psychic* reality of the little boy has been extracted from the mute, unconscious corporeality of matter. Psyche as psychopomp, as the guide of soul, is the active agency in this process. Somewhat as in the myth of Eros and Psyche, the psyche itself is seeking redemption from a primeval feminine principle and presumably this is why the manifest coniunctio takes place between Sol and Luna in her mercurial serpent-nous form. The reality of Psyche active in relation with Sol is meaningful, intelligible, and hints at final causes in this process, the affirmation of the reality and value of the psyche. Thus, as a whole, the painting points to a massive extraction of the psyche and the spiritual anima from the corporeality of Luna's sublunary world.

Presumably it is this redemptive orientation in the soul that brings Luna's dark side to light. Sighting through the poisonous aspect of our hermetic serpent-nous, looking down through the putrescence of Luna, we can detect her poisonous snake-like aspect, her "psychoid jealousy," her fearsome dragon nature, her typhonian animus in the fiery "forbidden sea". Here we find more repulsive children: a primitive "Dreadfulness-as-such," and melancholia, depression, hopelessness, and paralyzing sinfulness. All this characterizes nigredo in alchemical language. And it has all the concrete reality of a paralyzing hypnotizing serpent-stare. And this too, is "intelligible," if we look deeply enough into our serpent-nous.

It is difficult to enter into such a state of mind, since both orientations, the animal psyche and the anima as guide of the soul, are present to us only in impersonal biochemical or cosmological images. One, the psychic leads into a world of images and fantasies that have a solar character but which lack a compelling sense of reality and can disperse in capriciousness. The other, the animal psyche, leads back to a blackness and a sultry bitterness that has a reality, but that can only be approached through the content of a projection, the dread, the obsession, that obliterates the soul, and with it imposes the loss of an essential instinct.

Probably the schizophrenia has its origin in the toxic consequences generated from the tension between these two contrasting orientations in the archetype of life: the one psychic and solar, the other the blackness of the Rotundum lying hidden in Luna's shadow. And we can conjecture the traces of this tension in the ego symbol in our painting. For the ego appears as a random spark of red sulphur struck off from the signature. In this aspect, the ego is a "son of chaos," "son of the lapis," and "son of the mercurial serpent-nous." Yet the ego is also the "son of darkness," the "son of the rotundum," the son of terror, melancholy, despair, the son of a "blackened" lower brain and a poisoned nervous system compact of "wretchedness and vinegar and hyssop". This is the "unbearable dread" and the pathogenic toxin generated from this has emptied out the ego and punctured the psychic continuum, opening on nothingness.

Yet the way of cure, the discovery of an ego world, can only come from the rotundum. And it must be precisely the anima as psychopomp that must be the guide. For it is this aspect of psyche that has raised to view and carried in her reflective activity the blackness of the rotundum and the putrescent Luna, and has pointed to the logos-serpent as a panacea as well as a poison. She has revealed the intelligibility of the situation lurking behind the images of the painting. Practically, this would mean that a concentration on the psychic equivalent of a medicine is called for, and not the easier way of massive psychopharmic sedation.

The painting has given us an "eternal" picture of the factors present in this psychic situation. Nigredo, albedo, rubedo; unio mentalis, return of soul, and even *unus mundus* co-exist in a synchronous system of relations. It is this co-existence that constitutes the "eternality" pictured in our painting: and nascent in it, is the choice of the soul as psycho-pomp–the confession of finality.

Our young artist has illuminated a system of essential relations in the personality, rather than a causal system of origins. We have sought to view it in two ways, one: symbolizing neurophysiological activities underlying the psyche of the little boy; and the other: as alluding to archetypal tensions in the collective psyche. The whole work of redemp-tion the whole *opus*, must take into account these two dimensions, the physiological myth and the cosmognic myth. It must be the anima as psychopomp that, *Deus concedens,* will bring about this redemption.

"God willing!" This phrase raises a last factor in the alchemical model that is essential to the *opus*: that of psychological faith. For the alchemist was vividly aware of the poisonous terror of the *opus*, the blackness, the despair. He was vividly aware of the reality of the images of the *opus*, but also their delusive nature. Hence faith and prayer were absolutely necessary if emotion and *theoria* were to bring the *opus* to a successful conclusion. His attitude could well understand that of Saint Bonaventura who defined matter as a chaos of desires and as prayer. For this conative nature of matter becomes prayer in human experience, as the cry wrung from the very imperfection of all created beings apart from God. The alchemist laboured to save the vestige of God present in matter's conation, to transform it into a recognition of God's presence and so restore divinity to itself.

Here faith is fundamental: faith not as a system of codified beliefs, but faith as a function of symbolic apperception. Faith is not *what* is believed but that *by which* it is believed. The objects of faith are believed, but faith itself shines forth.

In our painting this psychological faith is as deeply split as are the two aspects of the anima which we have noted. It has turned negative in the form of dread and obsession. Its positive aspect is present in what we can detect of the psyche itself at work in this *opus*. And it is this aspect of the alchemist in ourselves that can abet the curative tendencies–if any–in the psyche's effort at feeling itself and understanding itself, and so, nourishing in her bosom a new image of wholeness.

Original Italian version to be found in "Oggi Jung," La Rivista di psicologia analitica, 17/78 pp. 127–142.

Fig. 1

Fig. 2

PRACTICAL APPLICATION OF ALCHEMICAL THEORY

Joseph L. Henderson, San Francisco

As Dr. Grinnell has told us, alchemical theory is made from "the formation of apperceptive symbols of a conceptual order," and this echoes Jung's method of arriving at certain psychological insights by the enrichment of dream imagery "amplified to the point of intelligibility". The alchemists called this *theoria*, in contrast to *practica*, which refers to specific transformations; but the two are continually represented by the philosophical alchemists as being identical. While the understanding of the personal, and to some extent the cultural, psyche requires the method of scientific testing, the archetypal experience is best understood with this attitude: that theory and practice are of one substance.

Most of you will recall an illustration frequently reproduced by students of alchemy (see JUNG, *Psychology and Alchemy*, vol. 12, C. W. Fig. 144, p. 278) of the title page to Maier's *Tripus Aureus* (Slide 1), showing what Jung calls "the double-face" of alchemy. The picture is divided in two parts, like the design for a stage set, partitioned to form two rooms–a library on one side and a laboratory on the other. In the center foreground is a round alchemical furnace, tended by a man clothed only in trunks, whose place is in the laboratory. On the other side, against a background of shelved books, are three richly attired men described as "an abbott, a monk and a layman," denoting three important alchemical philosophers: John Cremer, Abbott of Westminster, Basilius Valentinus, and Thomas Norton. Exactly in the center of the picture on top of the furnace we see a tripod holding a round, sealed glass vessel containing a lively winged serpent. Two plain serpents are stretched out on the stone surface below. One of the learned men is pointing out this phenomenon to the other two. How can we describe the meaning of this gesture? It would be all too easy, as James HILLMAN has warned us in his paper, *The Therapeutic Value of Alchemical Language*, to try to fit the image into one of our psychological concept-slots. In that case, the winged serpent could simply be described as the sublimated form of the other two, with the erotic overtones derived from early psychoanalysis. But if we stick to the actual imagery and refuse to turn it into a known verbal concept, we can, as Dr. Hillman implies we should, use a kind of craft language that describes what is actually there. Then I would say that if the serpent is equivalent to earth, and the bird equivalent to air, the union of serpent and bird as winged serpent miraculously transforms a pair of polar opposites, into the union of a pair of complementary opposites, where a sense of harmony replaces an impression of conflict. By achieving the unity implied in this symbol, the whole picture seems to say: "If you believe something to be true, then put it into practice, and if you practice something by all means try to understand the reason why."

On the basis of this analogy between theory and practice I have, close at hand in my bookshelf, a facsimile edition of a famous alchemical illuminated manuscript of the early seventeenth century, *The Splendor Solis*, by Solomon TRISMOSIN, one copy of which resides in the British Museum. It has for many years held a place in my life somewhere between a psychiatric textbook and a sort of Book of Hours, helping me in the work I do. Although I occasionally show my analysands one of the illustrations to demonstrate visually some problem and its possible resolution (and it is remarkable how one such picture can by itself fully amplify a dream!), I never felt like acknowledging this to any but my closest colleagues until recently.

Two years ago I was asked to present an introductory series of seminars for an electic group of psychotherapists at the San Francisco Institute, and I decided to risk mystifying them by taking the *Splendor Solis* as my text, with slides showing what I dared to call a pictorial view of a psychotherapeutic process illustrating the principles of Jung's psychology (as individuation-process). I expected the participants of this seminar to be intrigued by the pictures—especially the intuitive members who would have a midly inflating experience, while the sensation-oriented ones would be correspondingly skeptical and mildly depressed by them–and perhaps the two points of view would lead to fruitful discussion. What I did not expect was that they all seemed to find the series helpful as a practical method of learning what analytical psychology is all about.

In this brief time, I cannot begin to tell you enough to indicate why it happened this way, except that it seemed to convey to these participants, and to me, how true the "double-image of alchemy" is for our work, and how, invariably, we find in it the familiar landmarks of our conceptualism illustrated, elaborated and perhaps corrected, for us all to see in pictures that strongly expose the archetypal imagery shining through the cultural forms in which they have traditionally been embedded. In contrast to the language of the alchemists, which so often tries to explain the obscure by the more obscure, this visual imagery is exceedingly clear.

Let me describe the frontispiece of the *Splendor Solis* as an example: (Slide 2)

Two men are entering a building through a high, arched doorway. We are told one is the alchemist and the other his adept, or student. The alchemist is pointing out a sort of banner, bringing into focus, in bas-relief, a coat of arms of the art *(Arma Artis)* presumably the art of alchemy. This design consists of an old-fashioned, rather small leaden knight's helmet surmounted by a golden crown and a series of three crescent moons, above which shines a golden sun with human features, with its rays alternating straight and sinuous, spread out in all directions equally, but the lowest of all points downward, as if penetrating the upper crescent moon without actually touching it. Below the helmet is another sun symbol, also with human features, but the impression is as horrifying as the other is benign. The face is covered with pock-like markings, and in each of the eyes and the mouth another tiny demonic face peers forth. Instead of straight rays, the rays from this sun are like hooks that bend backward upon themselves regressively. The sun is further distorted by being placed on a shield at an angle to the vertical, in contrast to the upper sun, which is symmetrically placed in the center. On first sight, the design appears to be a stereotyped coat of arms, with a helmet embellished by several waving plumes and a crest composed of crescent moons. But, observing closely, we might say it is a coat of arms in a process of disintegration, with primordial elements tending to replace the old cultural image by a new archetypal image.

I took this scene as analogous to the beginning of a therapeutic encounter between analyst an patient, which allowed me to discuss in the teaching seminar the question of first interviews, initial dreams, and problems of diagnosis and prognosis before any therapeutic commitment has a yet been made on either side. The first and most obvious point was psychiatric in the old sense of the word when the threat to an overadapted persona might bring to light a latent psychosis. There followed discussion of the difference between these old fears and a more confident attitude of the modern psychotherapist in relation to the nature of emotional or mental illness, welcoming the opportunity to expose the shadow aspect of the patient and of therapy itself from the very beginning. We might say, with the alchemist: "There is a healthy sun and there is a sick sun. The sick sun is isolated, distorted, cut off from all relationship and morbidly subjective, suggesting a state of self-doubt and self-loathing." Is this not a true description of how a neurosis feels? The person so affected has been too long protected by an out-worn image of heroic over-achievement, represented by the knight's helmet. You see, these paintings were done in the early seventeenth century, when the age of chivalry had become an archaic mode, which, in the humanistic light of the Renaissance, appears over-protective or over-aggressive and, as Cervantes had told them, even ridiculous. So, the patient should learn from his therapist that there is a very specific danger in undertaking therapy, not just a generalized fear of madness. It is a true configuration of a certain schizoid condition that threatens to become paranoid. This is brought out into the open and, as it were, partially exorcised by being shown in the presence of the healthy sun above the helmet. Why is it healthy, and what in this sense is health? The painting is again quite specific.

The healthy sun is not alone; it shines by its own light but is in the correct archetypal relation to the crescent moon below. So it acknowledges the changeable, the related, the vulnerable nature of human life as well as the positive nature of human will. Summarizing, my seminar group and I saw this as a picture of an out-worn persona, represented by the helmet, about to be discarded or displaced and, as it were, transcended by the golden crown, referring to alchemy as the kingly art.

But this is not to be viewed as a unified goal but as the imagined union of two complementing opposites, solar strength willingly uniting with the lunar rhythm of change. In turn, this whole symbolism is to be seen as compensatory to the lower image embodying the raw psychic image of self-doubt to be processed and, perhaps, healed if treatment can be agreed upon by both therapist and patient, as adept.

What follows in this remarkable book is beyond the scope of this brief exposure. I can only indicate that it consists of three groups of pictures: The first series suggests the need for acceptance of the validity of archetypal imagery, with the precarious nature of the insights to be derived from it. The second series takes us through seven stages of the Great Work from the *nigredo* to the *solificatio*. The final series picks up loose ends and illustrates the fact that the process of psychic renewal is a symbolization that seems to include the personal life experience in such homely scenes as the play of children in the nursery, or the women washing clothes. But this simplicity is deceptive. It conceals a profound message from Hermetic philosophy in accordance with which the beginning is also the goal of the great work. As our frontispiece illustrates, whether in theory or in practice we are always trying to heal the split between spirit and matter.

THE THERAPEUTIC VALUE OF ALCHEMICAL LANGUAGE

James Hillman, Zürich

Jung's alchemical work has been relevant for analytical psychology in two main ways. I shall be suggesting a third way.

The first way has been excellently presented by David HOLT in his paper "Jung and Marx" (Spring 1973). There Holt shows that Jung imagined his work to be theoretically and historically substantiated by alchemy, and that Jung spent a great part of his mature years working out, in his own words, "an alchemical basis for depth psychology," particularly the opus of psychological transformation. As Holt indicates, it is to alchemy we must turn to gain the proper placing of Jung's entire endeavor. We need alchemy to understand our theory.

The second way has been profoundly elucidated by Robert GRINNELL in his book *Alchemy in a Modern Woman* (N. Y./Zürich: Spring Publ., 1973). There Grinnell demonstrates the incontrovertible parallels between the psychic processes in a modern Italian patient and those that go on in the alchemical opus. Where Holt stresses alchemical *theory* as background, Grinnell stresses alchemical phenomenology in *practice*. We see from Grinnell the continuity or archetypality of alchemical thematics in case-work. Thus, to work with the psyche at its most fundamental levels, we must imagine it as did the alchemists, for they and we are both engaged with similar processes showing themselves in similar imagery. We need alchemy to understand our patients.

The third angle which I shall now essay has to do with alchemical language. In my twenty minutes I want to make this one point: Besides the general theory of alchemical transformation and besides the particular parallels of alchemical imagery with the individuation process, it is *alchemical language* which may be most valuable for Jungian therapy. In brief, alchemical language is a mode of therapy; it is itself therapeutic.

To talk about therapy we must first talk about neurosis. Jung's general theory of neurosis is that neurosis is a "one-sided development of the personality" (*CW* 16, § 257), which I take to mean the unavoidable one-sided development of consciousness *per se*. I read Jung to mean that neurosis resides in the patterns of our conscious personality organization, in the habitual way we go about our days. Whatever we do here requires repression somewhere else: I do because I repress or I repress because I do. As Jung's own formulation states: "One-sidedness is an unavoidable and necessary characteristic of the directed process, for direction implies one-sidedness" (*CW* 8, § 138). Neurosis can be cognitive, conative, or affective, introverted or extraverted, for we can be one-sided in any direction of personality.

Jung's is a beautifully limiting idea of neurosis, keeping it to what some might call "ego-psychology". I wouldn't, couldn't, call it such for reasons we shall come to; but at least Jung's idea of one-sidedness keeps neurosis from complicated explanations in terms of socio-adaptive processes, developmental historicisms, intra-psychic dynamisms, bio-feedback mechanisms, and other jabberwockies. Neurosis is located right in one's conscious framework (*CW* 16, § 12). I am neurotic because of what goes on here and now, as I stand and look and talk, rather than what went on once, or goes in society, or in my dreams, fantasies, emotions, memories, symptoms. My neurosis resides in my mental set and the way it constructs the world and behaves in it.

Now the essential or at least an essential component of every mental set, of every personality, is language. So, language must be an essential component of my neurosis. If I am neurotic, I am neurotic in language. Consequently, the one-sidedness which characterizes all neurosis in general is also to be found specifically as a one-sidedness in language.

An important implication of this I will merely brush in passing. This implication is: to discover the specifies of any neurosis (i.e., analyze it), I must examine the specifics of the language essential to it, the styles of speech in which the neurosis is couched. Jung began on this path with his studies in word association; Charles Osgood's semantic differential and George Kelly's psychology of personal constructs could take us into further detail and practicality.

There is much to learn in regard to the rhetorics of the neuroses. For we all listen to the style of speech and not only to the contents of that speech and to the tone and body of its voice. Archetypal psychology has already begun to examine the language, especially the rhetorical styles of manifest speech whether in the hour, in dream reports, or written works. But all this we leave aside today.

The main implication of the proposition that the one-sidedness of neurosis occurs essentially in the one-sidedness of language will lead us directly to our goal this morning. To get there within the next sixteen minutes, let me clear the ground in a hop, skip, and jump. The hop: Since language is largely social, the one-sidedness of *my* language reflects society's collective language. Then, the skip: Jung has already defined collective language as "directed" ("directed process," "directed thinking"–CW 5, Chap. II), and I have attacked it in various places under its guises of "nominalism," "rationalism," "psychological language," "Apollonic consciousness," and "day-world concepts". Last, the jump: Conceptual language, which is nominalistic and thus denies substance and faith in its words, is the usual rhetorical style of "ego," especially the psychologist's "ego," and is the chronic locus of our collective neurosis as it appears in language.

You see that I am claiming, as have Freud and Jung in other ways, a general Western cultural neurosis of one-sidedness. However, I am locating this in our directed-process language which is *directed from within* (for, after all, who or what directs our directed thinking?) by its inherent syntactical, grammatical, and conceptual structures resulting in conceptual rationalism. *Horribile dictu,* this neurosis is reinforced by the academic training we must each have to become members of the psychotherapeutic profession. By conceptual rationalism I mean papers such as this that account for events in concept-terms rather than thing-words, image-words, craft-words, and also I mean our habitual use of identity verbs (such as "is") which unconsciously substantiate the very terms we consciously assert to be only nomina. Hence we hypostasize our hypotheses. A rift develops between theory and practice, even a theoretical delusion about practice. Like Jung we assert our conceptual statements are only heuristic; but, because of language, we cannot avoid in practice substantiating what our theory asserts is only heuristic, only hypothetical. We simply are caught in the literalism of our own language.

We speak in concepts: the ego and the unconscious; libido, energy, and drive; opposites, regression, feeling-function, compensation, and transference. When working with these terms, we curiously forget that they are concepts only, barely useful for grasping psychic events which they inadequately describe, let alone explain. Moreover, we tend to neglect that these concepts burden our work because they come freighted with their own unconscious history.

Not only, then, as Jung says, are psychological concepts "irrelevant in theory," but as he also says, the psychologist "must rid himself of the common notion that the name *explains* the psychic fact it denotes" (CW 8, §§ 223–25). Yet we psychologists imagine these concept-terms to be thing-words, for as Jung continues: "Psychology . . . is still afflicted with a . . . mentality in which no distinction is made between words and things." What is this mentality, this affliction?

Is Jung speaking of literalism, that one-sidedness of mind which experiences only singleness of language? In such a consciousness, there is no "as if" between the word and whatever it is conceiving. Then the subjects in our sentences become existing subjects and the objects become objectively real facts. Then such concepts as the ego, the unconscious, the feeling-function, the transference become literally real things. Substantives become substances. So much so that we consider these concepts able to account for personality and its neuroses, whereas I am arguing that these very same substantialized concept-terms–ego, unconscious, transference–*are* the neurosis.

As Freud began by de-literalizing the memory of sexual trauma into its fantasy, and as Jung began by de-literalizing incest and libido, we need to de-literalize a host of other substantialized concepts, beginning with "the ego" and "the unconscious". I have personally never met either of them, except in a psychology book.

Enter alchemy–thing-words, image-words, craft-words. The basic stuffs of personality–salt, sulphur, mercury, and lead–are concrete materials; the description of soul, *aqua pinguis* or *aqua ardens*, as well as words for states of soul, such as *albedo* and *nigredo*, incorporate events that one can touch and see. The work of soul-making requires corrosive acids, heavy earths, ascending birds; there are sweating kings, dogs and bitches, stenches, urine, and blood. How like the language of our dreams and unlike the language into which we interpret the dreams. When alchemy speaks of degrees of heat, it does not use numbers. Rather it refers to the heat of horse dung, the heat of sand, the heat of metal touching fire. These heats differ, moreover, not only in degree, but also in quality: heat can be slow and gentle, or moist and heavy, or sudden and sharp. As well, the heat of horse dung imparts to the heated material properties of horse dung itself. Heat cannot be abstracted from the body which gives it.

The words for alchemical vessels–the shapes of soul in which our personality is being worked–contrast with the concepts we use, concepts such as inner space or internal object, or fantasy, or patience, containment, suppression or relationship. Alchemy presents an array of different qualities of vessel, different fragilities, visibilities, and forms: condensing coils, multiheaded alembics, pelicans, curcurbits, flat open pans. One uses copper or glass or clay to hold one's stuff and cook it.

Finally, the words for the operations–that which one does in crafting the psyche – are again concrete. We learn to evaporate away the vaporousness, to calcine so as to burn passions down to dry essences. We learn about condensing and congealing cloudy conditions so as to get hard clear drops from them. We learn about coagulating and fixing, about dissolving and putrefying, about mortifying and blackening. Now hear psychology's craft-words: analyzing the transference, regressing in the service of the ego, displaced affect, supportive measures, showing hostility, syntonic identifying, improving, denying, resisting, etc. Not only are they abstract; they are imprecise. Because of this imprecision in our equipment, our concepts for grasping the soul, we have come to believe the soul itself is an ungraspable flux, whereas actually it presents itself always in very specific behaviors, experiences, and images.

Ever since Jung opened the door to alchemy for psychologists, we have tended to go through it in only one direction: directedly, our directed thinking is applied to its fantasy thinking, translating its images into our concepts. White Queen and Red King have become feminine and masculine principles; their incestuous sexual intercourse has become the union of opposites; the freakish hermaphrodite and uniped, the golden head with silver hair, red within and black without—these have all become paradoxical representations of the goal, examples of androgyny, symbols of the Self. You see what happens: image disappears into concept, precision into generality.

We could go through the door differently. We might try translating the other way—the actualities of psychotherapy and the language we use to conceive those actualities put into imaginatively precise alchemical words. Thing-words, image-words, craft-words. Grinnell's book does just this—and so, conceptually addicted minds find it hard to read. Heavy. It *is* hard and heavy precisely because it speaks in the concrete words of the *opus*.

We could also not go through the door at all. For if we see through the concepts to begin with, we do not need translations. Then we would speak to the dreams and of the dreams as the dreams themselves speak. (By "dream" here I mean as well the dream within behaviour, or fantasy.) This seems to me to follow Jung's dictum of dreaming the myth along. To do this we must speak dreamingly, imagistically—and materially.

I have introduced "materially" at this juncture because with six minutes to go we are close to the crunch, and the crunch of alchemy is matter. It is the crunch of our practice too—to make soul *matter* to the patient, to transform his/her sense of what matters.

Holt has already shown in his *Spring* paper that alchemy is essentially a theory of the redemption of the physical, of matter. If so, then this redemptive process must also take place in our speech, where the absence of matter is most severe, and especially because this deprivation is so close that it is unconscious to us even as we speak. We can hardly expect therapy—so dependent upon speech—to work on this massive curse of Western consciousness, our tortures over matter, if the tool with which we work, our speech, has not itself resolved the curse. Our speech itself can redeem matter if, on the one hand, it de-literalizes (de-substantiates) our concepts, distinguishing between words and things, and if, on the other hand, it re-materializes our concepts, giving them body, sense, and weight. We already do this inadvertently when we speak of what the patient brings as "material," when we present the soul life of persons as case "material," look for the "grounds" of his/her complaint, and also by trying to make "sense" of it all.

Re-enter alchemy. Its beauty lies just in its materialized language which at the same time we can never take literally. For us it is in the historical past, *in ille tempore,* and thus an extensive metaphor, a myth. I know I am not composed of sulphur and salt, buried in horse dung, putrefying or congealing, turning white or green or yellow, encircled by a tailbiting serpent, rising on wings. And yet I am! I cannot take any of this literally, even if it is all accurate, descriptively true. Even while the words are concrete, material, physical, it is a patent mistake to take them literally. Alchemy gives us a language of substance which cannot be taken substantively, concrete expression which are not literal.

This is its therapeutic effect: it forces metaphor upon us. We are carried by the language into an as–if, into both the materialization of the psyche and the psychization of matter, at once, as we utter our words.

My conceptual language, however, is not self-evidently metaphor. It is too contemporary to be transparent; we are living right in its midst; its myth is going on all about us, so it does not have a metaphorical sense built in it. I do not know, cannot see, that I am really not composed of an ego and self, a feeling function and a power drive, castration anxiety and depressive positions. These seem literally real to me, despite the experience that even as I use these terms, there is a haunting worthlessness about them. Nominalism has made us disbelieve in all words—what's in a name?—they are mere "words," tools, any others would do as well; they have no substance.

But our psychological language has become literally real to us, despite nominalism, because the psyche needs to demonize and personify, which in language becomes the need to substantiate. The psyche animates the material world it inhabits. Language is part of this animating activity, (e.g., onomatopoeic speech with which language is supposed to have "begun".) Unless my language meets the need to substantiate, then the psyche substantiates anyway, unawares, hardening my concepts into physical, or metaphysical things.

May I insist that I am not proposing to cancel our concepts and restore the archaic neologisms of alchemy as a new esperanto for our practice and our dealings with one another. That would be to take alchemical language only literally. I do *not* mean: let us start off now talking alchemy; I mean first let us talk *as alchemists, as if we were talking alchemically.* Then we can talk alchemy, even the old mad terms, because then we will not be using them as literal substitutions for our concepts, merely employing them as a new set of conceptual categories. So, it is not the literal return to alchemy that is necessary, but a restoration of the alchemical mode of imagining. For in that mode we restore matter to our speech–and that, after all, is our aim: the restoration of imaginative matter, not of literal alchemy.

Some eighteen minutes ago I said that the one-sidedness of neurosis perpetuates in our psychological language, its conceptual rationalism. One-sideness–that general definition of neurosis–now becomes more precise. It can now be seen to refer to the grasping nature of our grasping tools, our concepts, which organize the psyche according to their shape. Our concepts extend their grasp over the concretely vivid images by abstracting (literally, "drawing away") their matter. We no longer see the clay funeral urn or the iron pot-bellied stove, but "the Great Mother"; no longer the sea just beyond the harbor, the sewer blocked with muck, or a beech wood on a summer evening, but "the Unconscious".

How can we have faith in what we do if our words in which we do it are disembodied of substance? Here again I join Grinnell and Holt who take faith to be the key to the entire psychological and alchemical opus. But I would locate this faith in the words that express, operate–even are–this endeavor. Again: abstract concepts, psychological nomina, that do not matter and bear weight, willy-nilly accrete ever more hardening, leaden immobility, and fixation, becoming objects or idols of faith rather than living carriers of it. When we talk psychology we cannot help but become rigidly metaphysical because the physical imagination has been emptied our of our words.

According to Jung, neurosis is splitting, and therapy is joining. If our conceptual language splits by abstracting matter from image and speaking only from one side, then the as-if of metaphor is therapy because it keeps two or more levels distinct – whether words and things, events and meanings, connotations and denotations–even as it joins them together in the word itself.

Especially, our one-sided language splits immaterial psyche from soul-less matter. Our concepts have so defined these words that we forget that matter is a concept "in the mind", a psychic fantasy, and soul our living experience amid things and bodies "in the world". As Jung grew older he became ever more obsessed with this particular split, attempting to join it with ever new formulations: "psychoid," "synchronicity," "unus mundus". Even if defined as embracing both sides and even if presented ambiguously and symbolically, these words (unlike, for instance, the alchemists' own "soft stone," "hermaphrodite," or "Royal Wedding in the Sea of the Indians") only reinforce the splitting effect inherent in such one-sided language itself. For they too are concepts, without body or image. So psychology remains neurotic: we have a nominalistic psyche without matter (and therefore fantasy and image do not "really" matter, are "only" in the mind or must magically connect to matter in synchronicity), and a de-souled matter that solicits its redemption through body therapies, consumer hedonism, and Marxism.

We end up with a cultural statement about neurosis and its therapy, similar to ones made by Freud and by Jung. Our neurosis and our culture are inseparable. After Nixonian double-speak, Communist jargonism, and Pentagonese, after sociological and economic scientism and media management of speech, and all the other abuses—even those of Lacan and Heidegger and communications theory performed in the very name of language—that have drained words of their blood, brought into our day a new syndrome, childhood mutism, and made us in psychology lose faith in the power of words so that therapy must turn to cries and gestures—after all this I am simply suggesting a mode of recuperating language by returning to speech that matters. I am also harkening back to Confucius who insisted that the therapy of culture begins with the rectification of language. Alchemy suggests this rectification.

ALCHEMY, MARX, AND THE CLINICAL IMAGINATION.

David Holt, London

1.

In this short paper I want to give you an idea of how my interest in comparing Jung's psychology of alchemy and the work of Marx affects my clinical practice. I want to describe an imaginal activity which is both alchemical and marxist in its inspiration.

I start with the dream of a patient: a woman in her early fifties who worked with me over a period of four years while leaving a closed religious community in which she had lived since her late twenties.

"I am with a young man, near the Community. He is gentle, kind, a good friend, though by conservative standards he might be thought a long-haired drop out. He invites me to visit the place where he lives, which is a kind of Commune. He explains that a number of his friends are under attack by hostile authorities, who want to drive them out of the Commune.

As we go towards his house, I see a group of gunmen waiting to shoot someone. A young nun emerges from a house, and starts to walk down the street. The gunmen take aim. I see the nun duck, turn and run to safety, just as the men fire at her. This makes us realise how great the danger is, and we proceed with caution, even though my friend has told me he is not in danger himself.

We get to his flat, where he lives communally with three other couples. We are all discussing the danger. We realise that some of the gunmen, who are both terrorists and also secret service police, are at the rear door. We all have to leave. We let the two younger couples go first, then the older couple. My friend says I must leave now. I am worrying about him, but know I must obey. I listen as the footsteps of the gunman pass our door, then I crawl along the floor to the door. But at the threshold I must risk being seen, and stand to open it. As I do so, I see one of our small kittens, and call to her, but use the wrong name, the name of another kitten that is male. I call: 'Come on . . .,' and grab him/her, and dash out."

(In discussing the dream, the point was made that both the two kittens had been neutered, "so it does not matter which name I use".)

Now at the time when this dream was brought me, I was studying the text from Philalethes' "Intoitus Apertus" which inspired John TRI-NICK to write his book The Fire Tried Stone, and which JUNG discusses in Chapter III of Mysterium Coniunctionis. On reading the dream, my immedite association was with this text—the two seemed as it were to fuse in my imagination.

Let me remind you of the text.

"If thou knowest how to moisten this dry earth with its own water, thou wilt loosen the pores of the earth, and this thief from outside will be cast out with the workers of wickedness, and the water, by an admixture of the true sulphur, will be cleansed from the leprous filth and from the superfluous dropsical fluid, and thou wilt have in thy power the fount of the Knight of Treviso, whose waters are rightfully dedicated to the maiden Diana. Worthless is this thief, armed with the malignity of arsenic, from whom the winged youth fleeth, shuddering. And thought the central water is his bride, yet dare he not display his most ardent love towards her, because of the snares of the thief, whose machinations are in truth unavoidable? Here may Diana be propitious to thee, who knoweth how to tame wild beasts, and whose twin doves will temper the malignity of the air with their wings, so that the youth easily entereth in through the pores, and instantly shaketh the foundations of the earth, and raises up a dark cloud."

When I asked myself why I was associating my patient's dream with this text, I found the link in John Trinick's vivid amplification of the text, where he imagines the worthless thief patrolling round and round, first in one direction then in the other, but trying the door every time he passes. I was associating the winged youth-vile thief relationship of the alchemical text with the gentle, kind friend—terrorist/secret police relationship of the dream. This association stayed with me, and I recognised that it was influencing my reaction to the dream, and in particular to the dream's lysis about the two cats.

This is the cluster of images, drawn partly from a dream and partly from an alchemical text, round which I want to suggest the imaginative field within which I worked with this patient. The particular clinical theme on which I want to dwell is the relation between projection and the body imago.

2.

Jung's analysis of the Introitus Apertus text is in ways similar to Trinick's. But its feeling tone is strikingly different. One reason for this difference is, I believe, Jung's clinical experience of projection. There is a two sidedness to Jung's analysis, a sympathy for psyche's resistance to the withdrawal of projections, which is lacking in Trinick's book. This contrast affected my reaction to my patient's dream.

Much of our work together had been about a certain quality in her spiritual life which we had both come to feel was sentimental and off-centre. This dream started me thinking about this quality within the context of the contrast between the feeling tone of Trinick's book and Jung's amplifications of the same text. As a result, I came to believe that I understood better what was wrong with her religious stance. I put this to her in terms of the relation between spirit, body, and psyche. I had been arguing with her for months that she was ignoring the reality of psyche, and as a result trying to make the spirit-body distinction do work for which it was not made. She had been responsive, but had been unable to understand what I meant by psyche. Following this dream, and the way in which it opened my own imaginal activity into the world of Mysterium Coniunctionis, I found myself drawing on alchemical symbolism in arguing for the reality of psyche as distinct from both body and spirit.

During the next eighteen months or so this theme was at the heart of the analysis. The work she put into it generated a middle field of interpretation between her understandings of spirit and body. But this dilation of her imaginal field to include the three realms of body, spirit and psyche, did not seem to be enough. There was recurring evidence, in dreams, in affect, and in the accident prone history of car driving, of some principle at work in her life which demanded a more radical reappraisal of the way in which she understood the world and her embodied being in the world. This principle can only be described as one of terror.

Something of this terror could be located in events of her past life. But it retained a quality which stubbornly resisted interpretation in terms of her own biography. Waking and dreaming, she insisted that what she was afraid of could only be fully expressed in the imagery of Christian theology. Her terror had to do with some kind of crisis or drama between the Christian theology of creation and of incarnation. Between the act which created the world, and the incarnation of the creator as Jesus Christ, there was something which needed to be done. It was because she sensed a personal involvement in this need that she had gone into her religious order twenty years ago, and it was the same sense which was now moving her to renounce her vows.

The material through which we worked on her sense of personal involvement in this theological crisis organised itself round sexuality and money. In responding to the sexual expression of her theological concern, I found that alchemical symbolism gave me a standpoint outside her own conscious theological framework from which I could talk about her own imagery in a way she could use. But in talking about money, I found myself drawing on ideas which I knew were derived from a different source: the work of Marx.

3.

I have tried to explain elsewhere how I understand Marx's work as "about" the theological crisis of our modern technological culture. Here I limit myself to just one aspect of this crisis: how it affects the way we imagine the insideness and outsideness of body.

This metaphor of inside and outside is one which we use constantly with reference to the body. Our clinical use of the idea of projection depends on it. In the dream I have read you, being inside is represented both by Community and Commune. Being outside, by the street. The alternative male figures who made the link in my imagination with the Introitus Apertus text belong respectively to inside and outside. The dreamer is trying to choose between the containment of alternative insides. In the end, she must risk being seen on the threshold between inside and outside.

The immediate associations were with moving out of the closed community, finding somewhere to live, reactivating her previous professional qualification. Money was involved. Her community were generous and realistic in helping her make the transition, but it was help which reminded her of earlier patterns of dependence. She had to assess and prove her own earning power, and deal with bewildering questions of taxation coding and social insurance. The ideal of simple communism exercised strong attraction.

But behind these, centred round her accident prone driving, were more confused intuitions and sensations about the insideness and outsideness of bodies. Her car was like a second body. What happened to it compelled her to ask questions about the *whereabouts* of inside and outside. For months we worked on this. We came to admit that in talking of insides and outsides, and of projection between, we were making assumptions about the whereness of body which neither of us could justify.

To go further required a considerable dilation of our imaginal field. We had to find ways of imagining the whereness of body which allowed for our not knowing the difference between insides and outside. As a result, the relation between body and what I can only call the architecture of society became a central theme of the analysis. The work required us to admit the presence of two bodies: the personal and the social. Once this admission was made, we began to get a new understanding of the terrors which were proving so disabling in her life.

It was here that I found myself inspired by Marx. As we explored the space between the personal body and the social body, I drew on Marx's vision of modern man as alienated from his own nature by his own work.

Perhaps the best way of describing this to an audience used to psychoanalytic imagining of the body, is to ask you to attend to your hands.

Marx's theory of alienation is grounded in his analysis of how labour changes man's place in the world. Man's labour originates in the turn of his hands. It is grounded in the way our hands take things which are outside into their holding. Manufacture begins between the outside and inside, the back and front, of our hands. If we follow Marx through his historical analysis of what labour has done to both man and to the world, and of the alienation peculiar to our modern culture, we find that our mind returns again and again to that original and so easily overlooked turn between the front and back of the hand. That turn constitutes the beginning of a new phenomenology of body.

Within this new phenomenology, the distinction between the inside and outside of our personal bodies opens the way into argument about the social body. This argument is centred on, and generated by, the sharedness of body. When we engage with this argument, our images of inside and outside take their place within more comprehensive symbolic systems. As the anthropologist Mary DOUGLAS has written: "Natural symbols will not be found in individual lexical systems. The physical body can have universal meaning only as a system which responds to the social system, expressing it as a system. What it symbolises naturally is the relation of parts of an organism to the whole. Natural symbols can express the relation of an individual to his society at the general systemic level. The two bodies are the self and society: sometimes they are so near as to be almost merged: sometimes they are far apart. The tension between them allows the elaboration of meanings."

Marx's theory of alienation was an early attempt to analyse the tension between the two bodies as we experience it in an advanced, industrial culture. Since he wrote, much has changed, and we are now able to analyse this tension in ways which he never imagined. But for me, Marx is still saying something about this tension which I do not find elsewhere. He is saying something about the fear by which our shared body is terrorised.

He relates this fear to the bond between war and time. Standing as he did in the Jewish-Christian prophetic tradition, Marx taught that the body which we share presumes a war between opposing powers. This war issues from our failure to understand creation. Because it has to do with creation, this war stands in a double relation to time. It is both historical and dialectical. It both needs time for its completion, and yet proves its necessity in overcoming time. This is what revolution is about.

Marxism is how millions are today trying to remember what it is like to create. The tragedy, a tragedy whose consequences have yet to be realised, is that Marx denied the religious inspiration of his vision.

As a result, he failed to realise that his revolutionary insight into the power located in the turn of our hands, required reverence for that special terror which obtains between creator and creature.

This was the imaginal field out of which I came to meet my patient in the accident prone body of her motor car. We met where flesh and metal are experienced as sustained by a common labour.

For years she had been trained to imagine the life of the spirit as a constant war of light against dark, a war whose conclusion can only be imagined as victory of one over the other. This war, with all its consequences, was justified by the dependence of creature on creator. Together we talked of this war and of this dependence in terms of projection. On the one hand, the kind of projections which Jung describes in his interpretation of the Introitus Apertus. On the other hand, the kind of projections which underwrite the political bond between terrorist and secret police. As a result, she was introduced to imaginal activity of a new kind.

She began to imagine her own place in that war differently. Her place remained where it had always been: her body. But the whereness of the body was different. The testing of projections dilated her understanding of how body and world share a common cosmogony. Through this dilation, she began to realise that the war in which she was called to participate could be understood in another way: as the creature's obligation to prove the power of the creator. This proving emerged as equivalent within the realm of psyche to the idea of war within the realm of spirit. In recognising the creature's obligation to prove the creator, our work found its centre.

ACTIVE IMAGINATION QUESTIONED
AND DISCUSSED

Elie G. Humbert, Paris

Active imagination and dream interpretation are two techniques that are complementary. The former takes place in a diurnal consciousness which it tends to render more and more impervious to the unconscious. The latter, in the broad light of day, picks up on what has occurred during the night. The former seeks direct confrontation, whereas the latter goes through the mediations of which the conscious is made up: the concept of perception, amplification, associations and dialogue. These two techniques are both necessary in order to establish a working relationship with the unconscious and this is how they are presented in the life and works of Jung.

Nowadays there are signs of a certain reticence towards active imagination. As far as I know, relatively few analysts practise it and it is rarely the subject of study.

Such an attitude is indicative of a lack of consciousness somewhere, and so an attempt must be made to undertake a sort of analysis of active imagination, to question it and to specify its characteristics and its conditions.

1. *What active imagination brings.*

a) a relationship with the unconscious which does not involve speech.

Psychoanalysis is based on interpretation. It was developed in the various Freudian schools at the level of verbalisation, reaching its extreme in the Lacan school, for whom the unconscious is only accessible to analysis in language. Today when people talk of entering a post-analytic era, what they mean is a reaction against the imperialism of speech and an appeal to the experience of the non-rational. And it is precisely here that active imagination is situated. It is a path for the man who is seeking his identity today, below and above the purely mental.

b) the formation of the affects

The mental is that which is consciously worked out via language. It only allows the affects indirect expression. We know to what extent individuation assumes that the affects be verbalised. It is an essential condition for all psychic self-regulation and is the raison d'être of the different methods of regression. At the same time as it shows us the necessity and the meaning of regression, experience also shows us that we cannot allow the regression to flow along in just any old way, for if this happens we lose ourselves in emotional states which lead nowhere because they no longer comprise internal tension. Active imagination allows the regression to develop but at the same time obliges it to take shape. A model for this is what Jung lived through between 1913 and 1919. We can also see here the particular capacity of the image to organise a field of consciousness which presents with increasing clarity a life and perspective that go beyond the self.

c) Eros

The imagination tears the self away from its mirror. It forces it into situations that call for an immediate reaction. It does not lend itself as easily as language to narcissistic recuperation. Above all, it brings the self into contact with forces that are independent of it, forces which have their own origins and laws. Active imagination thus opens the self to the experience of a certain change.

So one can understand why it feeds the Eros. It assumes that the mental has released its grip and it brings in a world of direct relationships, there where the affects express themselves and where the subject is called upon to act according to his feelings or instincts.

1.1 *Questions.*

a) Isolation in relation to the other person and in relation to the body.

We speak of Eros, and practice shows that in fact active imagination supports and develops it. But what Eros are we talking about where the other person is not present? Is not active imagination a dangerously glib exercise since the affects take shape there outside of all relation to the object?

In any therapy that supports regression the other person is present, if only in the person of the therapist. Here the subject is alone in a sort of tête-à-tête with the unconscious. The pitfalls of such a relationship are well-known.

The body is also out of action, except in those relatively rare cases where active imagination is accompanied by gestures. Not only does the body not intervene, but is even expected to keep still so that everything can proceed as if it were not there. Is this not laying itself open to the criticism levelled at classical analysis: talking of the body, imagining it but not bringing it into play?

b) Pleasure of the image.

If there is Eros without either the other person or the body participating, does this not mean that the pleasure would derive from the image itself? Freud has demonstrated how the image can be the realisation of the desire. Even the most simple experiment shows that pleasure can be derived from imagination. This leads to one of the central questions of Jungian psychology—that of making the image erotic.

c) Reinforcement of the defenses and of the imaginary.

Is it not so that the pleasure that fixes the libido in the images then leads away from a dual reality—that of the impulses and that of the outside world? Would not active imagination be a way of evading both of them? In the face of the conflicts with the outside world and the frustrations that thereby arise, the imagination enables us to flee from the ordeal of reality and to seek some undefined solution in symboliation. On the other hand it maintains a screen against the impulses and dramas of early childhood. It does not regress as far as that and arrests the testing of the self in forms that are much easier to take because they are symbolic. By establishing the meeting with the unconscious at the level of the image, does not active imagination avoid real confrontations by weaving a cocoon whereby what happens only does so in the realms of the imaginary?

d) The Mother.

There seems to be a close link between the images and the Mother. In our society the Logos is related to the archetype of the Father, whereas the irrational and the image come from the archetype of incest and the return to the Mother. The image is made up of a homogeneous combination of concrete form and unconscious power. Unlike the word, it is not a means of separation but, on the contrary, one of participation. One can therefore well suspect it of belonging to the world of the Mother. If imagination allows one to return there and receive the capacity of re-creation, does it allow one to break free? Is it not, on the contrary, by its very nature, the trap which holds the prisoner fast? In other words, those who practise active imagination benefit from an enriching of the unconscious and a growth of libido, but do they not, by the same terms, remain under the spell of the Great Mother? Even the man who confronts the Mother in active imagination would not do it except in his own home.

e) Taking the image in accordance with the laws of the concrete.

What foundation is there for taking the image seriously to the extent of not letting it be transformed freely from one form to the other, but forcing it to keep itself in the form of concrete reality? It will be recalled that Jung said to the woman who saw a lion emerge from the waves and transform itself into a ship: "No lion can turn into a ship; what do you do when faced with this lion?" What does such a blocking of the image of the concrete mean? Does the role of both of them in the psychic not find itself modified by this?

1.1.1 *Characters and conditions.*

a) The Jungian approach.

In fact Jung refuses to measure the unconscious solely by its relation to the object. He sees the external world and the internal world as opposing forces, engaged in successive phases of the conjunction, and shows how the subject constitutes itself there in a dual confrontation. Far from treating the concrete as the term of reference, this analysis shows how the subject and the objective worlds (external and internal) form themselves reciprocally.

Anyone engaging in active imagination is putting into practice that which has been theorised about in the above metapsychological considerations. It should also be pointed out that the Jungian procedure is based on a suspension of judgement comparable to the phenomenological approach.

b) The confrontation/differentation.

The thing about active imagination is that the subject brings his own responsibility into play. The objective is not merely that images should emerge, but particularly that the self adopts its own position on the stage. Jung insisted strongly on "My life". It is not enough simply to allow unconscious contents to emerge.

c) Active imagination is not a substitute for something else.

It cannot take the place either of physical labour, the necessary analysis of the impulses or an external task. It is most frequently brought into play only at the end of an analysis, precisely when the defense mechanisms and the fixations in the imaginary have been rendered conscious.

d) Oedipus or paradox?

The question of the relationship with the Great Mother finds an initial element of response in the idea that active imagination must not be used to avoid separations. On a deeper level it is the Jungian model that is important. Whereas with Freud the development of the human subject is defined by the passage of the Oedipus, one condition of individuation is the ability of the subject to preserve the paradox, i.e. to live the conjunction of the opposites. It is quite clear that the involvement of the Mother is not the same in these two instances.

Conclusion.

If active imagination involves certain risks when it is practised outside the prescribed limits, it is nevertheless irreplaceable for maintaining a living relationship with the unconscious, and from this point of view it is essential to the affective and mental health of the analyst.

DREAMS AND PSYCHOLOGICAL TYPES
A Personal View

Thomas Kirsch, San Francisco

Two areas in Jung's work have a profound importance in our everyday clinical practice. They are his theory of dream interpretation and his studies on psychological types. This paper will attempt to describe how my attitude towards dreams has evolved in relationship to my own psychological type.

Dream interpretation was extremely important during my own analysis, enabling me to see hitherto unconscious aspects of myself, and being a good Jungian I thought this approach could be universally applied to all analysands. But my early practice was full of general psychiatric patients who did not know that I was a "Jungian". Most of these "non-Jungian" patients who remained in treatment did, however, finally report dreams. Three distinct groups of such patients emerged:

1. A group of patients who reported dreams, had relevant associative material, and for whom the dream analysis was meaningful to their lives.
2. A smaller group of patients who presented me with so many dreams that I became overwhelmed. We could not discuss any dream in depth, and thus these patients used the flood of dreams in a defensive manner.
3. A third still smaller group reported very few dreams, and usually they dropped out of therapy after a few sessions. Their failure to report dreams was not the cause of termination per se, but was usually symptomatic of a resistance to therapy.

It is important to emphasize the fact that in none of these groups did the patient know that I am a Jungian analyst. Those who have some knowledge of Jung enter therapy with a different set of expectations and do not concern us at this time. My percentage of "non-Jungian" referrals has varied from 20 %–50 % of my practice; how they become involved in their dream life has continued to fascinate me. It has been a challenge to interpret various complexes such as shadow, animus, anima, etc., without using the terms. (Naturally one tries not to use the terms in any analysis, but with people who have a reading knowledge of analytical psychology, it is hard not to slip into it from time to time.) It has often taken a great deal of effort to make the dreams come alive to these people.

Several techniques have been helpful in getting people involved in their dreams. I often tell the patient to imagine the dream situation as if it were happening in the outer world. For instance, a patient dreams of walking along the beach and there is a large wave approaching. I ask him to imagine himself there during the analytic hour. Often patients will then experience a great deal of anxiety, whereas in reporting the dream, not much affect was expressed. The patient begins to experience the reality of the unconscious, rather than viewing the dream as something happening out there to someone else.

A second technique which is often helpful in freeing up associative material is to ask the dreamer to pretend that he is talking to someone from Mars, who has no idea what the object in the dream is. This will often free the person to give a more naive and primitive association, and furthermore, makes it more interesting for the dreamer. An example of such an image is a patient dreaming that he is in a large department store looking for a sweater. When he is asked to describe the department store he has no immediate associations. When I proceed to ask him further about what one does in a store he hesitatingly states that it is a place to buy things, anyone can enter such a place, i.e. it is a collective place where one buys items such as a sweater. What is a sweater? An article of clothing to keep one warm. Therefore, this dream has to do with his buying some new protective cover to cope with the collective world. Sometimes if I express the thought to the patient, it will help him to associate further to the dream.

Thirdly, I try very hard to relate the dream to some affect-laden experience which has occurred in the previous day or two. When this is possible, dream interpretation becomes more immediately meaningful. An example of this is the following; young, single, male school teacher, thirty years old, recently begun analysis, reported an incident with his principal. Both had been wooing the students and there has been competition for their affection and praise. They discussed their respective power needs shortly before my patient had the following dream. He dreamt that he was close to his childhood home, but it was not actually his home. Suddenly, he saw his older brother standing in the door. He awakened, surprised. His associations to his older brother revealed that the patient had been favored over his older brother, who always had difficulties in school and career. The patient was seen as the great hope in the family. In a flash of intuition I realized that the dream had been triggered by the confrontation with his slightly older colleague. It turned out that the patient had unconsciously recreated the childhood pattern in his present situation at work. He had an "ah hah" reaction and became quite vulnerable for the next few minutes of the session. So far my handling of the dream is no different from what any analyst would do, regardless of type. Where the extraverted intuitive feeling reaction comes in is that I had sensed the sibling rivalry in the very first session, particularly in relationship to me. I did not comment on it at the time, because it was in the first session. Thus the dream corroborated my earlier extraverted intuitive-feeling hunch about the patient. This example demonstrates a dream interpreted primarily on the objective level. My guess is that generally extraverts lean toward objective interpretations, although it may have more to do with the sensation function than with the particular psychological attitude. Sensation types need the connection to the concrete reality and thus may tend toward the objective interpretation. This is a complicated subject and not one in which I feel competent to say more.

Besides the technical considerations in eliciting meaningful dream interpretations, there is the larger question of the dialectical procedure within the analytic process. One parameter within it which has not been emphasized is the effect of the psychological type of both analyst and analysand on dream interpretation. The Jungian literature has a pronounced tendency to emphasize the introverted intuitive analyst and an introverted intuitive patient, both being comfortable in the world of inner images. As I have become more comfortable with being an extraverted intuitive-feeling type, my response to patients' dreams has changed. Earlier in my practice I was much more circumspect in my reactions to dream material. I would restrain my own natural extraverted reaction, feeling and/or intuitive. Furthermore, I was oriented towards making interpretations on the subjective level. Other interpretations were not as "deep" or "Jungian". As I have become more accepting of my own psychological type, my reactions to dreams have changed. I am much more prone to show a spontaneous feeling reaction to some element of a dream. Secondly, the transference-countertransference and real relationship aspects of the dream have become more meaningful, as a way of dealing with the extraverted feeling part of the analytic process. In former years I had the tendency to deal with direct transference dreams in a more subjective manner. For instance, when a patient dreamt about me, I emphasized the symbolic inner healer and less about the transference in the flesh and blood. Now I am more apt to discuss the relationship between the two of us. Clinical judgement is necessary to decide which level of interpretation is correct in the individual situation.

As I think of dream examples from my "non-Jungian" patients I realize that those who stuck it out with me have features in common. They are introverted young women in their twenties and thirties, who might even be diagnosed as schizoid. They are extremely isolated from emotional reactions as a result of a deep maternal injury in childhood. The symptoms which bring them to treatment are those of depression: loneliness and isolation, a feeling of emptiness and worthlessness, often with suicidal ideation. They usually are quite successful in their careers, but feel a void inside.

Let me illustrate with a patient who used dreams defensively, presenting too many for meaningful analysis. She is a thirty-six year old single woman who came to therapy seven years previously with severe foot pain for which she had had two unsuccessful operations. She was extremely introverted and withdrawn and talked compulsively about inconsequential matters. When asked for dreams, she related long and complicated sagas, which I could not follow. Many of them revolving around the theme of masturbating in her childhood home with mother and grandmother in the adjacent room were lengthy sagas, and were presented with very little affect on her part. Early in her treatment I methodically tried to deal with each of them in turn until I realized she was flooding me to avoid her own affect. Although she rejected my attempts to reach her with my extraverted feeling, which seemed to overwhelm her, I persisted and at some level she felt validated by my interest in her, and this helped her to become less defensive against her affects. Gradually she began to respond to the content of her dreams, and she became appropriately uncomfortable when discussing masturbation, etc. Concomitantly she began to report less complicated dreams, and I experienced her as more genuinely involved in her analysis.

A second example is of a young woman who has used dream analysis in a therapeutic fashion. She is thirty-three, married, without children, an introverted sensation-thinking type with a successful career as a book editor. She was referred to me by her family physician seven years ago when she developed agoraphobic symptoms. Early in treatment she had several dreams in which she tried to meet with me, but I was not available or she had the wrong time, place, etc. This seemed to both of us to indicate that she was out of touch with herself in a deeper sense. The fact that we did not meet represented a resistance to going further therapeutically at the time. Except for her presenting symptom, her dreams were the major way of realizing her alienation from herself. Initially her ability to express affect of any sort was quite limited. In other typical dreams she was at home with her five sisters and mother and she was not able to talk to anyone in the room because there was too much noise. She sensed that she was caught in the *participation mystique* of the family and could not express her individual needs. These dreams have been most helpful in the reductive analysis of the mother complex. Furthermore, dream interpretation has been most helpful in releasing affects, particularly those of depression. At one phase of the analysis she would enter each session and immediately burst into tears for the first ten minutes. It seemed as if a dam were breaking which had been held in check by only the greatest of efforts. My extraverted intuition has been most helpful with this patient because her own associations to dreams have been so sparse. My intuition would raise several possibilities, and often would make the bridge to what she could not bring on her own. At that point she could continue with her own associations and a meaningful dialogue ensued. My feeling function has also been quite active in helping her to be comfortable. Again most dream interpretation has been on the objective level.

This paper attempts to demonstrate the effect of an extraverted intuitive-feeling response to dreams. However, I wonder if this can be done in reality. Firstly, I have left out any discussion of the influence of unconscious factors. Secondly, since we have all undergone our own analyses, we should have a healthy regard for our own inferior function, and be able to assess the patient from that point of view as well as to use the superior function blindly. For example, with the male school teacher, having obtained a detailed family history using my sensation function was most helpful in working out the meaning of the dream. In spite of these disclaimers, it is still important to examine the influence of psychological type and superior function upon the analyst's approach to dreams. Most Jungian literature emphasizes an introverted bias towards dream interpretation, and I have attempted to portray an extravert's orientation. In the course of this study it was noted that young introverted women seem to make particularly suitable analytic candidates for me as a young, extraverted feeling male analyst. I wonder if any generalizations can be made in this regard; that is, does a certain psychological type analyst attract and engage in analysis certain psychological type patients? If so, does it happen as presented here that the psychological type of the analyst is opposite to that of the patients described? Furthermore, I was most interested in those patients who did not know that I was a Jungian analyst and therefore were naive to Jungian theory. It seems that much more work needs to be done on this variable of psychological type in relationship to dream interpretation, and this paper is only a beginning.

THE USE OF THE DREAM IN CONTEMPORARY ANALYSIS

Kenneth Lambert, London

Introduction

A number of changes have taken place during the present decade in the significance attached by analysts to the phenomenon of dreaming as such and in their interpretative use of dreams in clinical work. These arise both from outside the analytical tradition as a result of considerations adduced by the work of the sleep laboratories and in neurophysiology and from within as the result of developments in psychoanalysis and analytical psychology. I propose to sketch out some of these changes mainly from the angle of analytical psychology – with illustrations from two cases.

The Psychoanalytical Tradition

The action of Emmy von N., nearly 80 years ago, in presenting her dreams to Freud lead him towards a point where he could begin to talk of the dream as "the royal road to the knowledge of the unconscious activities of the mind"–a revolutionary step for a mind of this time, rationalist and scientifically orientated, but too topographical and static for today. Much more dynamic was his theory that during sleep there takes place a lessening of the tension that arises out of the inhibitory control of impulses to action originating at the level of primary-process. That tension is further eased by the way in which dream activity manages to allow some expression to primary process impulses. These

provide the latent content of the dream and obscure it from consciousness by a manifest content that employs condensation, displacement
and the language of signs and symbols—a sort of "under-the-counter"
manoeuvre.

As a general theory of dreams, this is of course open to inumerable
criticisms and is of limited value only. For all that, however, Freud did
pioneer for psychology the notion of an inner world in which protective
and integrating processes can be furthered by dreams, whether considered as events in their own right or interpreted to enlarge ego-consciousness.

In the history of psychoanalysis, however, the widespread super-
session of topographical theory by structural theory and the rise of
Hartmann and the ego-psychologists brought about a lessening of interest in dreams for a time (ALTMANN [1]). More recently, however, that
process has again been reversed. Now, the language, images and feelings of dreams are being taken as valid and appropriate to aspects of the
psyche such as unconscious infantile phantasy; to vicissitudes in the
formation of object relationships and internal objects; to the interplay
between the patients' inner figures understood as whole or part objects; and to the interplay at deep levels between patient and analyst,
both in terms of transference and counter-transference, and in terms of
the analyst and patient as objects in their own right. In a word, the contemporary psychoanalytic approach is much nearer to that with which
we are familiar as analytical psychologists.

Some Contributions of the Sleep Laboratories

However that may be, Freud certainly held the view that dreaming
as such serves psychological health. It is implicit in his psychology of
dreaming and may be understood to be an expected by-product of his
way of interpretating dreams in analysis. That view of their function
has gained the well known support of workers in the sleep laboratories
like OSWALD (12), E. L. HARTMANN (6) and many others who
have established the distinction between rapid eye movement sleep
(REM, "paradoxical" or "D") and slow wave sleep ("orthodox" or "S").
Slow wave sleep is relatively dreamless, and mainly facilitates the

restoration of worn out and fatigued somatic process (Vide Redfearn 14); REM sleep on the other hand, by means of dreaming, sorts out and orders the impressions of the waking day and the interactions between the sleeper and his environment, certainly outer, and probably inner, to much of which he cannot give waking attention. In addition, Hartmann thinks that the repair of systems subserving attention, secondary process and self guidance may be involved in REM sleep as well. Richard JONES (7) in "The New Psychology of Dreaming" (sums up the psychological functions of REM sleep dreaming in the preservation and development of the human organism under five headings: 1. the *neutralization* of periodic psycho-noxious aspects of repressed infantile wishes; 2. the *stimulation*, through the imagery and more bizarre content of dreams, and by way of release, of the psyche cramped as it can be by the conventional and over-controlled thought processes of everyday rational life; 3. the *reorganization* of ego-functioning by increasing the cognitive grasp of the dreamer; 4. the maintenance of *optimal vigilance* in mammals whether in terms of potential danger to life and limb or, in more sophisticated terms, within the network of relationships in which the organism is involved; 5. the maintenance of *perceptiveness in depth* particularly in relationship to self knowledge and development.

One implication of all this independent work on dreaming, as W. C. M. SCOTT (15) has pointed out, is that analysts are further encouraged in being interested in the relation of their patients to dreaming. The experimental subjects seemed willing to tell their dreams to the experimenters. Sometimes children, too, wake up in the middle of the night and want to tell their dream to their parents. Are they told to go to sleep again as it is "only a dream"? Or are they promised they will be listened to tomorrow? Or are they listened to on the spot? What about parents on the other hand who are over-intrusive and try to drag the dreams out of their children, who then clam up and refuse to tell? Their dreams become their secrets. The same questions can be asked in principle about analysts and their patients. Quite an important aspect of the analysis of a patient, it turns out, is to consider, as an analytic point in its own right, vicissitudes in his attitude towards his dreams and his presentation of them, for dreaming is to be taken as being as significant as any other area of experience though not in principle any more or less so.

147

Furthermore analytical psychologists such Ernest ROSSI (14) and psychoanalysts such as Michael STONE (16) and R. M. JONES have begun to draw the attention of analysts to the research carried out, over more than a decade, by neuro-physiologists into the functioning of the cerebral hemispheres and the callosal bridge, that both separates and links them, and facilitates the working together as a whole of the cerebral basis of the psyche. Those studies arose out of work in the field of brain damage and the split brain, quite independent of any interest in analysis.

Michael STONE (16) has focussed as follows on the points, emerging from a mass of detail, that seem relevant to the interests that analysts have in dreams. In the more usual situation there is a fairly clear differentation between the type of capabilities that are based upon the left hemisphere and those based on the right. The situation may, however, be one of reversal or unclear distribution. Preponderantly it is found that in the left hemisphere are grouped together a number of rational capabilities—particularly verbalization and language facility. Also are included linear thinking using propositional and mathematical logic; aim directed acting according to a plan; capacities to analyze; and an exact adaptation to clock-time. By contrast, the right hemisphere processes feeling and emotion, musical experience, visual and spatial accuracy. It is the basis for a way of relating to reality within or without that uses *holistic* imagery which sums up situations in a way that is usually less available to the left hemisphere. The images may be beautiful, horrific, bizarre, humorous, cartoon-like, and may contain puns and playfulness of all sorts.

We are here dealing with the cerebral bases of human adaptation to, and relationship with, the environment, inner and outer, and it becomes clear how complementary the hemispheres are and how necessary both are for the organism to survive as a whole.

Stone goes on to cite D. B. COHEN (3) who found that REM dreaming shows all the features of right hemispherical activity, all through the night, but he also found that, as the night wears on, the left hemisphere seems to exert more and more control of REM dreaming so that more verbal activity comes into the dreams, suggesting a kind of growing cooperation. Stone also cites P. BAKAN (2) who elaborates in more detail. He note the similarities between dream experience and right hemispherical modes of expression, he reports "electro-encephalographic" evidence for relatively greater activity in the right hemisphere during REM sleep. He concludes that REM sleep "provides an opportunity for the exercise of the right hemisphere system while it is functionally disconnected from the left as a result of reduced callosal transmission," (during early sleep especially). He adds that the "relative ascendance of the right hemisphere system during REM sleep confers physiological and psychological benefits for the organism".

To sum up the contribution of the last two sections of this paper to the main theme, I would say that it consists in extending the scope of the theory of dreaming with which analysts can work. A good deal of it, we may agree, had already been adumbrated by Freud, though upon a different basis of observation. As it turns out, however, it was much more particularly and all-embracingly posited by Jung.

It does not deal, however with the problem of interpretation. That is a fundamental task for the analyst. It merely gives added validation to the analyst's interest in dreams and helps him to sustain a connection with the "somatic" basis of his work, however "psychological" or "spiritual" that may often be.

Analytical Psychology and Dreams

I shall now turn to attempt a short statement about dreams in classical analytical psychology, from which standpoint to discuss recent developments in the analyst's use of them. I propose to summarize a statement on the subject in a chapter on dreams in C. A. MEIER's "Jung's Analytical Psychology and Religion" republished in 1977 (10). For Meier, as with Jung, the dream is to be understood as a spontaneous and natural product of the psyche-soma. It has a language of its own which can in principle be progressively mastered. It often emerges into consciousness when, in the dreamer, an "abaissement du niveau mental" has come about. As in a drama, four movements in it can often be discerned—the presentation of the *dramatis personae*, the exposition, the crisis and the solution. Because the *dramatis personae* can be personifications or images of forces within the dreamer or in the outer world, the interpretation can be either an objective or a subjective one. Furthermore, apart from personal figures, typical archetypal motifs may appear such as that of the hero's journey, treasure in the cave, the crossing of the river, friendly animals and the *circumambulatio*. The language of the dreamer is largely that of signs and symbols and the form includes condensation, contamination and other distortions. Various kinds of relationship between conscious and unconscious figures are envisaged. Interpretation is related to a *circumambulatio* around associations of a personal and contextual nature, often taking a whole dream series into account, and mythological parallels are sought.

Now, that this classical Jungian approach to dreams is rich and impressive goes without saying. It both complements and is compensatory to the Freudian approach in a creative way. It enjoys a bonus of vindication from independent experimentalist work on dreaming. Nevertheless when it comes to the handling of their patient's dreams on the part of analysts in the daily clinical situation, the last quarter-century's experience has enlarged the range of understanding, interpretation and practice in a number of ways, a selection of which I group under four headings.

My first heading is about the eliciting of dreams from patients. A number of analysts find themselves, in contrast with earlier practice, not specifically asking their patients for dreams at least in the first instance. There is much to be said for this practice. A request for dreams, or indeed for any other specific kind of material, represents a real action on the part of the analyst and can run the risk of introducing an actual strain or resistance into the relationship. It can complicate the transference/countertransference. It may encourage either compliance or rebellion in the patient rather than facilitate communication of his real concern at any moment of time to an analyst who is able to be open to receive it. with neither prejudice nor the imposition of his own preferences upon the patient.

My second heading concerns the fascination that Jung's discoveries about dreams can exercise upon intuitive and imaginative analysts who may also have benefitted personally from dream analysis. It is possible for them to slip unconsciously into feeling themselves to be "dream interpreters" rather than analysts of their patients' dynamics. The dangers of that kind of over-subjective phantasying about a patient's dream has long been recognised. It was hoped that the study of dream sequences would achieve greater objectivity. A further step towards concentrating upon the patients' personality as such is to take his dreams, not so much as central, but simply as part of the flow of communication, with a nodal core, understandable as being meaningful. Thus associations to a dream can sometimes, with hindsight, be seen to have begun in sessions before the dream is presented and to have gone on for sessions afterwards. In addition there is evidence that archetypal themes may be discovered in the patient's material in many forms other than in dreams, i.e. in his reports of actions and events, in his descriptions of people, in slips of the tongue, in non-verbal communication and in the transference/countertransference situation. In this way the interpretation of the dream becomes part of the analysis as a whole. This is not, of course, to deny that many dreams can, in a striking and vividly experiential way, give the patient access to the emotional, spatial, non-temporal and holistic mode of the night hemisphere as part of the totality of his response to his situation.

My third heading has to do with the transference/countertransference, not only or so much in terms of its expression in the content of the dream, but more as it gets expressed in behavioural terms through the manner and mode of the patient's reporting of dreams to his analyst, together with the analyst's feeling-reponse to his patient's action–a response which may or may not be appropriate. When it is not, that may be due to a bias arising out of the analyst's psychological type, as elaborated upon by Thomas KIRSCH (8) or out of a countertransference that may be "neurotic" (RACKER [12]) or "illusory" (FORDHAM [5]).

Let us first postulate a situation where that last consideration would not need much attention. In it, the analyst is really open. The patient knows it. The transference has been enough analysed for the patient's use of his dreams to be relatively freed from transference distortions. When he remembers a dream, he will communicate it quite naturally as part of the flow of communication–and a useful interpretation, considerably influenced by the dream, can follow. Telling a dream represents an event in its own right, an action is taking place, similar to that of Emmy von N. The patient is performing an action towards his analyst and it is understood why.

Now let us envisage a distorted situation. Because most patients to-day know that dreams come into the work and interest of analysts, their transference can influence the way in which they present their dreams in therapy. The recognized countertransference can indicate to the analyst what his patient's action really is.

The following are examples:–

1. The patient presents regular dreams out of compliance and possibly a wish to divert the analyst's attention from the patient's real and feared problem. The analyst finds it all too suspiciously easy.

2. The patient brings a mass of dreams to each session. He is either tell-ing the analyst or boasting that he, the patient, is the kind of man who produces all these wonderful dreams, or he is swamping the analyst with them as if, according to infantile archetypal phantasy, swamping the analyst with too great a mass of material to cope with analytically. The analyst will feel either left out and underestimated or flooded, drowned, and oppressed.

3. The patient brings neither living material nor dreams. He is really saying "I'm not giving you what you want. You only want to in-trude on me and spy on me as my mother did. I don't want anyone to know about how bad I am, or rob me of any good I have." The analyst then feels starved and cold-shouldered.

4. The patient brings scraps of dreams and emphasizes how incomplete they are, or he throws them at his analyst in isolation and without a word of association. The analyst feels tantalized and tittilated or helpless in his countertransference which can indicate, among other things, that he has unconsciously cottoned on to his patient's wish to have, *by reverse*, his own interest tittilated into life, to the relief of his lifeless depression.

5. Then there is the patient who, flinging dreams at his analyst, makes sarcastic or destructively negative reponses to his analyst's attempts to understand the dreams and the material as a whole. That can arise out of envy, contempt and defiance of the analyst as the richly endowed one or it can represent a defence of the self, against the terrifying power of the analyst, (FORDHAM [4]). The analyst on his part feels the sting of the envious or defensive attacks upon him and his skills.

In all those situations, the analyst needs to focus upon the patient's *behaviour* with his dreams, while the *content* of the dreams, even if relevant, may have to be used for the time being for the analyst's information alone.

My fourth heading concerns some of the contents and actions in the dream. Recent psychoanalytic advance enables us to increase our understanding of the part played in dreams by unconscious infantile phantasy about "part" as well as "whole" objects and how images of that sort jostle side by side with internal objects and archetypal imagery, (LAMBERT [9]). The point is illustrated in some of the dream material I shall shortly present.

Cases

I now propose to give two highly compressed accounts of cases which bear out my main points.

The case of Robert

a) Robert, an intelligent and gifted young doctor, describes himself as the youngest son, by some seven years, as compared with his older brother and sister, both artists, whom he experienced as fairly trendy and chaotic in their personal lives. He felt that they had been openly contemptuous of his little penis when he was a small boy and physically rough with it. They still were so today in respect of his social and medical position, so "bourgeois," from their point of view, as compared with theirs. Robert's mother was a practical, ambitious, somewhat high-minded woman. She was well meaning but not very tactful and certainly not openly demonstrative of her tenderness. Robert experienced her as rather "nordic," but proud of her son who successfully used his educational opportunities to get him through to medical qualification. The father seemed very different–a warm hearted, sensitive, feeling type of man rather dark and "southern". He was experienced by Robert as a decent man, successful in his life and work as a financier, but too passive at home in relation to his wife. Robert managed the medical ratrace, with its ups and downs, successfully enough in objective terms, but always combined it with literary, poetic and musical interests. He could be dreamy but was gifted therapeutically and even capable of a streak of exact practicality in his medical treatments. Subjectively, he had always felt somewhat unsure of himself with siblings because of the phantasied small penis, and to compensate had developed his natural charm to aid him on his way. He had fastened onto the anthropological concept of "liminality" and felt himself to be perpetually in threshold situations, with few of the landmarks clear. He had also become pre-occupied at that time with the idea that he was "right-hand hemispherically dominant," and, seemingly to himself, more imaginative, pattern-conscious and intuitive rather than practical, aim-directed and logically exact in thinking and speech.

b) The Context of the Dream.

At the time of the dream I am about to recount, he had come to the end of a hospital appointment and found himself having to mobilize energy to secure a suitable new one as part of his career structure. He went to view a hospital post which, though interesting medically, also involved a good deal of rather demanding administrative work. He was describing this to me the next morning when he mentioned the dream he had awoken with:–

"I am in a house, maybe the parental home with a difference. I went to the top of the house where there was a large attic with big windows. In the room I found a strongly built housemaid with a plain, if not ugly, face. To my surprise, she became very sexually aggressive and implored me to have intercourse with her, yelling and shrieking at me to do so and jeering at my supposed impotence. I was not provoked into action but replied that I was perfectly capable of intercourse but did not intend to have it with her."

The context of the dream was therefore his mobilizing energy, his bracing himself up to going all out for a job that demanded administrative clarity and decisiveness. The dream emerged after 18 months communication of the material I have already described. In addition to that there was the theme of finding himself surprisingly competent when taking on jobs, despite the very considerable fear and uncertainty experienced by him in threshold situations. Thus, while he had been characteristically hesitating before entering upon analysis, he had feared –and that fear was spurred on by his friends–that he would be entering upon a really painful process of being held down to the grindstone with every minutia of his life being subjected to ruthless analysis. Indeed he had been half influenced in choosing Jungian analysis on the basis of a phantasy that it would not be so obsessively rigorous as psychoanalysis. Again he had found himself, with some surprise, enjoying his analysis and finding himself able to cooperate satisfactorily. My own countertransference enabled me to be spontaneously open and acceptant of all the facts of his personality as they came up—not favouring the imaginative any more than the practical and not asking specifically for dreams. Robert's difficulties stemmed back to the primal scene where in his phantasy his parents' marriage had been made difficult by his mother and father being such different kinds of people. Furthermore the effective practical but cool attitudes of his mother were often experienced by him as unattractive and repellent, while the easygoingness of his father, which he liked by way of contrast, reinforced that repellence. It was this, coupled with the phantasied small penis, that rendered Robert's awareness of his practical abilities and, indeed, physical strength, less clear to him than it was to others, including myself. There are traces of all distributed in the dream, such as the repellent features of the housemaid plus her vigour, his coolness, the taunting references to the impotence phantasy, and his defensive reply. It is therefore arguable that the dream had emerged out of a mass of prior communications that may be regarded as associations which made it easy for him to establish a view of its significance within the whole context of his problems.

c) The Nodal Point of the Dream.

The central point of the dream communication would seem to be that, faced with the demand of practical reality in the form of a post requiring administrative responsibility, he found it ugly and unattractive and rather haughtily and coolly drew back from it. On the other hand, the ugly maid's insistence suggests that deep down in him and despite his dislike of it there was another factor, an anima-figure potentially acceptable to him, that was interested in, and desirous of, practical work and insistent upon being allowed participation in his life. That side of his anima had become to some extent an internal object as a result of his experience with his mother. When he married, the repellent aspect of that internal object modified. Indeed his wife is able, practical—and also attractive. That modification was further fostered in the homosexual transference to myself in the sense that, while appreciating his darker intuitive and feelings sides, I certainly did not despise the other.

He was beginning therefore to get hold of the way in which early traumata had knocked him into a cool and negative, rather grudging, relation to his practical administrative abilities in which, nevertheless, a good deal of libido was present. A real grasp needed something like the surprise element and emotional content that was beginning to emerge in previous sessions, but was finally brought together and focussed by the dream in a way that was vivid and striking to him. In later sessions, Robert began to consider the liminal experience in general from two angles, i.e. (1) the normal anxieties accompanying it, as such, and (2) the extent to which liminal anxieties in his case had been intensified in an over-determined and indeed crippling way through exposure to them at an early and tender age without adequate support and understanding by the family matrix.

The Case of Charles

My second case is that of a young man whose life took an opposite turning from Robert's during his adolescence.

a) Charles' account of his history.

Charles was referred at the age of 20. According to his experience of his parents, he had had a beautiful but cool mother from an wealthy background, and a father, coming from an old family, who was often rather blustering and brutal in the use of physical violence but whose life had consisted of a series of failures in business, often at the expense of his wife's money. Charles was the eldest child with a brother three years younger, followed by a sister younger still. Charles changed when his brother was born and became possessed by hatred and rage towards him. At school he did well at lessons and in addition became a good rugby player, though for long years he had wished he was a girl. He had a memory that, when young, he would get depressed and cling to the skirts of a marble statue of the madonna for comfort. At eight, he disobeyed warnings and got himself very nearly drowned while sea-bathing. At 14½ he had become a sort of leader of the rebels at his boarding school and at 16 he "dropped right out," smoked a lot of dope and lived away from home without working. A venture at a university failed after the first few weeks. He began to discover in himself and to cultivate seriously transvestite phantasies, which he acted out so that he learnt to dress and look like a beautiful girl and become the object of lust in the boys and admiration in the girls. He also married a girl who had been an "au pair" in his parents' house. She left him free with his transvestite activities but began to oppose him when he turned his attention to becoming transexual. Before applying for the final operation he was beginning to think that his wish was really unobtainable. He felt too much of a man, to his despair and chagrin, and so he applied for an analysis, which had to be jungian, since it seemed to him to be more imaginative and feminine and valued dreams—important to him because he had good ones of which he was proud.

b) Charles' presentation of himself and the course of the treatment.

He presented himself as a feminized man—with all the girlish gestures well mastered. A leading feature that emerged in the course of the analysis was an intense envy of women. The wish to be a woman turned out to be really an attempt to fuse with the cool mother who, he thought, had rejected him for his brother. Furthermore, he wished to avoid the cruel frightening world of men, in which his father had been so unsuccessful. His bitter disappointments produced a nihilistic wish to turn everything upside down in bitter rage. He would choose sickness, impotence, evil, destructiveness and perversion. My acceptance of all that together with my interpretations started off a slow underground movement of change, which contrasted with both the nihilism and the self destructive anger.

The treatment had been intensive and unbroken by anything save the standard holidays. It was not very long before Charles began more and more to reiterate that he was sure that he was thoroughly male and that he was angry and heartbroken about this. Soon, by smoking less dope, he began to compare the subjective experience of being on dope with that of not being on it. He found new experiences with his wife as she really was an emotional woman—and primitive, as compared with his experience of her in a fusionary illusion of oneness when they smoked dope together. She too began to realize her disturbances and went into analysis. After a year, during which he sat in a chair, keeping his eyes fixed upon me, he started to try ways of using the couch. This meant for him a less negativistic transference to me as a parent figure and he could allow himself to feel more of a patient—more relaxed

and less watchful. The next stage came when, aged 22, he went to work for the first time and become really successful as a male nurse in a therapeutic community. Then, when he was 23, he got into a university, again five years after dropping out at eighteen. He followed an honours course in philosophy. It turned out well and, to his encouragement, he started being awarded alphas for his essays. At the same time, he, albeit rather unwillingly, agreed with his wife, who was keen that they should try for a child. She became pregnant and he was sufficiently in touch with his genital sexuality not to feel too badly about it. Thus by the time the baby was born, he was well on the way to being able to enjoy her as a father and to be something of a holding person for his wife and to support her tentative moves into maternal preoccupation. He was no longer gripped by his illness but could be conscious of conflict raging in him and could even tolerate the notion of repair. Accompanying changes in his physical appearance began to show. His face began to show some strength. His manner became more open. He could laugh and talk more freely and he decided to sit up and face me more often than to lie on the couch, while feeling free to do either with spontaneity.
c) A communication of four dreams.

As time went on, his dreams which, at first, he had compliantly brought as products of his imagination like poems, fell into the flow of communication in the midst of other material. A group of four are striking and the took place during a fortnight after four years of analysis:–

1. I go to a mediaeval castle on the top of a high steep pointed hill. It is cold and has no window panes. My family is there. It seems I had had an incestuous relationship with my sister about which my parents are angry with me. I fly into a rage over this and, to distract my parents' attention from the incest, hit out at a great sparkling chandelier. I smash half of it. We all, as a family, get down to picking up the pieces. I find that the sparkling glass is not smashed and disintegrated but rather is in its original tiny pieces. We gather them together to start re-assembling the chandelier.

2. The second dream goes as follows:–

I am in a mediaeval city. There is a destructive man about. With his friends he rushes through the city spraying it everywhere with a poisonous substance. This will kill every living person in the city. I find rising within myself a surge of almost demonic energy. I feel it will be either him or the rest of the world for survival, so, with this demonic energy, I attack him with overwhelming strength and tear his eyes out.

3. The third dream goes:–

I am in the waiting room. There is a see-through wall between it and my analyst's consulting room. I can see him treating a black girl. The scene changes and I am in a big tent, but I realize I am actually inside the skirts of a huge doll whose legs are near to trampling on me.

4. I meet my woman philosophy teacher. She has become a beautiful rather golden girl and emphasizes that I am good at philosophy.

d) Transference/Countertransference in the dream content and associations

If we take those dreams as a whole, we can hardly avoid noting the extent to which by now Charles was involved in them–not as a somewhat schizoid participant or watcher. His emotions were aroused. Two of the dreams being set in mediaeval times, could refer to adolescence. The other two are about youth anyway. In the first dream, he felt that the cold castle on the top of the hill represented his cool phallic home, so defensive (a fortress) and so vulnerable to the cold (no window panes), where incestuous feelings of warmth, in this case towards his sister, were condemned–according to his experience of it. He could acknowledge the fury this had aroused in him and how it made want to destroy everything symbolized by the chandelier and particularly to smash up the many facetted light and its sparkling vitality. And yet, even that was not mere nihilistic rage against the light as such. He insisted that it was a strategy, a guilty manoeuvre, to distract his parents' attention from the incest that he was determined to act out. In point of fact, that was by now masked as he hardly ever saw his sister. It was lived out with his wife in the earlier part of his marriage when he had "dropped out". He also thought that the cold castle and the cool chandelier light symbolized a feeling that he had had about my "cool" analytic interpretations which had made him feel more angry and more guiltily defensive than he had realized. For all that, however, according to the dream picture, he had only half destroyed the chandelier. And further, as a matter of fact, it was not even shattered but had simply come to pieces, that is the attacked half had, like the primal self, de-integrated rather than disintegrated, (FORDHAM [4]).

In the second dream, he felt his blood was up again. His associations were to his occasional violent attacks upon his own destructiveness. He had to put a stop to the destructive activity, even to take the law into his own hands–very surprising, as he was paranoid about the police. He realized that he was conscious enough to experience how violent the conflict had started to become as he got more aware of the destructive elements in the nihilistic side of his nature. Sometimes the battle seemed to be for life itself, during which time there was no opportunity to weigh up and integrate what was valuable in his nihilism. There is in this material a hint of Oedipus blinding himself as a punishment for incest, but, perhaps, too, it acted as a blinding realization of how deep down he really loved life. The transference element in the dream arose out of his sensing my capacity for an urgent discernment of crypto-destructive behaviour both internally and in the outer world. There was an element of identification or at least part agreement with me in this, but at that moment in his development he was tending to be still too violently repressive of his nihilistic side and would obviously need to become more deeply understanding of it. Not surprisingly, he was hardly mature enough yet to sustain within himself the tension of the opposites, shown as they are in the dream to be in a pathological condition of mutual destructiveness.

In the third dream, which is a direct representation of the transference, he sees me analyse a young black woman, i.e. his black instinctual feelings–his real ones as against his nihilistic destructive impulses, but they are split off still and "in the next room". This contrasted with his old habit of wishing to dress like a woman, expressed in the next part of the dream as finding himself inside the great doll's dress, but at the risk of being trampled on. He had an association with the tent-like cover. He had been taking part in a newly formed large group. He had felt the male leader to be rather an old woman and had himself remained rather anonymous in it. Transference/countertransference wise what he dreamt was correct. I did in fact steadily analyze all the time what was happening to his instinctual life and feelings as well as the signs of and the risks accompanying his longing for the mother.

The last dream seemed a bonus in the midst of his travail–the golden woman associated by him with his philosophy tutor, and validating him in his studies. We are here dealing with the anima as an internal object. The inner predisposition to expect and to meet a woman of a validating and inspiratory type, together with an internal image of this aspect of the anima, are matched and met by an appropriate woman in the real world, namely a real female philosophy tutor who was encouraging him and, along with other teachers, awarding him alphas for his university essays. It also had a reference to transference and counter-transference interactions, as I had found myself from early on spontaneously believing in his potential and ability and had pointed out signs of it as they arose. I regarded these responses as partly originating from anima aspects of myself.

Later dreams showed how he was beginning to integrate his angry nihilistic feelings, by no longer needing to destroy them and by finding, in a new way, a more suitable place for them.

Of course, it would not be supposed that Charles' story was now to have a "life lived happily ever after" quality about it. The child, a vigorous and lively girl, had been born. Charles' wife, under the strain of a brand new experience and not very far advanced in her analytic development, could and not infrequently did break down into an over-tired and unhappy infant herself. Charles needed to be on his mettle to hold things together in his little family side by side with doing studies and being financially responsible. The old nihilistic impulses could arise when his wife got low and Charles was out of touch with the incipient father archetypal capacities within him.

A dream illustrated the first problem:

I am in swampy land with a lot of shallow water lying around. I myself am paddling about lying flat on my stomach and on a sort of board. My wife is near me also paddling on a sort of board. I see an older man who is in a boat. He seemed to be paddling ahead as if he were leading me (or us) onwards. He seemed to have red hair and a round face, with a fringe of red hair right round the face, but with no moustache or beard. I say to my wife "This is the Wise Old Man," but I feel as if I am talking not quite directly to her–and, if anything, using the phrase to encourage her in the midst of these rather difficult circumstances.

When he brought me the dream, he said that he thought that the Wise Old Man referred to me as I tended his development and in a way lead him on. He thought that his wife in the dream represented an aspect of him as well as herself in person, for he thought that he was in a phase where things were not quite clear and differentiated in his life. He and his wife were in fact finding it swampy and hard going. He felt that a lot depended on him to keep on to their arduous path over against the temptation to give up and become nihilistic. Of course there were a number of archetypal internal objects in the dream—the swamp; the journey very close to the water on the flat boards; the boatman leading the way across the water; the psychopomp with the red hairy fringe around his face—a sort of sun-god. That showed how, in the transference and also in the reality of my dealings with him, I was being able to meet an archetypal predisposition on his part to seek and accept a psychopompic guide with a level of illumination sufficient to help him along with his journey. It meant of course that in his establishment of object relations with me as his analyst, the internal-object that emerged was fairly heavily influenced by imagery of a traditional sort which was archetypal in nature and function. The dream quite well illustrates Michael Stone's thesis (16) in the following way. The holistic imagery of the right-hand cerebral hemisphere provided for Charles a feeling grasp of his situation as a whole. That, coupled with his newly developing left-hand hemispherical capacities for verbalization and for representational logic (his philosophical studies) and aim directed activity (in practical everyday survival), could free enough energy to help him through the testing circumstances of his life at this stage.

The second dream opens out even more clearly his relationship to fathering, to inaugurating action and to taking a lead:— "I am with a Nigerian friend of mine. He could introduce me to a big black boss-man, but when he does so the big black boss-man takes no notice of me." The Nigerian friend was a writer and publisher and had suggested to Charles that he might be able to help him with his writing. The man had turned out to be largely a rather dull parasite or sucker. Charles wondered what he was doing that the big black boss-man could find no time for him and he wondered whether he was not still in conflict over fully taking on his new found masculinity and fatherhood with responsibility for family and career. If he was, then the boss-man figure could be alienated from him and hold him to be of no account. The figure draws upon the archetypal image of the "natural man," i. e. black and the boss. Charles had not had much experience of boss-men. There had been some authoritarian school masters in his life, though he dropped out before the completion of his school career. It left me as the object of a primitive archetypal transference, and obviously related to what he conceived of as my expectations for him and the possibility of my disappointment and alienation if he did not live up to them.

Those later dreams contain themes that are only to be expected during the vicissitudes and ups and downs of Charles' new way of life. The experience of them, and the interpretative process that went on between him and myself, greatly assisted in an integrative way Charles' movement on towards a repair and enhancement of life. He was recovering from a serious illness, that may be regarded as probably the sign of an immense vitality in coping with a strikingly non-facilitating environmental experience in infancy and childhood, and in defending the self from serious danger from both within and without (FORDHAM [5]).

Conclusion

I have tried to demonstrate ways in which dreams emerge in a useful and striking fashion, whether interpreted or not, in the midst of a general flow of material under the circumstances of; 1, their not being specifically asked for by the analyst; 2, their being taken as one aspect of a wide range of communications on the part of the patient, out of which central or nodal points of meaning can be isolated and interpreted. In other words, the patient is being analysed rather than the dream. And, 3, their being taken within the transference/countertransference situation.

Products to a greater or lesser extent of right hemispherical activity, though seldom entirely uninfluenced by the left, dreams can often be understood by patient and analyst to sum up in a remarkable way the psychological situation of the dreamer–his blocks, his dynamisms, perhaps the direction to be taken in his life. Above all, perhaps, they not only express archetypal themes and patterns in terms of images and internal objects, but also can introduce the dreamer to the beginnings of an experience of emotional intensity hitherto only latent or not-allowed to come into consciousness, and thus play an important part in the realization of the self.

REFERENCES

(1) Altmann, L. L. (1975) *The Dream in Psychoanalysis*. Revised Ed., 1975 New York. International Universities Press.

(2) Bakan, P. (1975) Dreaming, REM Sleep and the Right Hemisphere. Comments on D. Cohen's paper presented at the 15th Annu. APSS Meeting, Edinburgh 1975.

(3) Cohen, D. B. (1975) Lateralization of Functioning in the Cortex During REM Sleep: Preliminary Evidence from Dream Content, presented at 15th Annu. APSS Meeting, Edinburgh, 1975.

(4) Fordham, M. (1957) *New Developments in Analytical Psychology*, 1957 London, Routledge.

(5) Fordham, M. (1974) "Defences of the Self" in J. Analyt. Psychol. 19, 2.

(6) Hartmann, E. L. (1973) *The Functions of Sleep*, 1973, New Haven, Yale Univ. Press.

(7) Jones, R. M. (1978) *The New Psychology of Dreaming*, 1978, London, Pelican Books.

(8) Kirsch, T. (1977) "Dreams and Psychological Types," A paper given at the Seventh International Congress of Analytical Psychology, Rome, not yet published.

(9) Lambert, K. (1977) "Die Bedeutung von archetypischen Funktionen, Objektbeziehungen und internalisierten Objekten für die individuellen Erfahrungen des Kindes an der Mutter" in Zeit. Analyt. Psychol. 8.1.

(10) Meier, C. A. (1977) *Jung's Analytical Psychology and Religion*, republished in Arcturus Books, 1977 Illinois University Press.

(11) Oswald, I. (1966) *Sleep*, 1966 London, Pelican Books.

(12) Racker, H. (1968) *Transference and Countertransference*, 1968 London, Hogarth.

(13) Redfearn, J. W. T. (1975) Review of Hartmann's "The Function of Sleep" in Journal Analyt. Psychol. 20, 1.

(14) Rossi, E. (1977) The Cerebral Hemispheres in Analytical Psychology, J. Analyt. Psychol. 22, 1.

(15) Scott, W. Clifford M. (1975) "Remembering Sleep and Dreams" in Int. Rev. Psycho. Anal. 2, 253.

(16) Stone, M. "Dreams, Free Association, and the Non-Dominant Hemisphere: An Integration of Psychoanalytical, Neurophysiological, and Historical Data." J. Amer. Acad. Psychoanalysis 5 (2): 255–284

THE QUESTION OF MOTIVATION IN CHILD THERAPY

Mariella Loriga, Milan

A few months ago I received a call from a woman who wanted an appointment with me. When she arrived at my practice studio, she confessed that the person who really needed to be treated was not her: it was her oldest daughter. She had just turned eighteen and had attempted suicide on the very evening of her birthday. Furthermore, this had not been her first attempt. She had tried several months earlier and had come close to succeeding; so close that she had been hospitalized for some days and had received medical and psychiatric care. I told the mother that since her daughter was no longer a child I would rather have spoken with her directly and heard her version of the story, but the woman was already sitting in front of me, manifesting a remarkable amount of anxiety, so I decided to listen to her.

It was a long monologue: the story of a typical middle-class family with a fairly beautiful forty-year old mother and a businessman father, two daughters and economic well-being. The mother defined herself a "perfectly healthy and balanced person" and told me her husband was "the best father in the world," that her family had always been "happy". But suddenly and in a short span of time, something in the family mechanism had gone out of order. The older daughter, at the age of fifteen, started using her own head, wanting to choose her studies, her own friends, her own interests. "For her own good," her parents had not been able to let her do all these things. They had forced her to go to different schools than she had wanted and to live differently than she desired. She tried at first to rebel, but then gave in and let the others decide for her. The result was that she became abulic, listless, apathetic. She had gone through a period of intense anorexia (of which the family doctor had cured her by means of energetic physical treatments) and then, a few months later, she tried to kill herself for the first time. This was followed closely by the second attempt on the day she turned eighteen. At this point, her parents no longer knew what to do. They could not understand why their daughter was behaving this way and compared her to her younger sister, who was always calm and satisfied. On the other hand, they had let the younger one lead a much more independent life than her sister, justifying themselves by saying that her character was different and that they could trust her.

There was something peculiar about this mother's monologue which struck me at once while I was listening to her and wondering what she really wanted from me. There was a constant gratuitous justification of her past actions, a continued attempt to ask for my approval of what she had done; which was not, however, gratified. The fact was that she had come to me, not to have me treat her daughter, but only in order that I might assuage her sense of guilt, tell her she was right, comprehend her, perhaps offer her my compassion and create an "alliance between mothers" (she had found out from friends that I also had two daughters). I am certain that if I had given her all that she wanted from me she would have sent her daughter into analysis with me. But my silence, a few words here and there about the severity of the situation and the need to confront it as soon as possible, and probably my intimate comprehension directed not towards her but to that unknown girl who I could feel suffering because of all this manipulation; all this brought her to the realization that with me she would not be able to achieve her real aim: to make my supposed patient "normal"; i.e., to adapt her to the family's ideology. The mother went away from our encounter dissatisfied. A few days later I received a card from her to the effect that she had spoken with her husband and they had decided they could not afford so costly a treatment. It should be noted that no mention had been made of a fee or of the duration of any treatment, this having been purely an interlocutory encounter. They informed me that they would send their daughter to a community center which would certainly cost less.

I have chosen this case as the beginning for this paper because I feel it is quite emblematic of a whole series of problems which come up for therapists who work with children or adolescents and which relate to the patient's rapport with his family. When I first began my career, I tended to identify with my young patients and blame their mothers for their behavior. It is not at all difficult to understand the psychological motives for this attitude of mine if it is true, as I believe it is, that every analyst wants to treat his own suffering child component. Over the years, I have learned to see the suffering that exists in many families, sometimes reaching the level of desperation. This is even more evident in many women who, finding the meaning of their existence in the maternal role, are overcome with anxiety when this role is threatened by the coming of age of their children. On the other hand, in most cases men can substitute ambitions and success at work for family failures. I have also learned that only extremely rarely does a sick subject exist within a "sane" family, if it ever does. Often the child or adolescent for whom our help is required is only the exponent of a complex family pathology; i.e. the scapegoat. I am convinced that, even if we do not want to transform ourselves from child analysts into family therapists, we cannot refuse to see the effects of certain family ties and the consequences of the verbal or non-verbal communication which takes place among the members of the family.

In the case I have mentioned, the communication given to me by the mother was evident. She did not want to threaten the organization of a family she called happy and even less to threaten herself. Moreover, she was afraid that in recognizing the existence of problems in her behavior, she would cause the image of perfect mother, to which she needed to adhere, to collapse. She only wanted me to sympathize with her unhappiness and to speak with her daughter to remind her of the concept of the "crazy person," to show her all the sacrifices her family was ready to make to help her "be cured". I could not do this. Thus it seemed to me that the only possibility was to open a discussion about the mother's behavior, a tactic which might have been profitable in the long run.

I do not find it necessary to dwell on the present crisis in the family, which has been studied and analyzed often and from differing points of view. I do find it interesting to point out how intensely this phenomenon is lived out, even though the drive to break up the unit does not necessarily operate at the level of the consciousness. Beyond and despite each individual's awareness, the crisis in the family influences people and the surrounding social reality profoundly. I find that the contradictory way each individual lives out this reality is relevant, as are the often divergent reactions which co-exist in everyone's behavior.

It is not easy to identify the motives and causes of this process, which demolishes the traditional image of the family and puts all its aspects up for discussion. There is doubtless a series of factors (social, political, moral)which interact and contribute to unleashing or bringing out tensions which can no longer be hidden. The basis of this is the end of the family as the center of production and prime seat of education. Following the gradual deprivation of contents and functions, the family has become little more than a moment of refuge from the external reality which is more and more fractured, offering fewer and fewer moments of socialization and satisfying encounters. The family is used as an instrument of security and stability which allows us to reconcile all the conflicts accumulated without, in the social world. The role of the family and its function are further questioned when it becomes evident that the family institution cannot adequately handle these requests for protection. So situations which were once accepted are now experienced in a more or less conflicting light; the husband-wife and parent-child relationships, the legitimacy of family roles, are now subject to argument. The woman, in the role of both mother and wife, is especially torn by this conflict: on the one hand, she is driven to look for more autonomy and independence and to reject the traditional image of "hearthside angel". But on the other hand, she has trouble finding an identity which does not include this image which society still imposes on her. Unable to find the precise role or her correct placement within the family, she experiences a personal crisis of unfulfillment and dissatisfaction which has repercussions on the entire group and unleashes dynamics that may be impossible to control.

This is all part of the system in which we, as psychoanalysts, operate today. We cannot help remembering all this in our relations with our patients.

It is a known fact that the comprehension of motivation is of fundamental importance in the analysis of adults. But in treating children, we are faced with an almost paradoxical situation: the children may be the patients, but it is the parents who are motivated to analysis. But why? What are the reasons which lead two parents to decide to consult a psychoanalyst about their child's problems? And what attitude must the analyst have to make his intervention useful? These are the questions I want to try to answer.

Let us begin at the beginning: why does a family take a child to an analyst (and why that child, if they have more than one)? Often, within the family nucleus, there is someone who is willing to be the target of all the negative projections of the group, perhaps because his psychic constitution is more fragile or sensitive than that of the others; perhaps because situations in the family's history have placed him in a more difficult position. He is usually the one defined the "bad child" and it is he upon whom this rôle is pinned in family dynamics. These are the same dynamics which another child to be the "good" one. But the "good" child believes he will have a happy life, gratified as he is by the praise of those around him, and only later, as an adult, will he have to deal with the conditioning this role has caused him. On the other hand, the "bad" child lives badly, is unhappy and thus makes others' lives more difficult for them, too. It is usually on his account that therapy is required. This request for treatment may come directly from the family or be recommended by a doctor or a school. This is yet another element which is important for its own sake. Judging from the experience I have had, I would say it is preferable for a family to come directly to a child analyst with no intermediary help because in this case there has been the attempt, albeit confused or unconscious, to confront the problem. On the contrary, the cases in which therapy is requested after being advised by a doctor or the school are those usually destined to fail.

At any rate, the family's request is ambiguous. There is the obvious projection of shadow on the child who is considered "sick" so that the others can be called "healthy". Thus the reality is that the family has no real desire to cure the patient; his "illness" must maintain the fragile balance of the relations within the entire family nucleus. If he were cured, the others would have to confront their deepest problems. And it is here that one of the most complex aspects of child therapy lies: often, in consulting an analyst for its child, the family would like to hear its own projections and rôle play confirmed in order to assuage its own sense of guilt. In fact, as the child strengthens his own ego and his capacity for autonomy through the therapeutic relationship, the family is more and more threatened. The crisis of the rest of the family can sometimes lead to the decision to interrupt the child's therapy.

However, it is not always possible to trace the sole responsibility for a child's neurosis back to his parents. We know it to be a fact that within a child's unconscious there are archetypal images of parents which may not coincide at all with the real parents. The conflict with this inner image, or perhaps even the gap between the forms of these images and the flesh and blood reality of the parents with which the child must deal, can provoke the symptoms of neurosis which force a family to consult an analyst.

I would also emphasize the vast difference between neurosis in the child and in the adult. In fact, the adult can only live out and suffer from his own problems within himself, while leading a normal outer life. The child, on the other hand, knows no boundaries between the inner and the outer world: everything which anguishes him internally is immediately externalized in the most varied forms such as fear of the dark, bad behavior, lies, enuresis, stuttering, etc. It is thus inevitable that the family be affected by the child's anomalous behavior. There is the social image of the group which is attacked and should be re-built through the child's analysis.

Another point I should mention is the triangular relationship between child, mother, and analyst. It establishes itself in any child therapy and becomes particularly important in the case (frequent in Italy) that the analyst is a woman. It is extremely difficult for a mother to accept the fact that another woman has succeeded where she has failed. I am of the opinion that the mother's problems should always be kept in mind in the therapeutic relationship. She should never feel she is being alienated; her collaboration should always be valued.

The answer to the second question I posed for this paper refers to precisely this problem: that is, what should be our attitude toward the family of the child patient in order for our treatment to be successful? After many years of work, I have not been able to formulate a precise pattern to use, nor do I believe this to be possible. I prefer to decide from case to case depending on the situation which faces me, even though this attitude means more constant involvement. But I am sure this is the only way we can correspond to the communication the family sends us in asking us to treat its child and to the cry for help. Thus there have been cases in which I found it necessary to advise the entire group to take family therapy, in others I understood that the request for therapy for a child was really the request for the mother's analysis. At other times, we established a relationship of support for the family of the patient, with regular monthly or bi-monthly encounters with me. And sometimes, contrary to all this, the correct therapy for the family was treatment of the child alone, with all other relations reduced to a bare minimum.

Paolo's case was one of the latter. At the beginning of summer vacation the year he finished junior high school, he terminated analysis, in a decision we had made together with no help from his parents. Paolo had been sent to me for therapy by a neurologist four years before. He had gone through constant hard times: born during the eighth month of pregnancy, he spent the first few days of his life in an incubator and then rejected the maternal breast, a typical gesture of the severely disturbed child who is potentially psychotic. His growth and development were slow and difficult, his language retarded and incoherent. He was a dyslalic child with psychomotor disturbances, barely co-ordinated movements and stereotyped gestures. His I.Q. was low and at four he had been diagnosed as "difficult to recuperate" by a doctor who had advised an institution as the only solution. Fortunately, Paolo's highly anxious parents did not follow the suggestion and insisted that the child go to a normal nursery school, even though he was late in enrolling. They then sent him on to an elementary school where he repeated the first two grades. In the meantime, they had moved to another city and consulted a different neurologist. So Paolo came to analysis. He was still a child who behaved strangely, used absurd, gestures and felt misunderstood, unhappy and persecuted. He had enormous problems relating to his younger brother, the "normal" one in the family, who the parents always used as an example to be emulated. Paolo was tolerated by the family, supported because he was an accident. His parents' behavior toward him oscillated between excessive protection (the mother) and irked criticism (the father). I cannot narrate the child's gradual progress at this time. He is now almost fifteen and, through transference, has been able to gain confidence in himself and autonomy with regard to the family and, above all, his mother. Our

171

relationship went through different stages. From play therapy it moved to more and more involved conversation until it became real analytical sessions. But what I really want to point out is the way my relationship with Paolo's family developed. Given the serious nature of the case, at the beginning of therapy I thought it might be useful to conduct regular encounters with the boy's parents as well. They accepted this proposal with no difficulty. So for a while they came regularly. Sometimes they themselves asked for a meeting. But when they were in my studio, they never had anything to tell me or each other, except for a few rather banal criticisms about their son's behavior, or fairly tense discussions in which the wife accused the husband of too little collaboration and devoting too much time to work, thus leaving her alone with all the family's and children's problems. The husband seemed arid and rigid and the wife, who was younger, often had tears on her suffering, sensitive face. After about one year of therapy, some difficulties arose. The couple had the typical attitude of those who have to bring their child to analysis because "the doctor said so". Since they visited the neurologist twice a year for check-ups, they did not want to disobey him. Moreover, the wife began to say her son came to encounters against his will, she had to force him to come, maybe he could have gone to the pool or riding instead, all the things which would have been good for his health . . . Even Paolo began to say they lived too far away and that he had to give up seeing his friends to come to see me. I reminded the parents of the agreement made at the beginning of therapy when I had said that I would be the one to decide when to conclude therapy. I was firm about this with Paolo too, who really couldn't have wanted anything better. At the same time, as though a tacit agreement had been reached, the parents ceased coming except on rare occasions. I saw no more of the father, the mother stopped to say hello once in a while when she came to pay the bill. Until one day, at the front door (Paolo had stayed in my office), she said to me, "Sometimes Paolo is so strange; He says, 'Things would be better if I'd never been born!' and often I think so too." That terrible phrase struck me deeply and I asked the mother if she would like to come to talk to me alone sometime. A few days later, she called for an appointment; our encounter was quite different from the others. Free from the presence of her husband, this still young woman (36 at the time) was talking about herself, perhaps for the first time. She felt that I was there for her, to listen to her, that she could tell me everything she had never told me: her anxiety, when, at 22 and just married, she got pregnant the first time and wished she hadn't, the difficult pregnancy, the *dystocic* and traumatic delivery, the anguish of having an abnormal child, the refusal to realize it (as often happens, they had only understood that he was different from the others when they had taken him to school). Since that moment, she had begun the never-ending journey from doctor to hospital to special school and, at the same time, she plunged into a depression for which she had been taking tranquilizers for years and which she had only recently begun to come out of. Nothing had interested her for years and she had fervidly dedicated herself to the duties of a perfectionist houswife. She never shook off the anxiety that Paolo was different and every time he got sick she was terrified he would die. Having been able to express these experiences freely, it changed her attitude toward her son and she no longer contested his analysis. Ending the three-way encounters was probably a therapeutic intervention. This situation had kept the relationship formal and superficial, even though it was perhaps through those encounters that the wife recognized the fact that she could express herself differently, while the changes occurring in Paolo brought the family conflicts to light.

I have cited two cases, but I could describe countless others, all different, naturally. Some were successful, others concluded in failure when the crisis the parents had to overcome became unbearable for them. And yet I think it is always worth the try: often our job of child analysis gives results after lengthy treatment. On the other hand, if the problems of counter-transference are important in any analysis, they are particularly significant in child therapy, precisely because of the triangular relationship already mentioned (child–analyst–parents) which is an integral part of analysis in any case, even when the parents seem inexistent, even when we have seen them only once. This is the reality and we must keep it in mind. If we cannot comprehend the problems of the parents as well, it is better for the child if we do not accept him for therapy.

Original italian version to be found in "Oggi Jung," La Rivista di psicologia analitica, 17/78 pp 197–208.

THE DELUSION IN ANALYTICAL PSYCHOLOGY

Niel Micklem, London

As this paper is a contribution to the subject of "Analytical Psychology and the Treatment of Psychology" I want to begin by pointing out that the word psychosis is untidy. Its application is loose and there is a vagueness as to what it means. Maybe this has always been its tendency, but nevertheless the present uncertainty of its position is immediately concerned with the fact that it has become a "psychology word". Furthermore as psychology grows in importance so it makes greater assumptions of ownership on such words as psychosis and the way it uses or abuses them. I want therefore to introduce a reminder that psychosis is not just a term of psychology, but a very old word that is, and always has been in the service of medicine. Psychology is not medicine, even though the borders they share are ill defined. The word psychosis belongs in the vocabulary of illness and this too has ill defined borders, but is an area that remains the prerogative of medicine. Most people know when they are ill, though few could care to venture a confident opinion as to what was meant by illness. It is difficult to be precise about this state of morbidity, and the difficulty is not lessened as the expanding field of psychology in medicine confuses its psychopathology and contributes its own illnesses to the already existing range. In what follows here I am concerned with a psychological view of that state of illness called psychosis.

A considerable part of the untidiness attached to psychosis has grown during and since the last century through its need to be differentiated from neurosis. The ease with which these companions become identified and confused with each other is dangerously deceptive as well as being one of the interests in the history of psychiatry. On the whole psychosis seems consistently to have been associated with the word insanity, whereas neurosis has clearly not always carried such drastic inference. Today there are many syndromes of psychosis in the numerous classification systems and I want to move towards them by turning to the illness known as Paranoia. It is an important illness that has been eclipsed of late by other syndromes, especially by those of the schizophrenias which have caught the public's fascination. Yet of all the mental illnesses described through the ages few can be older or more closely associated with the word insanity than that known as paranoia. It was, indeed, one of Hippocrates' four part classification of mental illness, and even in those ancient times recognised as a condition in which delusion was central to the disease. Hippocrates and other writers tell how delusion has been accepted as the basic characteristic of insanity since the very earliest times. Today paranoia is recognised in its essence as a delusional system, a structure of faultless logical connections with no inner contradictions. Psychic functions appear unimpaired with an intelligent adaption, good and accurate sense perception and an undiminished critical capacity. Yet this structure is based on delusion and it has a logic that is not sympathetic or indeed acceptable to others. My purpose in this paper is to see what lies behind this state of psychosis wherein subjects are deluded and in an environment apparently offering a world of new meanings.

To make errors of one sort or another is surely the way of all mankind, and prominent amongst errors are those bearing the intellectual stamp of mistaken ideas like delusions. But are they necessarily delusions? There is the familiar experience of people who alienate themselves from their circle with the tenaceous assertion of some particular view they hold. Whether this view is acceptable or clearly mistaken, such people give an impression of healthy subjects with insight, receptive, related and open to change even if obstinate in their tenacity. How similar this seems and yet how profoundly different this is to the picture in the illness of paranoia. With the appearance of delusion in this syndrome there is a sense of error in the assertions, but with an incorrigibility that expresses itself in a real and fundamentally important manner. For psychiatry this is a psychosis, seen and experienced as a deeply disrupting event within the personality, apparently rendering the environment different. This transformation into a state of delusion is a moment of fixation that is an esential actor of inanity.

That there is an affect of terror and often an element of seduction associated with this time of fixation may be familiar to those who have observed the onset, even though the affect does not always communicate its presence. It is sometimes experienced in what is described as the delusional atmosphere (1), the affective forerunner of paranoia, a slightly uncanny state of affairs wherein perceptions are enveloped in a subtle and strangely uncertain light. The environment is rendered indefineably different. Vague and unexplainable though it may be, this affect for analytical psychologists is a reminder of the archetypal nature and image within the state of delusion. This image has a horror in its fixation that is deeply disturbing to the core of the personality. It is an archetypal confrontation that is in some way intolerable to the health of our being, mythologically expressed as if meeting the Gorgon, Medusa, where she dwells at the westernmost extremities of the earth in that far distant place of no sun and no moon, beyond the ocean (2). To meet this image directly is so terrifying that the beholder is turned instantly into stone. It is a moment of fixation which the image sees as a concrete, unchangeable immobility, as anyone will know who has ever experienced the unmoveable, stonelike rigidity of the delusion in psychosis.

I would like to look more closely at the psychology of this image and the place it holds in this difficult problem of medicine. To start with, this motif of horror and fixation is inseparably bound with the phenomenon of reflection. The considerable significance of this, amounting to a matter of life and death, is clearly expressed mythologically in the confrontation of Perseus with Medusa. He avoided the terrifying transformation by means of indirect gaze. Myth tells how the use of the polished shield as reflection in defence and the sickle with its moonlike reflection in attack were saving, health giving activities in a moment of peril. This indirection is apparently a health giving quality that belongs to a vital deviousness of the gods.

What bearing has this motif on delusion and the nature of psychosis? It tells that this image of the head of Medusa is the *image of no reflection*, and it is apparent that "no reflection" is a way of seeing that is intolerable to psyche. To be confronted with the image of no reflection is to be in some way most direly threatened with the loss of our most human characteristic which Jung speaks of as the reflective instinct (3). Reflection here is an indirection that can deflect an impulse into an activity of psyche. This vital and, as far as can be ascertained, specifically human characteristic is the way the psyche enters a bodily impulse and its physical reflex action. As psyche enters into the body in this activity so the image is incarnated and, by becoming psychological, the body is established as a living metaphor. Herein lies the meaning of the Gorgon's Head as the image that does not permit reflection. The essence of Medusa is, too, without body, for prior to any mention of this greatest of the Gorgon sisters there is mention of "the Head" (4), as if Medusa were this very head which Athene wears on her breast and which Persephone keeps by her and sends as the "gigantic shape of fear" to meet those who would seek to invade her Underworld. In fixation this is a psychopathic state of psychosis in which somewhere body is no longer metaphor, but has become the morbidity of flesh. The significance of this is itself reflected in Jung's last writings on psychosis (5) in which he intimated that schizophrenia—which like other psychoses, organic or otherwise, is a fixation in a delusional state—is an autogenous phenomenon conceived as the appearance of a toxin in response to an excessively strong affect. With this he was postulating the physical, biochemical changes of the body involvement in mental illness.

How this distant border realm of no sun and no moon, of no light and therefore no reflection, can present to conscious awareness may be appreciated in the dream of someone tormented with terrors and in that state so often diagnosed as being on the border of a psychotic illness. The dream is a simple image of looking in a mirror only to find there is nothing there. No reflecting image meets the gaze. Extremely disturbing though this experience was to the dreamer it nevertheless showed a psychic move in the direction of health, relieving rather than enhancing the psychic impotence, for this dream of "no image" was already an image with the possibility of psychic reflection.

The quest for further meaning in this event of the body and physical involvement with psychosis as a confrontation with this image of no body directs attention towards some related characteristics in the motifs of Medusa's natural sleep and the invisibility of Perseus. Both motifs express the same Underworld quality of death and the state wherein images are hidden and invisible by intent in the non-temporal, non-spatial world of Hades (6). The healthy state of psyche is invisible and Perseus as the one who dons that cap of Hades is making a move that leads from visible to invisible connections. Sleep too, like invisibility, is a way to death. It is a journey away from life and the literal representations of waking experiences.

Sleep is a deceptive study. The simple view of wakefulness at one pole and sleep at the other denoting the states of consciousness and unconsciousness does not allow a sufficiently comprehensive understanding, for now it is clear that sleep and wakefulness are not unitary states. They are progressions of repeated cycles represented in different phases of brain and body activity. The significance of this is reflected in the laboratory observations on the different states of consciousness throughout these cycles. Two main categories of sleep can be distinguished namely, varying levels of a relatively far away, "dreamless" sleep on the one hand, and on the other a paradoxical or "REM" (rapid eyeball movement) sleep of dreams in which encephalogram readings and neurovegetative manifestations indicate an emotional involvement of the body during this state of consciousness.

Scientific discoveries in this field confirm the importance that has been bestowed on the dream since most ancient times, for it is clear that dreams, like sleep, are in some way essential to our physical and mental health, even though they are not solely the carriers of health that might be supposed. Dreams are more than the guardians of sleep that Freud's early observations maintain. They are more, too, than compensations for a wakeful consciousness that the viewpoint of an ego psychology assumes. If dreams bring health, they can also be killers in the night (7), for the psychosomatic activities of the REM periods have their pathological side or, at least, are involved pathologically during disturbances of this rhythm (8). During REM sleep there is a particular working of the psychic images in the dream that is bound with an apparent activity of the autonomic nervous system. This is a matter of importance for the working of the dream (dream work), because REM sleep is not exclusively the state of consciousness in which dreams appear. It is, however, a special state of body involvement that appears in dreaming, being the activity of psyche entering body and the image becoming incarnate through reflection. Exactly what transpires in this important relationship between the images of dreams and the balance of health may be difficult to assess, but it is immediately concerned with the differing states of consciousness in sleep and the meaning of invisibility within these states.

These discoveries of the contemporary laboratory are a reminder of an earlier observation on illness by the Swiss physician, Paracelsus, whose writings sounded with overtones of depth psychology long before the concept of the archetype. Paracelsus spoke of the Ens Spiritualis (9) of disease within the visible macrocosm maintaining a state of health. The ens was both cause and cure of disease, and its influence under circumstances of illness brought about an intrusion of the macrocosm and a materialisation of the psyche which then became visible in illness. The very substance of psyche for Paracelsus was the "Astra," the supercelestial body which was also the "imaginatio" of alchemical study. This work speaks of imagination in a manner that is reflected in recent findings. That imagination is active during the various states of consciousness that are sleep is not new, but imagination in that particular state recognised as REM sleep is different. Reflection is awake in this quality of dream sleep. Reflection is at work as the images of dream in this period sustain and make the substance of psyche, the psyche of the body, rendering invisible what has become, or is threatening to become visible in the moment of fixation that is illness.

My endeavour has been to draw attention to an archetypal image in psychosis and through this image that is intolerable to psyche to see the pattern of delusion that is the essential ingredient of insanity. The fixation that is central to the alternation of personality is delusion. It does not imply, as is so often assumed, simply a matter of being right or wrong, but fixation in a different way of seeing that manifests through the particular loss of the capacity for reflection. Delusion, as the word says, concerns play (ludo). Jung says of this ". . . an unconscious product is the creation of sportive phantasy, of that psychic impulse out of which play itself arises" (10). This is also the movement of reflection, the innate human component that brings imagination to body. In the de-luded the imagination is un-played (de-played), un-reflected, and somewhere the vital play of life is incapacitated. In psychosis there are some areas of loss of this capacity for reflection as there are too areas of an involvement of the body that establish this state as an illness and therapeutically the responsibility of medicine. It is important to stress this because psychology, including analytical psychology, begins to distort its image through medical aspirations. Encouraging psychology over its boundaries has led to the assumption in many quarters that a psychosis is really something like a neurosis. It is assumed to be a movement of the psyche that is a sort of compensation and a somewhat vague and untidy attempt of psyche to transform itself. It is by no means certain that there is justification in viewing psychosis in this manner as similar to that of a neurosis. Psychosis is illness that, like all illness, touches the soul of the sufferer in dark, distant places, and does not readily behave in the convenient manner of compensation. It cannot be said that the methods and techniques of psychology have as yet any specific help in the treatment of illnesses, and so the corresponding limitation of their help in the illness of psychosis must be faced. A moment's reflection on the illness that is a state of fixation in certain cells of the body forming Cancer may show this more clearly. Cancer may be seen as one of medicine's physical counterparts to psychosis and a reminder that real illness on the borders of psyche and soma is a deceptively difficult phenomenon where the simplicity of the manifestations camouflages the depth of the roots.

This realisation of limitation does not mean that psychology has no part to play. Far from it indeed. Especially as analytical psychology it has a vital role, provided that it is clear where the psychology lies. Whatever happens to people is psychologically mediated always. This applies to the movements of psychology that meet illness in the deep, distant movements of the transference, as Jung has indicated in his work of untold value on this subject. The immense value of the dream in the methods and practice of psychology is widely accepted. Jung has surely contributed more than most towards an appreciation of the dream and how it may indicate an approach to therapy and the way towards involvement in the treatment of the individual. These, and many other ways of analytical psychology are not, however, *specific* in the treatment of psychosis even though they are central to healing in the process of individuation, which surely continues whether the illness of psychosis is apparent or not.

NOTES

(1) Jaspers, K. "General Psychopathology." Trans. J. Hoenig and M. W. Hamilton. Manchester Univ. Pres. 1963.

(2) Hesiod. "Theogony".

(3) Jung, C. G. Coll. Wks. Vol. 8, p. 117.

(4) Harrison, Jane E. "Prolegomena to the Study of Greek Religion." Camb. 1903, p. 187.

(5) Jung, C. G. Coll. Wks. Vol. 3, p. 270.

(6) For an appreciation of the Underworld in psychology see Hillman, J. "The Dream and the Underworld." Eranos Jahrbuch 42. 1973. Brill: Leiden 1975.

(7) Ziegler, A. J. "Rousseauian Optimism, Natural Distress and Dream Research." Spring 1976. Spring Publications. New York.

(8) Lairy, G. C. "Dream and Delusional Symptoms." Proceedings of the 2nd. European Congress on Sleep Research. 1974. S. Karger 1975, also, Snyder, F. "Sleep and Disturbances in relation to acute psychosis". Sleep Physiology and Pathology. Edit. Anthony Kales. J. B. Lippincott Co. Philadelphia and Toronto 1969.

(9) Paracelsus (Theophrastus Bombast von Hohenheim). "Paramirum Primum." Ed. Sudhoff 1, p. 215, see also, Hartman, F. "Paracelsus. Life and Prophecies". R. Steiner publication. Blauvelt. New York 1973. Jung, C. G. "Paracelsus as a Spiritual Phenomenon." Coll. Wks. Vol. 13 and "Paracelsus." Coll. Wks. Vol. 15.

(10) Jung, C. G. Coll. Wks. Vol. 4, p. 52.

THE DREAM:
IMAGINATIVE ACTIVITY VERSUS INTERPRETATION

Mario Moreno, Rome

The Jungian conception of the symbol, which Jolande JACOBI has elaborated and clarified in *Complex, Archetype, Symbol* (1), postulates the existence of archetypes, understood as significant structures which are essential to the *formation* of the symbol itself. "The unconscious," JUNG stated in this regard, "provides, as it were, the archetypal form which in itself is empty and therefore irrepresentable. But from the conscious side it is immediately filled out with the representational material that is *akin* to it or *similar* to it, and is made perceptible" (2).

It also seems possible to utilize the archetypal hypothesis in regard to the *decodification* of the symbol. This point strikes me as being especially relevant to the considerations on the dream I intend to submit to your attention, referring to JUNG's definition of the dream: "a spontaneous self-portrayal, *in symbolic form,* of the actual situation in the unconscious" (3).

If we admit that an emotion may determine a need for representation or, to put it another way, an *intention of meaning* which fails to find adequate representation in conscious denotative language, we may surmise that a specific significant structure, an archetype, activated by the emotion itself, proposes itself as a term of comparison in an intuitive process of comparison with the imaginative material presented by the conscious mind. The most adequate image analogically, based on this *intuition of similarity*, becomes a *symbol,* or the metaphorization of the original intention of meaning.

Let us attempt an example, the most elementary possible. One day, a young patient of mine quarreled with a girl with whom he had a sentimental relationship and he was unpleasantly surprised at the dominant and aggressive attitude his friend assumed, since she was usually sweet and understanding toward him. During the night, through the activation of the negative maternal archetype, the unpleasant emotion produced by the girl found its analogous representation in the image of a lioness he discovered in his garden and from which he fled, taking refuge in his house.

Relating this dream, I have already proposed the interpretation of the symbol contained therein which represents the essential nucleus of the dream, around which the dream itself is organized. What are the prerequisites of this interpretation? First of all, knowledge of the patient: I know, for example, that he had a dominating mother. Secondly, knowledge of the context and, in particular, of the meeting with the girl, which preceded the dream. But, in the last analysis, what is it that allows me to point out the meaning of the symbol? In my opinion, it is the possibility for me to share his emotion, my concordant countertransference, if you like, that is essential in enabling me to identify with the subject. This identification can, in turn, promote the activation in my unconscious of the very same significant structure which underlies the formation of the symbol. Connecting myself to this unconscious term of comparison, I can thus intuit the similarity between lioness and girl and so conceptualize the symbol, abstracting the common elements (for example, the female sex and aggressivity), establishing that lioness stands for girl, decoding the symbol lioness = girl.

Even though this model is not operating on every occassion, since the learning processes may permit the analyst an immediate decodification, it is to this model that we must turn, in my judgment, in order to begin a discussion on the use of the dream in analysis.

This hypothesis is linked to the psycholinguistic analysis of the *metaphor* and the differences between denotative and metaphoric language. In denotative language the conventional referentiality of the signs is respected; in metaphoric language this referentiality is broken and one that is no longer conventional but subjective and intuitive is created; in the latter imagination plays a fundamental part. As FONZI and NEGRO (4) call to our attention, the new referential bond between sign and meaning is not built on a lingustic law but on an intuition of similarity, which is tangible and not linguistic, between the two elements.

These scholars, following Jakobson, view the metaphor as a *capability*. They declare: "Precisely because it is creative the metaphor is not completely graspable. However much you may dissect it and analyze it, there always remains in the metaphor something that is unreachable through logical discourse and which consists precisely of that subjective evocation which pervades it and can only be felt and never proved . . . In this dimension the external stimuli are not only received or perceived, but also recreated by the subject, and this on linguistic as well as on deeper and more unconscious levels" (5).

Always in regard to the metaphor, LE GUERN affirms that it originates from the need to externalize emotional contents for which denotative language does not contemplate adequate terms. It is, however, one of the most effective means for transmitting an emotion: the associated image introduced by the metaphor is extraneous to logical communication and "impedes logical censure from rejecting the affective movement which accompanies it" (6).

To approximate symbols, in the Jungian sense, to metaphors, which however, are *conscious* creative acts of transference of meaning, seems to find confirmation in the concept of *metaphorization*. Fonzi and Negro use this concept to explain the unwitting transpositions of meaning which take place during childhood. Metaphorization would be a very primitive process, preceding even the syncretic and physiognomic perception of reality, the reflex of a situation of indifferentiation in subject–object relationships; a process preceding language itself, through which metaphoric objects, precursors of the real, permanent objects, are formed. Metaphorization would include, in their view, that intermediate area of experience which WINNICOTT speaks of and which lies between primary creativity and objective perception, regulating the relationship between the subject and external reality, and which "throughout life is kept alive in the intense experience which belongs to the arts, religion, imaginative living and creative scientific work" (7).

We may suppose, then, that in the dream the process of metaphorization reappears, freed from the inhibition exercised by logical thinking and denotative language, producing the symbol.

Indeed, as FREY-ROHN has recently pointed out (8), Jung attributed symbolic transformations to a natural "tendency to invent analogies," which he conceived of as one of the prerogatives of the psyche.

Even if other linguistic processes, such as, for example, metonymy, should perhaps be taken up in the study of symbolization, I feel that the essential role of the process of metaphorization cannot be ignored.

At this point it is interesting to note that several of the most recent psychoanalytical theorizations on the processes of symbolization permit us to verify a significant similarity to the Jungian conceptions and the model I have mentioned. FORNARI (9), for example, speaks of *confusive symbolization* to indicate the most archaic system of signification, set into motion by the *symbolic equation*, and which is most clearly expressed in the *transitional object*. He does not specify the nature of the connection between the two terms of the equation, external object and internal object, but, following Klein's hypothesis, which is Fornari's starting point, we may assume that this link is provided by those *phantasies* which, present from birth, intervene in the external world, modifying it in such a way that, through re-introjection, internal objects come to be formed. The external object would equal the internal on the basis of an analogy built on the evocation of the same phantasy. Here phantasy would have a function very similar to that of the archetype in my hypothesis.

Various psychoanalysts, such as Hautmann, Diatkine, Meltzer and others, on the other hand, have come to view the *entire* analytical process as a repetition of a *transitional experience*; they see, in other words, analysis as the "ludic container" of an oneiric experience. HAUTMANN (10), for example, maintains that the analytical process has as its object "the conscious and unconscious phantasy which is revealed by thoughts of varying degrees of concreteness and by elements precursory to thought" which "interpretation reformulates and translates into communicating language". This condition of *ludic container*, continuously fed by patient and analyst, would be made possible by the analytical *setting*.

Indeed, interpretation, although adequate in as much as it lays a bridge between the external world and the internal world, between present and past, between conscious and unconscious, between phantasy and reality, is still always an act which, since it claims to exhaust the meaning of a symbol in an exact conceptual formulation, contains in

185

itself a contradiction. It is, in fact, precisely at the moment we acknowledge the symbol's archetypal structure that the problem of the impossibility of circumscribing its meaning once and for all and completely arises. Interpretation should demote the symbol to a sign or to a logical linguistic (consensual) symbol, it should transform phantasy thinking into directed thinking, metaphoric language into denotative language. Instead, it risks interrupting the creative process of symbolization begun by the dream.

In his article *Imagination and Amplification in Psychotherapy*, HOBSON (11) subdivides the process of active imagination into four stages: passive phantasy, active phantasy, imaginative activity and colloquy. In passive phantasy the image occurs as an involuntary intrusion, representing dissociated psychic elements, antithetical to the conscious attitude. Dreams would be precisely an example of passive phantasy. My patient, although badly stung by the quarrel with his girlfriend, had sought to maintain a positive attittude in her regard, minimizing the episode's importance. All the same, in the dream his negative maternal complex had emerged involuntarily and compensatorily.

Active phantasy, asserts Hobson, is encouraged by an expectant intuitive attitude, by an urge to let the images emerge. In imaginative activity, then, "the conscious attitude remains open and receptive but it is now more active in the sense of viewing the phantasy process critically, by the use of directed thinking". Colloquy, finally, would involve "an even more active participation of the observer by means of a dialogue with the phantasy image".

On the basis of this subdivision Hobson describes *subjective amplification* as the process promoted by the conscious attitudes adopted in active phantasy, imaginative activity and, occasionally, in the colloquy stage. Here the phantasy image is confronted with a *symbolic attitude* which "endows it with value as an intimation of something important which is as yet unknown," and makes it possible for *analogous images* to emerge. Then, according to Hobson, in *objective amplification* the analyst adds *analogies* to the products of subjective amplification, so that the symbol's meaning is extended and enriched.

In effect, the process Hobson describes in the stages of active phantasy, imaginative activity and colloquy, and which underlies what he calls *subjective amplification*, does not seem, in substance, to differ from the process of symbolization already at work in the dream. Here, too, analogous images emerge through the intuition of similarity between the oneiric image and the additional imaginative material supplied by the conscious mind. Here, too, it is likely that the unconscious term of comparison is supplied by the archetypal significant structure operating at the moment. The activation of the archetypal element could be helped by a lowering of the mental level, i.e. by that symbolic attitude which, foregoing immediate identification of the symbol's meaning, admits the need for its further representation through images.

Perhaps we can say that the interpretation of the dream begins with *objective amplification*, or when another person (the analyst) connects the images, as Jacobi puts it, "with analogous material in kindred images, symbols, legends and myths in such a way as to comprehend all its shades of meaning, all its different aspects, until its meaning shines through in perfect clarity" (12). It is here, in fact, that the passage from an intrasubjective level to an intersubjective one occurs, where, nevertheless, the transference–countertransference relationship make intuition of the unconscious term of comparison, the formal structures on which to base the analogies, possible, and permits, therefore, communication. It is as if the analyst continued to dream the patient's dream: he continues to use oneiric, metaphoric language. The interpretation takes shape only when he connects the meaning of the oneiric symbol to the material supplied by *association* and the knowledge of the dreamer's psychic situation, i.e. with external reality.

Actually, we know that Jung spoke of *context* to indicate the "interconnected associations objectively grouped round the images of the dream" (13) and *amplification* to indicate the material supplied "by association and analogy" (14), and this could lead to a certain confusion. Perhaps a more precise distinction between associative and analogical material would be desirable, reserving only for the latter the term amplification.

"The essence of hermeneutics," JUNG wrote in 1916, "consists in adding further analogies to the one already supplied by the symbol: in the first place, subjective analogies produced at random by the patient, then objective analogies provided by the analyst out of his general knowledge. This procedure widens and enriches the initial symbol, and the final outcome is an infinitely complex and variegated picture" (15).

In any case, at this point we may pose ourselves the fundamental question: for therapeutic purposes would it be more advantageous to favor the creative symbolic process begun by the dream, or imaginative activity, or, if you like, subjective amplification, or would it instead be better to propose interpretation of the symbol, attempting to circumscribe its meaning, offering the conscious mind the chance to reduce to a logical discourse what one only vaguely feels?

We know that in the realm of interpretation Jung distinguished interpretation on the objective level–analytical, causal-reductive–and interpretation on the subjective level–synthetic-constructive. Already in this distinction a kind of reply to our question is implied, since it is clear that interpretation on the subjective level tends to foster the transcendent function, the symbolizing capacity, the individual synthesis of the parts of the Self. Interpretation on the objective level, instead, tends to connect what is lived to external reality, to offer a logical explanation of behavior, weaving it into a comprehensible causal network, reinforcing the ego. Jung proposed that the analyst from time to time choose one or the other type of interpretation, basing his choice on the states of the subject's conscious mind.

But our question, arising from many analytical experiences, would like to be more radical. Would it at times be more useful for the analyst to give up every type of interpretation so as not to interfere in the creative process the dream has set in motion? Would an attitude that favors the activity of subjective amplification be, on the contrary, more fruitful?

Indeed, in many cases, suggestions such as the invitation to fantasize the dramatic evolution or the lysis of the dream, or to identify oneself with one of the characters in the dream, lending him one's own voice so that he may express himself, or to design an oneiric image or mime the behavior and emotional reactions of the dream's protagonist, seem to have a therapeutic effectiveness superior to any interpretative proposal. In these cases imaginative activity is promoted, which, in harmony with Fordham, I would hold distinct from real active imagination.

In his essay *The Transcendent Function* (16) JUNG declares that in the confrontation of the fantastic unconscious material with the conscious mind, two tendencies emerge: one advances in the direction of *creative formulation,* the other in the direction of *understanding:* "The ideal case," says JUNG, "would be if these two aspects could exist side by side or rhythmically succeed each other ... It hardly seems possible for the one to exist without the other, though it sometimes does happen in practice: the creative urge seizes possesion of the object at the cost of its meaning, or the urge to understand overrides the necessity of giving it form. The unconscious contents want first of all to be seen clearly, which can only be done by giving them shape, and to be judged only when everything they have to say is tangibly present" (17). And he further specifies: "Often it is necessary to clarify a vague content by giving it a visible form ... By shaping it, one goes on dreaming the dream in greater detail in the waking state ... Aesthetic formulation leaves it at that and gives up any idea of discovering a meaning ... The desire to understand, if it dispenses with careful formulation, starts with the chance idea or association and therefore lacks an adequate basis ... The less the initial material is shaped and developed, the greater is the danger that understanding will be governed not by the empirical facts but by theoretical and moral considerations" (18). I uphold the validity of Jung's argument even though we speak of analogical representation and interpretation of the oneiric symbol.

On the other hand, in *The relations between the Ego and the Unconscious* (19) JUNG asserted: "In many cases it may be quite important for the patient to have some idea of the meaning of these phantasies produced. But it is of vital importance that he should experience them to the full and, in so far as intellectual understanding belongs to the totality of experience, also understand them. Yet I would not," JUNG goes on, "give priority to understanding. Naturally the doctor must be able to assist the patient in his understanding but, since he will not and indeed cannot understand everything, the doctor should assiduously guard against clever feats of interpretation. For the important thing is not to interpret and understand the phantasies, but primarily to experience them" (20). In using the dream in therapy, then, beyond asking ourselves when we should use interpretation on the objective level and when on the subjective level, we must ask when we should use interpretation and when, instead, we should forego it, at least temporarily, to foster the imaginative activity which can be stimulated by the material of the dream.

At the very least this imaginative activity can also be furthered by the analyst's objective amplification, provided that this does not aim at an immediate interpretative conclusion, but is offered, instead, as a contribution to the imaginative game which takes place between analyst and patient, especially where the patient himself tends to propose more or less reductive interpretations, as expressions of resistance.

I would like to conclude with an example designed to illustrate this dilemma between imaginative activity and interpretation in the use of the dream in analysis.

A patient of mine was deeply disappointed by a sentimental relationship in which she had made a large affective investment. Several days after the relationship had come to a negative conclusion, she related this dream:

I have a necklace with a puppet made of beads as a pendant; the necklace has been turned around so that the puppet hangs down my back.

She associated with the beaded puppet a small purse embroidered in like fashion which she discovered as a child in a trunk in the attic and which she often returned to admire. The beads, she added, are given to the savages as barter. At this point, I silently formulated an interpretation of the dream. I was tempted to tell the patient: the puppet is something others manipulate by its strings; this is her infantile part which she lets others manage, just as occurred in this relationship. The dream warns her that the puppet is behind her back and that she must now, therefore, accept responsibility for its existence. I did not follow this impulse, probably dictated by my hyperprotective maternal counter-transference, and perhaps vaguely intuiting the greater richness of the symbol, I said to the patient: "Now try to take this puppet in your hand and tell me what you see." The patient, after a few bewildered moments began to speak: "The puppet changes color according to how you look at it, no, it has a little bit of every color, it is like a harlequin. . . . Then at a certain moment it resembles a crucifix, but also a dummy, one of the kind painters use, which can be made to assume any position. It is something pliant, malleable, without a rigid form . . . But, of course, it is something full of possibilities . . . Perhaps now I am beginning to understand . . ."

At this point, I, too, understood the substantial difference existing between the interpretation I had been tempted to give and the meaning that was emerging from the patient's analogical amplification. Now the puppet took the form of an evolutive potentiality, as a capacity for transformation and renewal. My interpretation might have silenced this extraordinary messenger of the Self.

NOTES

(1) Jacobi, J.: Complex Archetype Symbol in the Psychology of C. G. Jung. Routledge & Kegan Paul, London, 1959.
(2) Jung, C. G.: Der philosophische Baum, in: Von den Wurzeln des Bewußtseins, Rascher, Zürich, 1945, p. 491.
(3) Jung, C. G.: Collected Works, vol. 8, p. 263.
(4) Fonzi, A., Negro Sancipriano, E.: La magia delle parole: alla riscoperta della metafora. Einaudi, Torino, 1975.
(5) Ibid., p. 16.
(6) Le Guern, M.: Sémantique de la métaphore et de la métonymie. Larousse, Paris, 1973, p. 75.
(7) Winnicott, D. W.: Gioco e realta'. (Ital. trans.) Armando, Roma, 1974, p. 43.
(8) Frey-Rohn, L.: From Freud to Jung. Putnam's Sons, New York, 1974, p. 168.
(9) Fornari, F.: I processi di simbolizzazione tra mondo interno e mondo esterno. Riv. di Psicoan. XXIII, 1, 1977.
(10) Hautmann, G.: Pensiero onirico e realta' psichica. Riv. di Psicoan. XXIII, 1, 1977.
(11) Hobson, R.: Imagination and Amplification in Psychotherapy. Journ. Anal. Psychol. 16, 1, 1971.
(12) Jacobi, J.: La psicologia di C. G. Jung. (Ital. trans.) Boringhieri, Torino, 1949, p. 107.
(13) Jung, C. G.: Coll. Works. vol. 16, p. 148.
(14) Jung, C. G.: Coll. Works. vol. 12, p. 289.
(15) Jung, C. G.: Coll. Works. vol. 7, p. 291.
(16) Jung, C. G.: La funzione transcendente, in La dimensione psichica. Boringhieri, Torino, 1972.
(17) Ibid., p. 113 (Coll. Works. vol. 8, p. 86).
(18) Ibid., p. 114 (Coll. Works. vol. 8, pp. 86–87).
(19) Jung, C. G.: L'Io e l'inconscio (Ital. trans.) Boringhieri, Torino, 1967 (Coll. Works. vol. 7, p. 213).
(20) Ibid. p. 133.

IL SOGNO: ATTIVITA' IMMAGINATIVA VERSUS INTERPRETAZIONE

Mario Moreno (Roma)

L'ipotesi archetipica è utilizzabile nel concepire non soltanto la *formazione* del simbolo, ma anche la sua *decodificazione*. L'archetipo, inteso come struttura significante, potrebbe funzionare come termine di paragone in un processo intuitivo di confronto tra materiale immaginativo e l'intenzione di significato originaria. L'attivazione controtransferenziale dell'archetipo permetterebbe all'analista l'intuizione di similarità che collega l'emozione all'immagine.

Questa ipotesi collega is simbolo al processo di (italics) quale risulta dall'analisi pscolinguistica.

Alla luce di questa ipotesi, mentre l'amplificazione soggettiva sembra portare avanti il processo di simbolizzazione già operante nel sogno, l'interpretazione comporterebbe il rischio d'interrompere questo processo creativo.

Ci sarebbe dunque da domandarsi, rispetto al sogno, se talora non possa essere opportuno che l'analista rinunci, almeno temporaneamente, all'interpretazione, sia essa a livello dell'oggetto o a livello del soggetto, per non interferire col suo intervento nel processo creativo messo in moto dal sogno, per favorire invece l'attività di amplificazione soggettiva o magari contribuire al gioco immaginativo che si svolge tra analista e paziente, con un'amplificazione oggettiva che non miri ad una immediata conclusione interpretativa.

Un esempio adatto ad illustrare questo dilemma tra attività immaginativa e interpretazione nell'uso del sogno in analisi, conclude l'intervento.

PSYCHOSIS AS VISIONARY STATE.

John W. Perry, San Francisco

As we embark upon this discussion of schizophrenia I am sure we are all mindful of the fact that this was the area in which Dr. Jung wrote his first two classic studies: *The Psychology of Dementia Praecox* formulating the complexes of the personal unconscious, and *Symbols of Transformation* investigating the primordial images of the collective unconscious. It thus became the launching platform for his explorations in inner space. He kept up his interest in this condition throughout his life, as many of us do since we find that it touches upon most of the central issues in the psychology and psychotherapy that deal with dimensions of depth. We will find from the various members of this panel that the work that Dr. Jung began is being carried forward.

There are many mysteries around the phenomenon called "acute schizophrenia," its cause, its treatment, and its outcome. It appears from our recent experiences in San Francisco that in the therapy of schizophrenia, what is crucial not only in effecting a favorable outcome, but even in determining the nature of the syndrome itself, is the attitude toward this condition.

Let me specify at the outset exactly which condition I am speaking of here: this is only one among many syndromes that pass under the name "schizophrenia," namely that one which gives all the appearance of being the most grossly psychotic, with deep withdrawal and regression, delusions, hallucinations, and with active production of elaborate symbolic imagery and ritualistic gestures, often denudative, usually angry behavior.

Oddly enough, as has long been recognized by psychiatrists, this highly disturbed state is the one that shows the most favorable outcome. The old figures before the days of phenothiazine medication indicated a 12–15 % spontaneous recovery. It has long been assumed rather broadly in this field that medication has improved the chances of good recovery and long-term outcome, yet recidivism has become a gigantic problem (National statistics show 65 % rehospitalization by the second post-hospital year). However, in our carefully controlled random selection study of 103 cases at Agnew State Hospital five years ago we found medication not to be clearly beneficial. In a double-blind experimental program in which placebos or thorazine medication were given to alternate cases, those who were medicated showed better results only during the in-hospital stay. In the three-year follow-up the results on 80 of the cases were to a startling degree opposite, both in terms of recurrence requiring rehospitalization and of further psychological development. Those given placebos in hospital and no medication afterwards showed only 8 % recurrence in three years, those on medication during and after hospital stay, 73 %! Those without medication showed continuing growth curves on the psychological scales, while those on medication plateaued, without evidence of further growth!

When the Agnew Project was finished, my Jungian colleague Dr. Howard Levene and I established a residence facility as a preferable setting in which to handle the acute psychotic episode with optimal conditions for proper therapy. It became part of the community mental health system of San Francisco. In the short life-span of our operation under this funding, shortly under a year, we handled thirteen (13) cases with a three month stay. We gave no medications. Our expectations were high, but we were astonished at the results. The most remarkable feature was the rapidity with which these persons made their come-back from the psychotic state: most "came down" into a coherent, rational state of mind within one to five days, and the longest anyone took was nine days. Their recovery was not only becoming symptom-free, but going out into fruitful living and growth afterwards. Of these 13 cases, 12 were grossly psychotic upon admission, yet 11 made good recovery, which is 85 %.

Any attempt to account for exactly how this came about must necessarily be inadequate, since there are many unaccountables in this therapeutic method. However, there are a few certitudes to point to. First and foremost is the attitude of the staff toward the psychotic state. These were paraprofessional counsellors who were not educated in psychopathology, and their agreed point of view was that "labelling" with psychiatric terminology has destructive effects upon the clients in the form of disqualifying their experience and even their nature. Therefore there was a strict policy among them not to "label". They were characterized by a general demeanor of caring, encouraging, supporting, and giving affection. The atmosphere in the residence was in consequence warm, buoyant, and open and free in personal self-expression.

Thus far I am describing the phenomenology of the therapeutic experience on a somewhat external level. On the inner dimension, the essence of the process seems to be that the self-image is undergoing a profound reorganization; that is, on the personal level the self-concept and self-esteem, on the archetypal, the affect-image of the center and its renewal processes.

In the personal process of the reconstruction of the self-image, the crucial factor seems to be the "labelling" issue, that is, the question of how the client and his/her experience is viewed both by the client and by the therapist. The archetypal process that goes on meanwhile has a generally prevalent ground plan with parallels in myth and ritual of early antiquity which I have described elsewhere (in *Lord of the Four Quarters*): the principal features are activation of the center, death and rebirth, world destruction and recreation, clashes of opposites, their reversal, and their union in marriage imagery, and a messianic calling and program for society.

There is a dynamic of the psychotherapeutic relationship that is crucial to the transformation of the self-image. Perhaps the most remarkable feature in this state is the instant recognition, at the start, of the therapist's openess or lack of it, whether he/she is accepting and cognizant of the myth world in which the client is dwelling. If the client senses a negative feeling toward this nonrational inner experience, there results an immediate clamming up and withdrawal, sometimes irrevocable. Equally impressive is the fact that if the therapist addresses the client's ego that is so totally submerged in the psychotic turmoil, just as though it were still clear and in its rightful position of mastery, a coherent and natural response follows very soon. Quite similar is the finding that if the staff gives over to the client the full sense of responsibility to look after himself, take care of himself and the property, with unlocked doors and full permission to go in and out of the residence at will, this responsibility is accepted and the ego soon finds itself back at the helm.

Whenever on the contrary, the client is addressed with even the faintest hint of a patronizing tone as being sick and out of control, or childlike and incapable of the usual rational behavior, he/she will render back exactly what is portrayed in the negative expectation. Therefore if a staff member regards a client as insane, incoherent, or confused by nonsensical notions, the client thereupon feels insane and out of control, and behaves accordingly. Even such subtle implications of sickness as white clinical coats may be devastating.

It might seem as if I were portraying the "schizophrenic" individual as highly suggestible, as a hysterical one might be. However, despite this superficial resemblance the dynamics of this interaction are quite different here. We are dealing here with a marked tendency to identify with any highly charged affect-image that presents itself from outside in the setting or from inside in the psyche. Thus the individual in this state "becomes" a savior, a madonna, a second coming, or an emperor, when such affect-images are activated in the psyche, or "becomes" a crazy "nut" if such an image is imposed emotionally from without.

I view this tendency to identify with these inwardly or outwardly derived affect-images not as a character trait of the schizoid make-up so much as a characteristic of the altered states of consciousness that are marked by activation of the lower centers, that is, the so-called "high arousal states".

If the affect-image coming from outside is demeaning, causing the individual to feel wrong-headed and nonsensical, an exasperated rage wells up which is utterly shattering to the psyche. Madness is indeed a state of being "mad" in both senses of the word. This rage needs to be released into expression and communicated to someone who can receive and understand it, so that it may be integrated into the relationship and thus into the personality. Even more, it is imperative that the occasions for rage be reduced to a minimum by a mode of reception of the individual's experience that is validating.

If the affect-image coming from outside is favorable and accepting in this fashion, allowing the individual to feel as human and authentic as anyone else, then we discover the utterly remarkable clearing up of the insanity in a matter of days. Not only do we find, then, that validation of the inner psychic experience is essential for the clearing up of the psychotic turmoil, but even more impressively we find that invalidation becomes an equally essential factor in the production of the psychopatholgy that marks the syndrome we call "schizophrenia".

This leads us to the question, what therapy is like when the psychotic turmoil has subsided. In a word, it may be said that the same features prevail as in ordinary psychotherapy when working with archetypal activation, only multiplied tenfold.

The therapist must be at home with unusual dimensions of experience in death, without anxiety, fear, or mistrust, that is, with confidence that the psyche knows what it is doing and how to do it. The therapist has to enter upon a mutual experience of transformation with an open, warm, and caring relation on the part of both toward each other. Thus the transference is of the essence, as it usually is in psychotherapy when it involves archetypal depth. In this case, the processes that usually take place over the course of two or three years now come tumbling upon one another in the space of a few weeks. Many of the basic issues of the transformation of the self take place *in potentia,* that is, in symbolic imagery. The more the therapist is aware of the significance of these various dimensions of experience, the more they can come to fruition in consciousness. This is because they come into mutual recognition in the therapeutic bond between the two persons.

Here I am assuming that the relationship between the two persons in the psychic process is the element that effects integration. That is, all that needs to be dealt with is first integrated into the relationship, as the transformative vessel, and thence assimilated into the growing ego and its life experience.

Hence is it any wonder that when the processes of the renewal of the self are under way, validation of the person is as urgent as it is?

I have been speaking of "labelling" as if it signified only a negative item. More strictly, the term ought to be "diagnostic labelling" in the sense of pointing to a psychopathological syndrome. The condition still needs a name so that it can be spoken about, obviously, but a validating name in this case. The closest cultural and historical parallel to this turmoil is the high arousal state that seers, prophets, and messiahs customarily undergo on the way to formulating their newly conceived mythologies. These occur typically in turbulent times of acute, rapid culture-change, and their role is to experience inwardly what the entire society is suffering, but in such a way as to discover the creative potential in the destruction of the waning culture. Visionary states have commonly been the source from which new myth and ritual forms have sprung throughout history. Our clients are less grand in their scope and less articulate in their expression, but I see the fundamental process as similar. I therefore like to call this condition by the term "visionary state" in the interests of validation.

CURRICULUM VITAE
John Weir Perry, M. D.

Doctor John Weir Perry studied medicine at Harvard where he also had his A. B. degree in History and Literature. During the war he served with the Friends Ambulance Unit in China. Aiming to do research in psychology and religion, he received a Rockefeller Foundation fellowship to train in Analytical Psychology at the C. G. Jung Institute in Zürich. In recent years he has been Assistant Clinical Professor in Psychiatry at the University of California, and Lecturer in the C. G. Jung Institute, both in San Francisco. Besides his analytic practice, he has worked with schizophrenic in-patients, and on this experience has written several articles and two books, *The Self in Psychotic Process* and *The Far Side of Madness*. He has recently been engaged part time in an NIMH-sponsored research program, the Agnews Project, on new developments in the handling of schizophrenia, and is co-founder of Diabasis, a residence center for this purpose in San Francisco.

Publications:
(1953) *The Self in Psychotic Process.* University of California Press, Berkeley.
(1966) *Lord of the Four Quarters: Myths of the Royal Father.* Braziller, New York.
(1970) "Emotions and Object Relations," *Journal of Analytical Psychology, 15,* 1, pp. 1–12.
(1971) "Societal Implications of the Renewal Process," *Spring,* 1971, pp. 153–167.
(1972) "The Messianic Hero," *Journal of Analytical Psychology, 17,* 2, pp. 184–198.
(1974) *The Far Side of Madness,* Prentice Hall, Inc. New Jersey, Spectrum Books.
(1976) *The Roots of Renewal in Myth and Madness,* Jossey-Bass Publishers, San Francisco.

ACTIVE IMAGINATION IN TWO ANALYSANDS
OF DIFFERENT FUNCTION TYPE

Faye Pye, London

Active imagination is both a form of expression and a technique of encounter-and-reciprocal-relation between the consciousness of an individual and his unconscious. It therefore seems probable that the dispositions of functions (1) in consciousness (according to Jung's typology) is a factor in the use of the method.

I had the opportunity of observing this in practice when two analysands were working with me concurrently whose superior functions were converse (2)–that is to say, one had superior introverted sensation and the other had superior extroverted intuition, with the corresponding inferior functions. From the point of view of an observer, the type contrast was made more striking by the fact that they had some similarities of background: both were women; in their fifth decade; practising Christians; in the same profession; both English, and both involved in an individuation process.

Both have generously allowed me to use their material.

It seemed to me in retrospect that the two processes vividly illuminated each other, and illustrated the different manner of active imagination peculiar to the type. In selecting examples much has obviously had to be omitted. Material has been taken from an early and a late stage, to illustrate in each case the emergence of the fourth function, confrontation with it, and its integration leading to transformation. In each case a dream relevant to the practise of active imagination is also given.

I. First pair of examples

The first examples consist of events, which happened before either analysand was consciously aware of the process in which she was involved. It seems that each of them experienced unconscious death-and-rebirth phenomena at the symptomatic level, which very nearly had fatal consequences. Although these events as such were remote from active imagination, they represented a psychic aspect which was later to reach its goal in active imagination.

Already in this early stage the peronality type determined the mode of experience. What happened was as follows–:

a) The sensation type analysand (whom I shall now call Miss S), some time before she began her work with me, took a lethal overdose of drugs. She immediately reported it, so that medical intervention saved her life. It seems probable that she was acting out concretely, in terms of her sensation-reality, the as-yet-unrealised meaning of her unconscious extroverted intuition.

b) The intuitive analysand (whom I shall now call Miss I) suffered repeated heavy menorrhagia, severe enough to require blood transfusions. This occurred in the first few weeks of analysis. No medical grounds for the bleeding were established. It is possible that she was living synchronistically in her body the content of her unconscious introverted sensation. This is the more likely since she had many striking synchronistic experiences during the later course of her analysis.

Interpretation of these events as death-and-rebirth phenomena is in both cases speculative, but it seems justified in the light of future psychological transformations. At that time, in neither instance could there yet be any extension of conscious awareness, or renewal.

II. Second pair of examples

a) The second examples come from a period of time following several years of analysis (3½). Miss S was now seemingly trying to find her intuitive experience in various collective forms in the outer world. She attended yoga classes and took instructions in transcendental meditation. Both of these disturbed her physically. She was admiring and envious of a friend who could "speak with tongues," and longed to have the experience herself. "Speaking with tongues" has been interpreted by JUNG as the symbolic use of language to express contents that are

Miss I's Drawing No. 1. June 1975. "White Winged Horse"

Miss I's Drawing No. 2. March 1976. "St. Therese throws down the Glove"

Miss I's Drawing No. 3. December 1976. "The Source"

too strange and remote from consciousness to be formulated in current cultural terms (3).

Difficulties in self-expression and communication are characteristic of introverted sensation (4). Miss S hung on the fringes of self-expression, frustrated by her sense of inadequacy in this regard. She had fantasies of becoming a skilled calligrapher so that she could make perfect, aesthetic lettering.

Eventually a breakthrough came, apparently initiated by the unconscious. Over a period of several weeks, on successive independent occasions, her consciousness was flooded with meaningful ideas and images. She worked on these to give them form as poems. In one of them she became aware for the first time of the unity of all things and of her own potential wholeness.

b) In a corresponding phase (2½ years) Miss I was expressing herself, as she had done from the beginning, in vivid visual and verbal imagery with considerable talent and insight. But there came a time when she had to face reality problems which could not be overcome by intuitive flights. She communicated this experience in the following fantasy:–

A white winged horse came from the sky and invited her to ride on his back. He carried her away into the clouds. An "Eros/Mercury" figure wearing a winged helmet appeared and shot a barbed arrow which pierced her heart. The horse came down to earth. In distress she said to him, "I am alive and dead at once–how can I get it out when it is barbed?" The horse replied "Only he who can heal the wound can draw it out." She thought of the sword in the stone–an image of initiation and of concrete reality.

Here the intuitive is earthed by material reality (which is thrust on her by the unconscious itself). She is faced with limitations and conditions which irk her free and active spirit. Her only recourse is to enter into dialogue with the unconscious, whose image here is the talking horse.

III. Third pair of examples

The final examples are 2 dreams which were followed by active imagination. Each analysand had a dream which led her into direct confrontation with the central unconscious numen.

a) Miss S dreamt that an old bearded monk who was an icon painter was pursuing her. She was afraid of him and was doing her best to escape. But he persevered from a distance. Eventually she found herself in a high barn-like building. She was standing beside one of its walls in which there was a large opening leading straight on to a precipitous drop outside. She could go no further. As she stood there a car drove past her and deliberately ran over the drop. She looked down expecting to see disaster, but instead she saw the car turn a somersault, land on all four wheels, bounce a little, and then go off down the road. She then knew that she must meet the icon-painter, and at the same time she found that she no longer feared him.

Miss S's response to the dream was terror. For one thing she was disturbed by the unreality of the leaping car. She also felt the icon painter to be somehow awesome. She was deeply impressed with his holiness. He was an "older" whose state of spiritual advancement was such that he could create icons: that is to say, incarnations of the holy spirit, a union of inner and outer (3).

She angrily denied my suggestion that she might herself go to meet and converse with him. But to my astonishment some two months later she began to do psychological drawings. Her sensation had transcended itself in its encounter with the unconscious vis-a-vis (5).

As an example of type-contrast it is interesting that Miss S's drawings were on the whole abstract, whereas Miss I's were vividly representational. This points to their compensatory nature. It is as though Miss S expressed intuitive insight in her drawings, and Miss I expressed sensory awareness of her inner images.

b) Miss I's dream was as follows:–

St. Theresa of the Child Jesus (6) came from death into life to visit the dreamer and others. She came because she wanted to. She was able to do it because she was such a powerful saint ("she had a will like steel"). At first she was present but not visible, and the sign of her activity was a red glove poised on the tip of its index finger. Then she appeared in person, young and laughing behind a desk, in her Carmelite habit. The dreamer asked her whether there were presences or persons to guide and welcome those who arrived in death. The Saint said, "Not at first, but later there would be people."

Two episodes of active imagination followed. In the first St. Theresa was recalled and asked, "Why the glove?" She replied by taking the glove and throwing it to the ground saying, "She throws down the gauntlet and stoops to conquer." Miss I picked up the glove. A gust of wind blew in through the window behind the desk, fluttering the curtain. In the second episode the Saint said to Miss I, "Live your myth with the same fidelity as I lived mine." Miss I interpreted this as, "Make *your* myth as real as I made mine."

The image of St. Therese appears as one to whom body and bodilessness, spirit and matter, life and death, are all equally available as dimensions of being. Like the icon-painter she unites opposites of spirit and matter. Like the icon-painter too she made actual in specific form, her spiritual insight. She was the exponent of her "Little Way," which transcended-by-accepting the limitations and conditions of material reality.

General Comments

At this point for reasons of time it is necessary to leave the developing process, and turn to some general considerations.

Sensation and intuition are both non-rational functions of perception. A consciousness that is orientated by either of them is close to the archaic levels of the unconscious. In such circumstances an individual has to develop a means of dealing with the archaic powers. Intuition does this by offering multiple ever-changing symbolic forms into which the unconscious dynamism can flow. Sensation in its turn carefully delimits clear and precise boundaries in fact and in matter. When however the movement towards wholeness and the union of opposites become dominant, consciousness in each case is confronted with the threat of the other mode of reality. Consciousness then has to sacrifice its defences and, by embracing its opposite, risk a symbolic death, from which only the transcendent function (7) can deliver it.

At this critical time, active imagination provides the way for a gradual extension of consciousness and assimilation of the unconscious. When the numinous transpersonal centre has been personalised, as in the icon-painter and St. Therese the dialogue between consciousness and the unconscious has become potentially available.

When I began to study the material of Miss I and Miss S I had expected to uncover a gulf between them. Instead I found that their experience, though different, was intimately related. Doubtless this was due to the facts that both were concerned with the non-rational functions of perception, and each was grappling with her inferior function.

In practise their talents in active imagination were very different:–

Miss I had a continuity of imagery and a symbolic flow which might suggest greater ease. Miss S was handicapped by her problems of expression and by the intermittent nature of her encounters with the unconscious. Yet when it came to the critical issue, when ethical commitment meant the difference between success and failure in confrontation with the unconscious, Miss S was perhaps even at some advantage. She was for instance less likely to be carried away by compensatory inflation or to be seduced by aesthetic irrelevances. On the other hand in the intervals, when the unconscious did not provide her with stimulus, she felt herself to be "empty," or dependent on the inspiration of others, in a way Miss I did not.

For both of them the practise of active imagination was decisive. It led Miss S out of her inner isolation towards a capacity for conscious communication with inner and outer persons. It also released her from the narrow concrete prison of religious fundamentalism into the symbolic life.

Miss I on the other hand pursued the task of "making her myth real". In a series of imaginative experience she developed the Symbolism of rock and stone to a point at which she was able to declare, "Now I feel that I have substance in myself."

Freedom to choose the manner, mode, timing and dimension of their imagining seemed to be essential in both analysands. It was necessary to them, both as "types" and as individuals. The unconscious drove ruthlessly towards its goal, even though when once its will was achieved, it bore the face of inner guide and friend. Active imagination was the means by which the maturing ego could "lead its captivity captive".

REFERENCES

(1) Letter to Dr. E. V. Tenney. C. G. Jung Letters, Vol. 2, p. 228. Trans. R. F. C. Hull. pub. RKP. 1976.
(2) Coll. Wks., Vol. 6, para 241.
(3) Letters to Dr. E. V. Tenney. op. cit. p. 227.
(4) Coll. Wks., Vol. 6, paras 650 and 664–665.
(5) The Orthodox Church. Timothy Ware. A Pelican Original. 1963, 43–50.
(6) Autobiography of a Saint. Therese of Lisieux. Translated by Ronald Knox. Fontana 1958.
(7) Coll. Wks. The Transcendent Function. Vol. 8, p. 131–193.

THE ENERGY OF WARRING AND COMBINING OPPOSITES: PROBLEMS FOR THE PSYCHOTIC PATIENT AND THE THERAPIST IN ACHIEVING THE SYMBOLIC SITUATION.

J. W. T. Redfearn, London

I want to discuss some of the problems the therapist may have in coping with conflicting opposites in his "psychotic" patients and in the psychotic parts of his "normal" patients and of himself. Of course, the psychotic patient may often impute evil motives or intentions to the therapist when an impasse or frustration arises, but it is not always as simple as that. The patient may actually need to unload pain or evil into or onto the therapist. For the patient this may be a matter of survival or at least of bodily health.

The level at which psychic and psycho-physical interactions of this type take place I am going to call the level of the primal relationship. It is in many ways similar to that which exists between the mother and her baby. At this level we are sensitive to emotional atmosphere, even to a quite detailed and specific degree. So-called narcissistic needs *are* bodily needs. The need to *unload* badness and later to *project* badness is a physical as well as a psychic necessity.

Using the terminology of Erich NEUMANN, we are dealing with the uroboric stage of psychic development and the early part of the great mother stage when we have a life-giving all-powerful world-or great-mother and a world-destroying and annihilating great mother.

If we keep in mind the image of some such awesomely powerful part of the self presiding over the situation between the psychotic patient and ourselves, we are more likely to give due respect to the relationship.

Many of us are familiar with the untreated psychotic patient who apparently *has* to act out violently, even murderously, in order to obtain relief for himself. For this reason we as therapists may need to distance ourselves, or at least share with other helpers the bad or destructive projections and the physical effects of these bad feelings "put into us" by our psychotic patients. And so the problem becomes a wider social one.

At the level of the uroborus, we are dealing with undifferentiated psychic energy and an undifferentiated cosmos. Later, we are dealing with the differentiation of opposing drives and with the corresponding opposing emotions and images, and we are up against forces of the most powerful and elemental kind, in both creative and destructive relationships with each other. We must not forget that there is a disintegrative process in the human psyche which is itself the opposite of the creative synthesis of opposites which we associate with the symbolic process. Ignoring the death-dealing, implacable, maiming aspects of nature and of ourselves is a perilous and suicidal attitude. In dealing with psychotics, we explore these levels in ourselves, in our patients and in society.

This primal psychic level has much to do with the archetypal aspects of union and separation, and with the immense creative and destructive energies involved. Union has to do with love, merging, linking, feeding, the *coniunctio oppositorum*, and creation. In a less positive form it has to do with hallucinations, delusions and ideas of reference.

Separation in its positive aspects has to do with differentiation, with the avoidance of distress, pain and over-excitation. We avoid the pain of conflicting feelings by separating. We discontinue unions which are unbearable—too depressing, too much of a strain, bad for the health, poisoning or debilitating or depleting or injuring us, or which are simply too confusing and chaotic. We avoid being painfully penetrated, or invaded, or swallowed up, or taken over, or annihilated—treated as a non-person. But the psychotic person in his need to survive does all these things to us, and he has to, or else suffer these things himself. For brevity we use some such term as splitting *defences* in the patient. They are experienced as extremely *offensive* if they are at all effective.

The healing of splitting defences is always painful to patient and analyst. It requires, in order of priority, survival, recognition, concern, and even love on the part of the therapist. Fortunately the patient often teaches the therapist how to provide these things.

The containing and holding aspects of the mother or therapist and later of the ego.

If we take the alchemical image of opposing psychic forces or substances coming into contact inside a container, with the absorption or creation of energy, we can use this image as a model with which to understand some of the phenomena of psychosis.

First of all, let us consider the symbolic process, the process involved in therapy and in individuation. A personal conflict or life crisis will result in the activation of conflicting unconscious tendencies–opposing archetypal activities. In the working-out of such conflicts, the healthy person will be able to use some containing element and the energy produced will be harnessed and used creatively rather than being wasted, or producing destruction, explosion, or disintegration. In other words he will in the course of maturation have learned how to sustain and resolve conflicts within himself. The capacity to sustain and resolve conflicts is usually regarded as an important aspect of the ego. In the early months of life the mother and the environment subserve this holding function, and the maturing ego introjects the mother's particular ways of holding and containing, of restraining, delaying, and delimiting conflicting instinctual patterns. The symbolic attitude is normally dependent upon the introjection of the mother's holding capacity. It can be learned later, from the therapist for example.

If the holding capacity of the ego is not adequate to enable the conflict to be sustained and result in the emergence of a life-enhancing symbol or in creative activity, various makeshift vessel-like functions may be used. A parent or parent-substitute, a friend or analyst, the analytical situation, conventions, rules, moral principles, rituals, a persona function, dramatisation, turning the conflict into a play activity, or the framework of aesthetic activity, all these are in universal use for providing the structure, the limits and the inhibitions within which the ethical conflict can be resolved. All these are therefore versions of the alchemical vessel, or are parts or fragments or miniature versions of it. They could be called ego-aids or ego-substitutes in this context.

This "alchemical vessel" in the mature person corresponds with a sense of personal identity based on the body image. In other words the vessel has basically a human form. At this basic level the vessel, the body of the great mother, and the body-self of the individual are not differentiable (cf. NEUMANN, The Great Mother).

As I have said, this containing function, although innate, is normally experienced and differentiated through the experience by the baby of its mother's affirmative, recognizing attitude towards himself as a person (see NEWTON and REDFEARN, The Real Mother and the Ego-self relationship).

The mother-vessel-self archetype is at first coterminous with the cosmos and is at first relatively unbounded and undifferentiated. The containing and limiting of excitation is done by the actual mother. Later the mother, her insides so to speak, are experienced archetypally as paradise, a treasure house, or as hell, depending essentially on whether she is experienced as giving herself or taking herself away from the baby.

Later still, the mother acquires more human dimensions and the containing function is located in the individual's own personal bodily self. In the joys and sorrows of the personal relationship between mother and infant there still goes on the sharing of treasures and the pangs of hurt in the give-and-take of feeding, playing, and communication.

Going back to the idea of the alchemical vessel's being an analogue of the body-ego, we must understand that the "vessel" of the strong mature individual can contain and transform large amounts of the energy produced by the meeting of opposites. On the other hand, the "vessel" of the weak, schizoid individual can contain and harness little energy. He is easily over-excited. Energy soon reaches the level where it is experienced destructively. It soon assumes omnipotent dimensions and it tends readily to be experienced either as an attribute of the "ego," or to be projected and thus to be alienated from the ego. The situation in either case involves an absence of real responsibility in relation to the forces concerned.

Thus for the borderline person the approaching "Other" has often to be pushed away or else to be experienced as part of oneself or completely under one's control. If incorporated, the "Other" may become bad and have to be extruded. All these phenomena are consciously experienced in the body-ego of the stronger person. The body-self of the stronger person can contain large amounts of love and energy, whereas the body-self of the weak person can contain little before spilling over in premature ejaculation, metaphorical or literal, or in acting-out or in anger (see LOWEN, Love and Orgasm). On the other hand we hear of holy men capable of actually taking into themselves not only the problems but even the bodily diseases of friends or others, of suffering them and of getting over them. Whether these stories are strictly factual or not, they illustrate my concept of strong vessels.

Now, as the heirs of Wilhelm REICH assert, the amount of containable energy depends on the absence of neurotic "armouring" and the aliveness of the body. I myself am not however equating aliveness with absence of suffering or even of disease.

For example, the bodily pseudo-health of many eccentrics, ascetics, schizophrenic and hypomanic persons may be achieved at the expense of relatedness rather than through suffering and transformation. And this can apply to the "narcissistic" person who is well within the range of the normal.

This hypothesis, namely that there is such a thing as apparent health based on projection of the bad, and another kind of bodily health based on acceptance and transformation, is at present just a suggestion for medical and bioenergetic research, rather than an assertion of undoubted fact.

According to my hypothesis, it is not the ego which is doing the unloading or projecting of the bad but an archetypal function of the body-self. Later, it has to do with the narcissistic self-image, or egotism; not, I suggest, with the ego.

In the case of patients functioning at this level, an affirmative primal feeling in therapist or attendant is very sensitively picked up and reacted to. However, an affirmative primal attitude may have to be patiently worked towards during many months of therapy, and is not necessarily the "instinctive" response of the born therapist. One's "instinctive" response tends to be similar to or the opposite of that which the real mother originally had or developed towards the patient. One may have to learn from the patient over the course of time how to be able to take an affirmative or recognizing attitude towards his "evil" or "destructive" impulses particularly when these involve *actual* loss and sacrifice by the therapist.

At this schizoid level of mental life, both approaching, getting closer to the patient, and separating or distancing, have to be handled with great sensitivity. For the schizoid person, the excitement which we all feel on increasing closeness tends to be experienced as invasive, destructive, or deleterious. Conversely, the withdrawal of the wanted person brings about extremely negative and destructive images or impulses, which are often projected. Thus the withdrawing loved mother or beloved person becomes a loathsome witch, a murderess, someone who ought to be got rid of. The other person has to be omnipotently controlled or becomes the object of intense energetic feelings or impulses. Thus "I want to be closer to you" becomes "you have sexual designs on me," or "We are going to be married" "I hate you for refusing to be close to me" becomes "you are going to murder me," and "I hate you for leaving me after such a short visit" can become "you are Satan," at the level of the primal relationship. Not only is natural and correct distancing important, but unforced timing. At the primal level of caring the mother is able to take her timing from the baby and his natural functions. Forcing her own time on her baby constitutes a gross disturbance, particularly of the autonomic system and may result in a precocious ego-self relationship, a false, compliant ego-like structure rather than one truly related to the self and the unconscious, autonomically-based bodily functions.

At this level the symbol does not exist, the metaphor is the experiental reality, because the excitement of the conflicting opposites cannot be contained and transformed. There is no "as if," no sense of humour, no tolerance of ambivalence, and so all these functions have to be carried by the therapist.

"Primal scene excitement" in its most basic archetypal form belongs to this sphere of experience. In its more archaic forms the engulfing interacting parent-creatures are represented in imaginal monsters and in very primitive muscular and autonomic patterns. These experiences are prehuman and prepersonal and antedate the emergence of the human self-image. This is why as the persona and the shadow are analysed, the primal scene or the coniunctio oppositorum, and the link between the "I" and one's body, may assume bizarre and monstrous forms on the one hand, or sublime or god-like forms on the other.

Both the persona and the shadow are partial body-selves, at least to the extent that they remain as unadaptive and stereotyped patterns relatively alienated from the ego. I prefer to use terms persona-function and shadow-function, to describe the healthy, ego-available forms of these bits of the self.

The uncontainable opposites may of course originate in the environment, in the form of a psychotic or seriously disturbed parent, incessantly warring parents, or insupportable double-bind situations. I am reminded of a patient who in her psychotic state complained of not existing in her body and of a feeling of being situated outside her body. When I met her mother with her lying self-deceptions I felt precisely the same feelings as my patient complained of, and I knew exactly why the patient felt as she did. R. D. Laing in England and Harold Searles in the United States have convincingly described massive introjections of psychotic parents and psychotogenic situations and so there is no need for me to elaborate on these. Jung was possibly the first to emphasize how parents in a sense force themselves, their world, and particularly their unconscious complexes on their children.

At the schizoid level, bodily impulses and affective discharges are experienced as cosmic events. Later in life, unintegrated patterns of affective discharge, when they are alien to the ego, are experienced in the same way, i.e. as alien forces. Patients describe their unintegrated discharges as mighty winds or as elemental forces, etc. Jung gives an excellent example in his dream of his own struggle against a strong wind with his shadow going before him. He observes that the shadow is thrown by the tiny light of consciousness. In a paper read last year in Berlin, Kate Newton and I have described how in a borderline patient her pregenital bodily impulses and her infantile rage were at first experienced in this way, i.e. as uncontrollable elemental forces, and how through the affirmative primal relationship with the analyst these parts of the self were gradually contained by and functionally related to the now more friendly ego.

"Containment by the ego" should not be confused with the concept of mastery and control, which is a manic or obsessional defence, as illlusory as mastering the wind or controlling the lightning. Premature and stereotyped posturing in relation to these archetypal forces are rife in collective psychology and certainly should not be added to by the analytical psychologist. All "techniques" constitute illusions of this sort. Premature reductive interpretations as well as naive introjections and idealizations on the therapist's part may both be damaging, because both increase splitting defences. If there is a split between the bodily and the spiritual we should not make matters worse with one-sided interpretations.

So much for the pre-personal level of psychic functioning. An analyst who is not aware of this level of functioning in himself could not be expected to cope with patients in whom things were wrong at this level. A mother who was not functioning well at this level, not being a person, could not help her child become a person with a personal sense of identity.

Manic and depressive parts of the self.

Whereas the schizoid or paranoid person splits and tends to project the bad in order to survive, we might say that the depressive person takes in the bad in order to preserve the loved Other, and the manic person denies his feelings of badness and dependence upon the loved Other. The depressive person tends to take the Other into himself whole, denying the bad parts and denying his anger for fear or loss and fear of damaging the Other. So one can say that affective psychoses represent premature attempts to attain whole-person feelings. They are premature because the goodness or badness are not fully assimilated before being transformed. Manic denial is short-cut transformation, depressive introjection is defensive incorporation of the bad. Using an oral metaphor, there is a yet no chewing and taking in only the good while spitting out the bad.

By about the age of eight months, as all parents know from experience, the baby is able to relate to his mother as a person, to distinguish between her and others, to differentiate her from himself, and even to care for her in a loving way. We think that his love for her causes him to feel sad or ill, rather than to hate her when she seems to be cross with him. Paranoid and splitting mechanisms are replaced by depressive ones in which aggression begins to be contained by the child because of the value to him of the loving primal experiences he has had with her. The normal infant can begin to delay or inhibit his impulses. He remembers his mother in her differing aspects, coming and going, giving and witholding, loving him and being angry with him, and so on.

The good and bad great mother now has a much more human form, the infant is more outside the mother, more an individual person, provided that his mother has affirmed him as such and continues to do so. We are now entering NEUMANN's patriarchal stage, the beginning of Margret MAHLER's stage of individuation and separation from the mother and from the symbiotic capsule containing mother and child in the dual unity of the primal relationship. In the second year of life the child, copying its parents, learns to say "no" to them, thus becoming less vulnerable to penetration by bad outside forces.

Both depression and mania, it seems to me, involve premature and unsuccessful attempts to swallow the loved Other whole, with opposite but equally ineffective ways of dealing with bad or unacceptable feelings.

As far as treatment is concerned, I suppose one's main pre-occupation in treating depressive patients is to protect them from their own self-destructiveness and help them dare feel angry with the loved Other. One's main pre-occupation with manic patients on the other hand is often to assert and maintain one's own identity and point of view, because one feels constantly in danger of being swallowed up and taken over by him. The depressive patient feels devoured by the self, the manic patient feels he has devoured the self, as JUNG in his "two essays" so well understood. The self includes the archetypes in projection, including the mother and often the combined parents. I well remember the excited and omnipotent state I was in when I first felt I had devoured my analyst, and he coped by relying non-analytically on my good feelings and on the established relationship between us. Where this does not exist therapy of manic conditions is not possible in my experience. The patient usually terminates the relationship as he feels perfectly well.

It would be hardly conceivable to me to deal analytically with depressed patients without using notions about anger, bad feelings, swallowing and incorporation, feelings of being overwhelmed, and so on. It would be hardly possible for me to relate to the manic parts of my patients or myself without, I hope using similar, well-digested concepts of denial of dependence, control, triumph, and contempt.

I hope I have managed to give some indication of how I am always trying to relate the so-called symptomatology with his behaviour, his body-self, at the level where we can understand these so-called defence mechanisms in terms of unconscious fantasies and, fundamentally, to archetypal processes and to the self, which includes the actual functioning of the digestive system, let us remember. To become caught up in the patient's fantasies without relating them to his actual behaviour or to things happening to him is to become swallowed up in him and in his psychosis, which is abandoning him in a very real sense.

Counter-transference towards psychotic patients.

The infectiousness of manic patients is of course well known; one tends to be swallowed up by them in the sense of being taken over by their mood and viewpoint, until the snapping point is reached where one can no longer go along with them and one may have to take over, to contain *them* in other words. For example, they may be spending all the family's money or refusing to pay one's fees. This snapping point in several patients in my case was a real "gut" reaction. I found that to go along with them in their world was an increasingly gut-twisting, gut-tightening exercise until I asserted myself and my own viewpoint. I am quite sure my intestines were actually involved in the way these words indicate. Incidentally, one of my manic patients expressed herself very pertinently one day just before she had to be hospitalized by telling me that her fondest wish at that moment was to rip out my guts, and it felt as if she were doing just that at the time.

Of course the therapist who cannot lose himself in, i.e. allow himself to be swallowed up by, his patient is not much good either, although he may be good for certain moods and conditions. Although one must be prepared to struggle to maintain one's identity and values rather than be overwhelmed by the patient, one must also be prepared at all times to have one's values and identity shattered in some sense by new evidence, new circumstances, new aspects of the patient.

Counter-transference feelings, or the awareness for the archetypal atmosphere at any moment, are the best guide to the psychopathological level and nature of the situation between patient and therapist being constellated. Although relatedness at a primitive level is a sine qua non of therapy, I myself find that when a patient has got into me to such an extent that he or she is having striking telepathies or clairvoyant dreams about me or seems to be exerting a disturbing influence over me of this kind, it is time to consciously summon suitable resources to counteract this state of affairs. I have always found that a simple effort of awareness and will has been sufficient to effect the necessary distance or separation. Feelings of being "got into" or "got at" or "swallowed" are for the experienced therapist an accurate guide to the patient's unconscious wishes and fantasies, and can give valuable information about where the patient wishes to enter you and about the amount of sadism involved in the entry or penetration. It is not the words of the personal question or remark that matter, but the way in which it is asked and the amount of discomfort caused in the therapist.

(The counter-transference feelings which I have experienced most frequently with psychotic patients are perhaps worth listing. I have often felt dismay and sadness when a patient seems to be slipping away from where one can be with him; indignation when a patient is everything good and I am all bad, and often a feeling of being robbed in such cases; I experience cold horror at schizoid callousness, for example at a description of so-called love-making when schizoid defences are prominent, I have often felt completely overwhelmed by the flood of unconscious material from patients in danger of psychosis, and have found that it is often wise to say so; I have sometimes been frightened when a patient is splitting off his fear and making me feel his fear for him; tightening and twisting of the guts is a commonplace particularly in potentially violent group situations, or when it is becoming imperative to "cut off" from the patient for his sake or one's own; I sometimes experience numbness or weakness in the arms when a strong impulse to strike the patient is being inhibited; murderous feelings when a witch anima is being constellated. I have listed negative feelings, but the primally deprived patient often elicits impulses of primal love in the therapist–impulses to hold, stroke, caress, feed, and so on which are more embarrassing to enumerate than the negative ones.)

Now the energy with which the psychotic defence, e.g. splitting or projection, is invested is the amount of energy which has to be held and harnessed if therapy is to take place. This is the energy of the warring and combining opposites to which I have referred. It is a moving experience when the patient's holding and balancing ego replaces the patient endeavours of the therapist, and when the alienated, dreadful forces of unintegrated instinct become accepted as part of the inner world of a responsible human being. Sometimes for example in children, this can happen quite quickly in therapy. In other cases it is a matter of months or years of patient work against the gradient of one's own instinctive nature.

The symbolic attitude requires giving full value to the unconscious and to the psyche, including visionary and numinous experience and so-called fantasy. Expressions such as "acting-out" seem to me an expression with a bias in danger of under-valuation of the psyche. What the patient with the symbolic attitude achieves is a synthesis of acting-out and not-acting-out—a new attitude towards the impulse and the emerging symbol. We as therapists try to achieve a similar attitude towards the patients and his visions. Just as a mother who is too realistic or too autistic can kill or distort the vital magical omnipotence in her baby, and can destroy all the joy of living, so the therapist who is too "realistic" or too autistic can prevent the therapeutic process from taking off at all. Yet he must also be true to himself and sincere in his transactions particularly with the psychotic patient, so that if the therapist has not coped with the primal forces in himself he cannot have the necessary empathy and integrity to cope with them in his patient. This applies to the persona of course, but with psychotic patients it applies to the shadow and the anima and splitting and differentiation between good and evil at the deepest levels of the psyche, where psyche and body image and bodily activity are no longer distinguishable.

The Organization of Therapeutic Environments.

Psychotic patients demand that the relationship with the therapist be right, or got right *at the primal level*. Neurotic patients have it right anyway more or less.

The frustrating thing about treating psychotic patients is the difficulty of providing enough treatment at this level. It is obviously not enough to merely see patients even daily if the rest of the time they are in a psychotogenic environment. This is why the Agnew project, places like Chestnut Lodge, and the Philadelphia association in England are so valuable and important. We need an analogous institution for the London group of Jungian analysts.

We in London have no residential centre in which we can look after our patients in analysis at times when they need such an environment. We have a few friendly hospitals, particularly where our members work, which go some way to providing this facility, but none where the whole staff are involved in this kind of approach to psychosis. The classical medical training and approach, and the classical psycho-analytical approach, are both highly schizoid and the emphasis on the 19th century scientific approach and the selection of doctors in key posts for academic brilliance exaggerate splitting between feelings and behaviour, feeling and thinking, patient and therapist, rather than healing these splits and humanizing the therapist and through him the patient. However the younger generation of doctors do not seem as badly affected in this way as our own in this respect, and we can probably look forward to a greater understanding of the matters I have discussed in this paper by the medical profession.

PSYCHOTHERAPY IN DEPRESSIVE PSYCHOTIC STATES

Augusto Vitale, Milan.

Psychic life is constituted through an energic flow (libido); no flow of energy can be maintained without the tension between two opposite poles.

The image or symbol that, almost always unconsciously, covers the polarization and relationship between the two poles (described by the incorrect term transference, which is now irreplaceable through usage) is always the relationship between two subjects and not between a subject and an object; an I and a Thou then, whose complicated interrelations of give and take have been mentioned by JUNG in his paper of the Psychology of the Transference.

Primary structures of the transference with their parental images (of which the Oedipus complex represents the most famous example but which irremediably must limp because of the absence of the "fourth" . . .) operate often or nearly always even during adult life, generating that complex which is interconnected with psychological affective "values". Some aspects of these "values" could be: estimation of oneself, sense of guilt, and fundamental disposition of "libido" to gather itself or to extend itself (the root of its nature according to Freud and also the root of the Jungian attitudes of introversion and extraversion). Depression has as its opposite exaltation. At a more normal level, we might say the polarity would be found in boredom compared with vitality; and at an extreme level, melancholy compared with mania. Depression, in general, indicates the energic level, the quantity the tension of the flow of the symbolic image of transference, which operates more or less unconsciously in each subject.

It seems then obvious that "depression" is a quantitative term indicating energetic, psychic "tone"; But this has to be considered as the result of an energic "balance" connected with a particular primary transference structure.

Generally speaking, a depressive transference relationship occurs when the subject spends more libido than he produces; in this way we have before us an element of a deficit situation, with an constant activity which tends to balance the accounts; this shows itself through an instability of the energetic tone, through an instability of the estimation of oneself and even of ego identity; at the same time these are also all expressions of the vicissitudes of the transference relationship which attempts to seduce and blackmail the Thou through illusions and disillusions; through euphoria and depression. The energetic situation fails when the ego throws off its mask and starts searching furiously in the wound with an obsessive need both to verify the relationship and to find proof of abondonment and betrayal; it then starts looking for the guilt and begins to punish, to expiate, to revenge itself until it gets to the fifth act of the tragedy ending with parricide and suicide. Melancholy, since it is an extreme psychic degree of the depressive situation, contains a new dynamic characteristic element: the arrest of the energetic flow and the unbearable concentration of energy in the ego; the unbearable sense of guilt, unworthiness and remorse which finds suicide as the only way out in order to bring about expiatation. In these elements we find the evidence of the secret; namely that the I has succeeded in destroying the Thou.

There is another possibility for suicide, more often realized in a symbolic and demonstrative way, where the I mortifies itself in order, through a retaliation mechanism, to punish the Thou with that same pain-inflicting weapon which was constellated through the abandonment.

The study of the transference quaternio in a depressive situation, which is required for the understanding and comprehension of every single case, reveals a variety of psychodynamic motifs around the enantiodromic relation between the archetypes of the Great Mother and Saturn.

As far as therapy in depressive states is concerned, the strong concentration of the I in the typical pathogenic transference relationship generates a particular "impermeability" at different levels with which the psychotherapist always experiments; but in extreme psychotic situations it would appear that psychotherapy is totally powerless. Only this consideration can substantiate the reason for the success of shock therapies. For the latter violently deflect the libido from the vicious self-consuming pathogenic circle of the depressive stasis and activate energetic channels which are different from those constellated by installation and reinforcement of the depressive transference: the I can then turn away from its rival which had enormously narrowed its field of vision and can perceive new possibilities.

Therapy is centered in the first phase upon surprising the I which is in a state of unawareness by showing it other possibilities of existence than its former obstinate concentration; the instruments used to effect this change range from physical and chemical stimuli directed at the central nervous system (electroshock therapy or LSD) to more general psychotherapeutic techniques. A laugh is as every analyst knows, a valuable little shock for the I–Pinocchio's doctor would have known this–and a depressed person who laughs must be on the right road.

Before or after a psychotic crisis, psychotherapy should lead the subject to discover the cause of his depressive transference situation where part of the Thou has been taken over by people, by situations or by the more diverse "things".

The libido, which is finally being withdrawn from these projections, should find new channels, and at this stage it would seem that group therapy offers positive possibilities through the re-education in interpersonal relationships and through the "invention" of new forms of relationship with the collective conscious; for there is now a psychic state which is ready to receive in a constructive way much of the energy which had been heavily invested in the primary transference structure.

Original Italian version to be found in "Oggi Jung". La Rivista de psicologia analitica 17/78.

ESTABLISHING CONNECTIONS BETWEEN TWO WORLDS
A contribution to Active Imagination.

Edith Wallace, New York

Working with groups means departing from the original practise of active imagination. However, maintaining its spirit offers a valuable approach to evaluation of images different from most schools which offer courses in "art therapy". I have been practising this approach for over seven years, always reluctant to talk about it. I am now ready to offer some descriptions, although there is in it that which defies "definition". As JUNG says:

Spirit that can be translated into a definite concept is a psychic complex lying within the orbit of our ego-consciousness.

Spirit that can be defined only touches the surface, and we are dealing here with depth and meaning. I am impressed time and again how quickly such deeper layers are touched even in a weekend workshop.

I came to the method I am using through my own work with painting materials. Sometimes it was active imagination, sometimes it was painting and I puzzled over the connection between the two for a long time. I do consider the *source* for both to be the same. The distinction becomes necessary when we are using the imagery that has been produced, not only by naming what is *not* art as such, but also in recognizing when something that may have started out as active imagination turns into art. The aim is often to discover creative potential through art media, whether the potential is painting, music, literature or any of the arts, or any of the sciences or other creative potential. It aims at bringing out potential.

Of course there are other things that happen as well; I want to give here two examples from a weekend workshop. When there is a break-through it can be spectacular. Often I do not see the follow-up, though I know that in most cases someone will. One of the two examples here gave me the chance to see what had happened in the intervening year; on a number of occasions I have heard years later.

First example: A woman found her shadow in a most unexpected way in a collage* done in her "favorite" colours. She was apparently in a most affable mood and chose to do a tissue paper collage in rosy colours. The collage turned out to look like a wallpaper of what might have been pink flowers and could have suited a nursery. The first un-expected thing was that she became unhappy to the point of tears and depressed for the rest of the evening. The depression did not lift the next morning until she decided to do a collage in colours she did *not* like–what she called "ugly browns" (and other earth colours). The finished product made her extremely happy, once more much to her surprise.

Through looking at the collages together and evaluating just the collage per se, it became very clear to her what had happened. Those colours she loved turned out to be a sham like her life where everything was pleasant and polite, but without meaning or substance. Without any conscious knowledge at first, the second collage gave her hope that her own depth still existed somewhere and could be tapped in spite of a conformist and superficial life. "Likes" and "dislikes," "beautiful" and "ugly" seem to be criteria on a surface level only, while on the level of meaning, that which we like and dislike is no criterion.

In the *second example,* the reaction of the group, myself included, was "ugly," while to this woman it represented a beautiful friend. In the lower left corner of her collage a brown animal appeared which could have been Leviathan, but for her it was a representation of an animal in the zoo, who was her friend, whom she went to visit in order to talk to him. In her extraverted way she *had* to represent an outer image: it took a year for ther to see that I was trying to evoke *inner* images. I had to be content with the validity of the "inner" dialogue she had with this animal, her "friend," whom one could of course also

* I speak of *collages* rather than paintings because I use mostly translucent coloured tissue papers as my first choice medium. S. the illustrations in the *Exhibit.*

consider an exteriorisation of a much-needed friend. When she returned to my workshop the following year her life had changed considerably and so had she. She had freed herself from a restricting marriage. The collage with the monster/friend hung on the wall in her home!*

The Play Element

In the beginning of the sessions I always make sure to say that this is "play"–Kindergarten–and I add: drop everything you *know* whether concepts or known forms like forms in nature or even forms seen previously in a dream or vision. This is to shut out unwanted interferences. It sets the ego aside without eliminating it.

I do set the rules of the game; I step in where I see the need; but always in favor of the ongoing *process* whatever it might be, and never interfering with it. There is a guidance in the same way as we use it in analysis, but it is far from the *rêve eveillé* kind of guidance; or anything resembling those methods that aim at "altered states of consciousness," methods which operate at times with a deliberation that seems so often manipulative in an area where we must leave the guidance to the Self of the person involved. In order to make sure that the process be left to the wisdom of the unconscious of the involved person, therefore the person him/herself needs to be given a chance to step aside and *allow* the process to happen. This is what I am trying to help along for "building channels to the creative," for making contact with the non-personal, the "treasure hard to attain".

I am inviting the making of connections, not fantasy play. This may mean the setting of rules and seeing to it that they are enforced–in a loose and non-obvious way. Since there are "don'ts" involved, antagonism can easily be provoked. Since they mean letting go of control it can be a threat to "safety". Therefore when it is established that the general attitude is supportive, more often than not the reservations fall by the wayside.

In the Play-Element there is a basic and profound meaning. It has been said that all art is meditation. Play has the fascinating capacity to produce utter concentration. Thoughts and preoccupations seem to leave the mind as long as the game is on–the desired state for medita-

* For further examples see description of *Exhibit*.

224

Fig. 1

Fig. 2

Fig. 3

Fig. 4

tion and for the opening phase of active imagination. No wonder that when we "play" with coloured tissue papers the images are apt to come from the deeper layers of the unconscious, because the playing has opened that road and has gotten ego interferences out of the way.

In *Play* we allow ourselves to speak another language, a language which is more closely connected with that of the unconscious and therefore brings with it a more direct connection with statements from and expressions of the unconscious. It is a kind of connection that cannot be reached when we are "serious" and logical only. This creats a dilemma because so often the emphasis on that kind of "seriousness" and logicality outweighs the manifestation of the "Play-Element," which creates more tolerance for the one and not for the other.

HUIZINGA says: "Play lies outside the reasonableness of practical life;"—true enough! But then he goes on: "has nothing to do with necessity or utility, duty or truth." (2)

My contention is that it has to do with all these things. Necessity: granted it has nothing to do with "necessity" in a so-called practical way. In a way of integration and of healing the play-element is of utmost necessity and it therefore has an element of utility as well. By way of duty to our growth and self-development it is the highest duty, and I have stated already that there is no truth without the Play-Element.

I am talking about the use of play in a specific situation, not random play, play much closer to the Greek idea of games. It can mean a return to ritual—one reason why it works so well in a group—an easy and acceptable way to reintroduce ritual into what could be a barren culture. And for these reasons it can work only—if I may express it paradoxically—if we take play seriously.

The necessity of play is recognized by those professionals who are called "art therapists," working in an evergrowing field not yet clearly defined but well distinguished from what used to be called "occupational therapy". For them art in its various forms is considered the healer and this not merely by contemplating art and enjoying its beauty or pleasant rhythm, but by being actively engaged in it, opening up to inner "creative sources" and being healed by this opening. However, without a knowledge of the reality of the psyche no true understanding can occur. As JUNG says:

It is serious play ... it is play from inner necessity. That is the ambiguous quality which clings to everything creative ... The creation of
something new is not accomplished by the intellect, but by the play-
instinct from inner necessity. The creative mind plays with the object it
loves. (3)

We know today how much of Jung's own experience of the "necessity" to play is contained in these statements.

Another point: How can we make the best use of the knowledge
that energy needs to be contained in order to "create", to produce gold?
The process already in action can be spilled again if we start emoting;
wanting to "share". It is like standing with another person in a beautiful landscape in silence, or having a companion who continually says:
"Oh, look! Isn't it beautiful?"—this kind of sharing is neither sharing
nor communicating. Being gripped by the event is the communication.
I often invite participants to get into a concentrated meditative state
and see that quiet is maintained so that energies are not squandered.
Mostly, when people get into what they are doing they become so totally concentrated that there is no such danger—they are in touch with
something truly of value to them; even children become quiet when
this kind of concentration takes hold of them. But there are also moments of excitement and that can get spilled easily in a group in a
spirit of wanting to share and wanting to share prematurely. At the
risk of arousing opposition and rebellion I do step in at that point and
stop the externalising of energy forces which are needed for the process
of creation.

As an example, I will start with the end result (no slide available,
therefore sketch of outline):

This was a very stirring image, quite powerful and a clear statement
of what was to her a Priest performing a primitive ceremony. It was
easy to be taken into the atmosphere of ritual and worship, the priest
standing high in an atmosphere of red fire while "hooded figures" (her
words) were looking on and partaking. During her description she was
also telling this story: "I got very excited doing it, and I wanted to
share it, have everybody take part in it." It may have been then that I
cautioned everybody to be quiet. She said I stopped her, which at first
she resented, but then saw very readily that what she could offer for
communication with the finished product was "real," far superior to

raw emotion and deeply moving for all of us. It is not to share the emotion but the "event," and the "event" was not finished at the first moment of wanting to squander the emotion.

Immediately after this showing another woman in the group presented her collages, a series which ended with this one:

In contrast to the other one, this was high up in the air, not surrounded by fire and in an enclosure, but open: you could almost feel the wind blowing. Here it was a feminine figure like a priestess. The two pictures, it seemed to me, were an interesting juxtaposition: in the first one a male priest performing close to the earth, representation of the feminine, while in the second one the feminine figure performing in the sky, the masculine element.

The Play-Element acts as a bridge builder between two worlds, just like the symbol. The language of the world of infinite possibilities is quite different from everyday language. Every time we have spoken it, for instance by producing images, we have spoken the language that connects to true understanding.

To arrive through play in the place of infinite possibilities, concretely being confronted with an archetypal image always relevant to the individual's life and task, is a miraculous occurrence. It can be an opening and the beginning of a whole long process. (S. pictures and letter from Cambridge in the *Exhibit.*) It can happen to people who are apparently unprepared (non-involved in any way in depth psychology) but of course ready for the experience, and for them it often means starting an analytical experience.

Involvement of the body.

Since we are now encountering the world of the "imaginal" which is a non-corporeal world, it is well to experience it in body language to make it a living reality. I have emphasized the "drama" of the psyche itself by inviting bodily expression of the image; for instance, we may *look* at a painting or collage and *see* things and understand, and one can train this seeing and thereby understanding, but something else happens when we *feel* the product in our body. I invite people to step into the collage–after having looked at it for a long time and "taken it in"–and dance it: every static and every moving moment in the collage becomes part of the dance. Sometimes while the group is looking at someone's collage I have them get up and enact a movement they see in it. The difference in grasping a meaning through the body experience in this way is remarkable. We have another bridge between the non-corporeal imaginal world of infinite possibilities and the physical, tangible world of limited varieties. In this way we not only gain better understanding but prepare the way for making it usable. And it has a liberating effect.

We repeat the cosmos when we dance our "creation", Shiva's dance created the world—and destroyed it.

We think—and this happens to all of us—we are "only playing" when in reality we are establishing contact with the world of "reality" and truth, what CORBIN (1) calls the world of the "imaginal" *(Mundus Imaginalis)* as opposed to the world of fiction (mere fantasy) of which JUNG says:

A fantasy is more or less your own invention, and remains on the surface of personal things and conscious expectations (4).

This I am trying to avoid and circumvent by saying: no known forms, no concepts, nothing that is in your conscious mind and ego-directed, no musts and shoulds and efforts, just "play" (which for some has proved to be the greatest effort of all!)*

Concepts, JUNG says, are negotiable values, images are life (5).

The consequence of what started out as mere play are far-reaching and they go from the mundane of solving an immediate problem to contacting the deepest sources of one's potential and even experiencing the possibility of wholeness with the stirring of the Creative Source within.

Timing means Listening. Means letting go of control. Timing means *waiting*, waiting for the right moment, waiting for something to break through. This is the agony of the creative process, this having to wait, but unless we do, we have only a meaningless production rather than a significant creation. Significant in the sense of meaning, sometimes meaning just for oneself. And this waiting sets the stage for the kind of connection that constellates synchronicity and with that the connection between the two worlds has been established.

Conclusion.

Connections to the depth of new potential can be established through excluding extraneous interferences in a process of art work done in a playful spirit. In setting the stage for it and in evaluating, I am treading a middle ground between total non-interference on the one hand and labelling, analyzing and giving rational explanations on the other. It is this middle ground which I believe Jungian psychology has to offer to a training program for art therapists.

* Schiller: "Accordingly he must in some way return to that negative state of pure non-determination which he enjoyed before ever any sort of impression was made upon his senses. But that was a state entirely empty of content."

NOTES

(1) Corbin, Henry, *Mundus Imaginalis or the Imaginary and the imaginal* (New York and Zurich, Spring-Publications, 1972).
(2) Huizinga, Johan, *Homo ludens, a study of the play element in culture* (Boston, Beacon Press, c. 1950).
(3) Jung, C. G., *Psychological Types*, C. W. 6 (New York, Pantheon).
(4) Jung, C. G. *Analytical Psychology, Its Theory and Practice* (New York, Pantheon Books, c. 1963), pp 192.
(5) Jung, C. G., *Mysterium Coniunctionis*, C. W. (New York, Pantheon, 1963).

EXHIBIT

The following examples deal with the appearance of an archetypal image:
(1) Constellation of the central archetype in the group setting (joint collage).
(2) Search for the center–two collages in progression.
(3) Transformation of the feminine image, with the appearance of what I could see as *Demeter*, one among a long series of collages (of which I am showing two). This was done in a group of people who were working together for 10 months; my course extended over approximately five weeks.
(4) Collage of what the doer called "Poet Laureate" which sparked off poetry writing in someone where this capacity had lain dormant. The appearance of the poet-animus in the collage encouraged the activity.

ON DEPRESSIVE DELUSION

H.-J. Wilke, Berlin

The syndromes of mental disorder differ widely in the reactions which their delusional content arouses in the persons around them. If the syndromes are ranked according to these counter-transference reactions, then paranoid delusions come off best. Because delusion and reality are often so difficult to distinguish, these patients tend to be tolerated by their environment. Acute hallucinatory schizophrenic conditions, by virtue of the rich variety and peculiarity of their delusional content, have always held a fascination for the therapists, and as a result they have inspired an extensive literature.

Not so the "affective psychosis," whose depressive delusions show a quite different pattern. Their stereotyped themes of guilt, worthlessness, impoverishment, hopelessness, and sometimes apocalyptic doom have aroused much less diagnostic and therapeutic interest. This is clearly not in keeping with the respective prevalence of these syndromes. The World Health Organization (WHO) estimates the incidence of depressive illness at no less than three to five percent of the population (1).

In terms of counter-transference, it is likely that the affective aspect of these depressive disorders calls forth the corresponding affective reactions on the part of therapists. The "affect" in question seems, in general, to consist in a kind of disinterest, frequently expressed as therapeutic resignation accompanied by a tendency to invoke the timeworn endogeny hypothesis. This renders the depressive less suitable as an object of scientific study than the paranoid or schizophrenic, for the simple reason that the affect involved itself inhibits the research motivation.

Historical Background

"Melancholy" is one of the few terms carried over from the ancient pathology of humors. It designates a bodily condition, the surplus of black gall, held to be responsible for various physical and mental illnesses ranging from epilepsy to melancholy as we now conceive of it. It might seem strange that the motor discharges of the epileptic should have been attributed to the same principle as the oppressive gloom of the depressive, but this becomes clearer if we consider that the Greek word for gall also means anger, as is still evident in the term "choleric". It is almost as if ancient medicine had here grasped the latent destructive tendency of the depressive. Black gall in moderate admixture is an acknowledged constituent of the sound mind and body, but it has also been recognized always as a substance charged with destructive energy and quite capable of causing death. Thus, Sophocles uses the term *melancholos* to describe the toxic blood of the Lernaean Hydra, used by Heracles to poison his arrowheads. The centaur Nessus succumbed to its venom, as did Heracles himself.

The ancient physicians responded to this pathogenic principle in kind by treating it severely. Celsus (30 A. D.) mentions chains, chastisement, and shock treatment. In the Middle Ages, standard treatment included trepanation, the ever-popular bloodletting, and application of red-hot irons to the head until the bare bone was exposed (2). Aggressive treatment has continued unabated down to our own time, as witnessed by electroshock therapy and the recent technique of sleep deprivation (3). Even the 2,000-year-old standard treatment of purging with hellecore root *(Helleborus niger)* implies a tendency to fight fire with fire, at least in the pharmaceutical imaginings of the ancients. The *actual* pharmaceutical effect of the herb is to induce tarry stools through inflammation of the intestinal mucous membranes–clear proof to the ancients that black gall was being eliminated.

These examples demonstrate quite clearly the virulence attributed to melancholic disorders, as well as their emotional impact upon patient, therapist, and fellow-man alike. A havoc-wrecking pathogenic principle provokes correspondingly aggressive therapy, and the result is an emotionally tinged rejection of the patient by this therapist. The continued existence of this pattern is borne out by some modern critiques of psychiatry (4).

The modern nomenclature "affective psychosis" is merely a contemporary rephrasing of the older idea of emotional threat. In analytical psychology, affect and emotion are a direct expression of the energetic charging of pathogenic complexes (5) and of unconscious energetic processes. Jung often stressed the dangerous nature of these processes and the considerable risk of unconscious contamination *(unbewußte Infektion)* inherent in them (6).

It is my contention that the epidemic spread of depressive mental contents can be historically documented (7). In the medieval religious movements and sects, the feeling that the end of the world was near attained epidemic proportions, helped along by the threat of plague and the pressure of bad social conditions; the concrete manifestation was the flagellant processions of the thirteenth and fourteenth centuries. These were condemned by church, state and society alike and sometimes even came under the scrutiny of the Inquisition, though their ideas were actually quite in keeping with the Christian thought of the time. The flagellants saw in the profligacy of the world, and of the clergy, a sign of the approaching end, to be met with self-castigation. These apocalptic fears, however, carried with them great hopes of salvation, as manifested in widespread chiliastic speculations, or, on the secular level, in the common expectation that the emperor Frederick Barbarossa would somehow return. Such hopes of salvation and bliss are often hard to detect in the depressive patient, even though their presence is to a large extent responsible for the magnitude of depressive suffering.

Despite the considerable historical distance, parallels between these old apocalyptic concepts and those of our depressive patients can be drawn. Similar dynamics can be observed. These are references throughout history not only to the ominous, destructive aspects of depressive disorders, but also to their positive side. Thus, Aristotle considers melancholy an attribute of distinguished minds, a companion to the hero's calling. The positive aspect remains effective in Western thought, from the medieval clergy's special attention to melancholy to the broad popular development of the concept in the Romantic period, with its intellectualization of melancholy as a kind of *Weltschmerz* to which geniuses are prone. We should not overlook the creative and prospective potential always assigned to this seemingly destructive clinical picture. Thus, the modern philosopher Romano GUARDINI, in his essay on melancholy, builds his argument not only on the ancient and medieval traditions but finds parallels also in such modern figures as the melancholic philosopher Sören KIERKEGAARD (8).

Depressive Delusion

Although recently there has been some discussion in psychiatric literature about the historically changing forms of clinical pictures and their accompanying delusions (9), the content of depressive delusion has remained surprisingly constant. The lamentations of a world-weary man recorded in an Egyptian papyrus shortly before 2,000 B. C. are quite similar to those of our present-day patients (10).

H. K. FIERZ (11) has urged us to "keep our eyes and ears open" in order to get a clear picture of the event being confronted by the psychiatric patient. This admonition is particularly apt in the case of depressive delusions, since they lack the color and expressiveness of other types of delusion and, being by nature gray, monotonous, and unprepossessing, they are peculiarly susceptible to being overlooked or not being taken seriously. FIERZ (12) and W. ALEX (13) have shown that psychotherapy can have surprisingly positive results even in depressive psychoses.

One reason that depressive phenomena are easily overlooked may be that, in addition to being for the most part quite unimpressive, the actual delusional *content* is rather sparse. The pathological manifestations of affective psychoses are most evident as changes of affect. That is to say, the emotional values are more often altered than the ideational content. What we encounter most frequently is a delusional *mood*, a somber, disconsolate tainting of the patient's view of the world. However, it is often evident that the treatment of depressive delusion is strongly affected by counter-transference. The therapist's defenses are easily projected onto the patient whose very real troubles then tend to be misunderstood as resistance (4). As in the historic precedents, we find aggressive and destructive counter-transference reactions even in present-day analytical therapy, the more so the more severely depressed the patient is. Instead of emotionally going along with the patient in his depression, as HILLMAN suggests (15), the therapist, unable to bear his own *therapeutic helplessness*, may seek to break down the patient's protective wall of silence. At the same time, the patient often perceives the therapist's undertone of fear and aggression more clearly than he himself does. Such aggressive counter-transference especially hinders one's cognizance of the depressive dynamics and of the delusional phenomena in their prospective or salutary aspect.

Case Material

I. GALEN (16), born in 131 A. D. in Pergamum, tells of a patient who suffered from the delusion that Atlas, weary of the weight of the world, was about to shake off his burden and thus destroy not only the patient himself but all the rest of humanity. However absurd and "crazy" this notion may have appeared to the people of the time, it nevertheless served to illustrate the burden that the patient felt to be weighing upon him, or descending upon him, threatening to destroy his world.

Seen in historical perspective, this idea may be taken as prophetic, reflecting the great upheavals that were then in the offing. One is tempted to equate Atlas' burden not only with the ancient world, but with the whole ancient world-view, which was beginning to crumble. The socio-cultural ramifications of delusion are especially evident here. We may assume, taking the prospective point of view, that GALEN's patient was struggling toward the kind of reorientation achieved by the patient of the Egyptian papyrus through his dialogue with Ba (17), stepping out of the severe ritual framework of his culture to face it as an individual. The collapse of old cults and ways of thinking is not only a destructive event; it also provides an opportunity for new creative possibilities and a new orientation of consciousness.

II. A woman in her mid-forties with the diagnosis of endogenous depression had spent several months of each year, over a period of five years, under psychiatric care in a clinic. Her somber world was portrayed to the therapist in black and bitter terms calling to mind the old meaning of "melancholy". Her seemingly abrupt mood changes were clearly of a delusional nature. Her laments of lonelineless and isolation finally culminated in the distinct feeling that she had been" born alone". Several sessions later, apropos of her unstable relationship with a strongly mother-dependent partner, she complained that if she were to lose her lover, too, there would be nobody left "to hold her hand at the grave".

"Born alone" is a contradiction in terms, since the idea of birth presupposes someone giving birth as well as someone being born. One must revert to early myths of creation and the orgin of man to find analogies to this idea of solitary birth. Only the primeval Gods gave birth through self-impregnation, their progeny being identical with themselves. The Egyptian scarab is a symbol of the "self-born" and is regarded as the creator of the Gods (18). The patient's idea that someone should hold her hand at the grave is an obvious variation on the idea of sickbed or death-bed hand-holding. The grave, of course, lies beyond death, and in Christian terms it is only Christ who offers His hand in salvation there; the only ancient analogy is Hermes, Guide of Souls. If one pursues both analogies, one can clearly glimpse alongside all evident pathology the creative and transforming aspect of death—"dying" carries with it the idea of "becoming". And indeed, the patient's depressive self-reproaches soon changed unexpectedly into reproaches directed against the therapist, and the dissatisfaction with the analytical situation became the motive for further change and for an emergence from the phase of stagnated lamentation.

Summary and Discussion

Depressive delusion is a specific manifestation of depressive illness. In keeping with the nature of this illness, it appears predominantly in the form of delusional mood and only relatively rarely as specific delusional content. The delusional mood carries the patient into his own deep, dark places—areas that are as a rule he has long repressed and has, indeed, fearfully avoided.

Often this obscure region of the soul is devoid of words and images at first. To find its key we must depart from psychopathology and seek clarification in the historical approach, with an eye to the postive potential of melancholy and its role as a normal constituent of existence. GUARDINI (19), in his role as Christian philosopher, speaks of an "urge toward shelter and quietude, the inner gravitation of the soul toward the great Center, a surge toward inwardness and depth". In terms of analytical psychology, the goal formulated here is that of individuation. In view of the impaired prior development and neurotic thought-patterns of most depressives, this tendency toward individuation is highly perilous and may even be fatal; the self is constellated predominantly in negative and destructive images. Often, it is only at the end of a dark pathway that we are able to see that the patient, in his distraught traversing of precipices and sloughs, has been trying to find a firm footing all along (20). If he succeeds in reaching this firm ground, the experience usually acquires a religious dimension, as GUARDINI forsees when he defines melancholy as the unrest of man in the proximity of the eternal (20). When the delusional mood coagulates into an image, especially one so much at variance with external reality as to be termed a proper delusion, then considerable progress has been made. The soul has hit upon a vehicle whereby to convey a true picture of its condition, usually with clearly archetypal components. The nonverbal, nonvisual darkness of the mutistic depressive condition is lifted, and the depressive, heretofore merely "lived out," is formulated into an experience that commands the full attention of the therapist. The destructive, hopeless, and somber material that now comes to light requires his sympathy and participation, so that the latent creative and constructive possibilities may gradually come into their own.

The frequently reported increase of depressive illness in the Western civilization points to its increasing significance as the reflection of a collective malady. The rough outlines of this problem can be easily recognized. There is a general tendency to repress depressive experience as an evocation of the dark side of life (death, destruction, disease). Foremost in the collective consciousness is the belief in technological progress, combined with untrammeled optimism as to world-betterment and attended all too often by hypomanic self-aggrandizement. The ideology of affluence and the confidence in a forthcoming general happiness are best understood as the outward projection of unconscious paradise fantasies (22). Depressive experience, by shifting the emphasis, can help to restore the proper perspective; thus, it may even be regarded as a wholesome element. For the ancients, "melancholia" was a necessary component of the *mens sana in corpore sano*, and in medieval times pictorial and other admonitions toward *memento mori* served as ample reminders of the dark side of life. In our day, an increasing tendency to ques-

238

tion technological progress can be noted. It seems quite possible that the incidence of depressive illness will diminish when the collective consciousness admits of more latitude for depressive thoughts, and for posing questions in general.

FREUD commented thus in 1916 (23) on the delusional self-reproach of the depressive: "He must, in some way, be right, and he must be describing something that actually is as he imagines it to be." If we are prepared to regard all depressive phenomena as serious statements about a hidden reality, if we can even see depression itself as a reality-principle, then, if we are very patient, we may succeed in introducing some light into its darkness.

Many points have only been hinted at here. But the analyst who is experienced in the treatment of depressive patients and aware of the broader context will easily be able to fill in the missing links: the connections between therapeutic helplessness and masochistic triumph, between depression as a reality-principle and hope, which is often an illusionary principle too easily applied to patients such as these.

The history of therapy shows that melancholy has always been thought to harbor a highly aggressive and destructive pathological principle, and this has long been combatted with draconian methods, which today are abetted by the analyst's own counter-transference aggression. Thus, the prospective aspect of what is going on in depression cannot be uncovered without the therapist having to endure his therapeutic helplessness and integrating his aggressive counter-transference.

Interpreting depression (its dynamics and its content) in the light of ancient concepts of melancholy enables us to view it as an essential constituent of existence, as a component of psychic reality. In terms of individuation, its "heaviness of spirit" *(Schwermut)* may help the mind to acquire a necessary substance and depth. Depression leads to realms of the soul where the question of meaning and the religious dimension of experience are of vital importance.

Translation from German by Lee B. Jennings.
Original German version to be found in the Zeitschrift für Analytische Psychologie, 9: 123–131.

REFERENCES

(1) Kielholz, P., "Indikationen für die Pharmakotherapie der Depressionen," *Diagnostik* 9 (1976), 257.

(2) Friedrich, J. B., *Literärgeschichte der Pathologie und Therapie der psychischen Krankheiten* (Würzburg, 1830; reprinted: Amsterdam: Bonset, 1965), pp. 116 f. For this section see also: Ackerknecht, E. H., *Kurze Geschichte der Psychiatrie* (Stuttgart: Enke, 1957); Starobinski, J., "Geschichte der Melancholiebehandlung," *Documenta Geigy, Acta psychosomatica* (1960); Wyrsch, J., "Über Depressionen," *Documenta Geigy, Acta psychosomatica* (1958).

(3) Pflug, B. and Tölle, R., "Therapie endogener Depressionen durch Schlafentzug," *Nervenarzt* 42 (1971), 117.

(4) Lomas, P., "Taboo and Illness," *Brit. J. Med. Psych.* 42 (1969), 33.

(5) Jung, C. G., *CW* 8, 18–19.

(6) Jung, C. G., *CW* 16, 501, 503.

(7) Erbstosser, M., *Sozialreligiöse Strömungen im späten Mittelalter* (Berlin: Akademie-Verlag, 1970).

(8) Guardini, R., *Vom Sinn der Schwermut* (Zürich: Arche, 1968).

(9) Glatzel, J., ed., *Gestaltwandel psychiatrischer Krankheitsbilder* (Stuttgart, 1973).

(10) Jacobsohn, H.: "Dialogue of a World-Weary Man with his Ba," in: *Timeless Documents of the Soul* (Evanston: Northwestern Univ. Press, 1968).

(11) Fierz, H. K., *Klinik und analytische Psychologie* (Zürich: Rascher, 1963), p. 210.

(12) Fierz, H. K., "Psychotherapie der Depression," Zeitschrift für Analytische Psychologie 4, p. 1.

(13) Alex, W., "Depression in Women," Professional Report of the 16th Annual Joint Conference of Jungian Analysts of Northern and Southern California 1968.

(14) Wilke, H.-J., "Die Bedeutung des Widerstandskonzeptes für die Behandlung Depressiver," Zeitschrift für Analytische Psychologie 7, p. 286.

(15) Hillman, J., Suicide and the Soul (Spring Publ., 1976).

(16) Starobinski, p. 28.

(17) see note 10.

(18) Lomas, pp. 32 ff., p. 256 f.

(19) Guardini, pp. 43 ff.

(20) Neumann, E., Ursprungsgeschichte des Bewußtseins (Zürich: Rascher, 1949), p. 93.

(21) Guardini, p. 52.

(22) Wilke, H.-J., "Neurosentheoretische Überlegungen zur Struktur und Dynamik depressiver Erkrankungen," Zeitschrift für Analytische Psychologie 5, p. 81.

(23) Freud, S., Gesammelte Werke (Frankfurt: Fischer, 1963) X. 432.

THE TREATMENT OF CHRONIC PSYCHOSES

C. T. Frey-Wehrlin, R. Bosnak, F. Langegger, Ch. Robinson, Zürich
Klinik und Forschungsstätte für Jungsche Psychologie, Zürich.

As it is now more than thirteen years since the Zürichberg Clinic opened, we welcome the opportunity to report to this Society, on our experiences with psychotic patients and to follow it up with some reflections based on these experiences.

To begin with, a brief description of the setting: the Zürichberg Clinic is a State-accredited, closed psychiatric clinic. It houses thirty-five patients in two buildings. Although in the annex boarders are free to come and go, the main building is run as a closed nursing home, the centre of which is a closely supervised eleven-bed ward.

The team looking after the patients consists of the following: five analytically trained physicians and seven analytical psychologists who provide individual psychotherapy, usually three times a week. (All twelve work with outpatients as well.) Two art therapists introduce the patients to drawing, painting, and modelling in clay. There is also a weekly general discussion group as well as a Gestalt group, psychodrama, a group for physical education and another on music; a therapist for breathing technique is available when required. The nursing team consists of a dozen nurses (male and female). A further six people do the housework and kitchen work. The director, and the administrator who also works as a therapist, are assisted by two secretaries. Contact among the personnel is assured by regular conferences several times a week as well as by frequent personal conversations.

Patients with all kinds of psychiatric diagnoses, except severe organic illness, are represented; one-third suffer from schizophrenia, one-sixth from manic-depressive psychosis and the rest mainly from severe neuroses and addictions. More than half the patients are under thirty years old. About half are Swiss. In addition, about twenty nationalities have been represented, mainly from Europe and the United States, and psychotherapy has been conducaed in ten languages. This mixture is fortuitous; admissions are in no way selected.

It would be tempting to try to convey an impression of the variety of our lives to you—the routine day, interrupted by feast days and holiday camps, the empty boredom which repeatedly afflicts the whole community, the silent or noisy despair of individuals, natural death by old age, or suicide, and the successes, sometimes after long and arduous labour, sometimes sudden and unexpected. Surely almost all modern psychiatric private nursing homes are familiar with such events which offer nothing new. How often, for example, are spectacular successes, on closer investigation, reducible to average expectations?

In this paper we should like to focus on one aspect of our clinical work which, however peripheral, nevertheless makes constant and insistent demands on our attention. We should like to discuss the dark side of the healing process, that of the chronic and incurable. As early as 1861 Griesinger had noted in his text-book that while one-third of the inmates of psychiatric hospitals in Germany get well and one-third improve, the other third are incurable (GRIESINGER [5]). Do these figures differ essentially from those of today?

Pschyrembel's medical dictionary defines "chronic" as "slow to develop, slow in its course". But this is not the meaning the term has for us. "A case has become chronic" means that our therapeutic efforts have been of no avail, have become ineffectual. "Experience teaches that active treatment is of no further use." The patient is then removed from a therapeutic institution in order to make room for another who may be helped; he is transferred to a "care-taking" institution where less effort is made because it is no longer worth it. "Chronic" means no further development, final standstill. It means unchangeable—hopeless.

How do these patients come to us? Maybe one of our collegues has been working with a patient for a longish time as an out-patient when the condition worsens, thus necessitating admission. Or, again, a case is admitted because treatment at another clinic has failed to bring about the desired result. The experienced clinician sometimes knows that it is a hopeless case. Nevertheless, we respond as if we did not know this and proceed to treat such cases, in our usual way, in tacit expectation that "progress" will be made. Nor are we strangers to ambition in therapy; we like the challenge of a difficult case.

New surrounding and the therapist's enthusiasm have a stimulating effect on the patient: his condition improves. Nonetheless we know the improvement will not last and deterioration, when it comes, is therefore not unexpected. But renewed improvement brings new hope: relapses can be "explained," e.g., by the unfavorable effect of a visit by a relative.

But there comes a time when all this changes. The therapist leafs through the patient's records kept by the physician in charge in which the condition and behaviour of the patient are recorded. This is how the therapist experienced the patient in the last session–but, alas, the entry was made four years ago. It is now that the therapist comes to realise that, from the clinical point of view, four years of intensive work have been wasted. Furthermore, he must reckon that possibly, or even probably, nothing is going to change in the future. He is treating a chronic case.

This realisation changes the situation in a fundamental way. The joint efforts of therapist and patient hitherto were based on the expectation that sooner or later, the patient would get well. This fundamental assumption has now been demolished. The disquieting question arises whether the attitude which aimed at an ultimate recovery was ever really appropriate. This can hardly have been the case since it left out a reality–the chronic nature of the case. On the contrary, the expectation of a cure had prevented the therapist from completely accepting his patient; he had put him under pressure of becoming a success and the patient could not live up to this expectation.

Paradoxically, it is at this point that, sometimes, a ray of hope appears, which, every now and then, may be fulfilled. Now liberated from the pressure to succeed, the patient finds he can breathe freely in the new atmosphere, and thus may still find his own way to recovery (RUPP [10]).

If we remind ourselves of the original meaning of the word *therapeia* –"tending"–psychotherapy continues even when there is no success in sight. Thus "to accompany" takes the place of the "urge to heal"–a more modest approach. "The great departs; the small approaches' is the essence of the sign P'i, Standstill (Stagnation) in the *I Ching*. This finds expression in the method of the analysis. It remains analysis in the strict sense, inasmuch as the unconscious continues to lead; the patient reports phantasies, dreams, hallucinations. But the interpretations become more modest. They are limited to integrating the unconscious products into the framework of the patient's by now restricted existence (and thus, perhaps, opening it up a little). Often the interpretations are limited to what Fierz, with reference to Klaesi, once called "valuing"— that is, the value of the unconscious products is recognised (FIERZ [3]).

An example may serve to illustrate that this too may be meaningful. A patient has been in the Clinic for ten years. He is completely absorbed in observing his stomach and in the scrupulous observance of a self-prescribed diet. At times he is bedridden; then again there may be times when he feels more free and can even do regular errands for the Clinic. One day he decided to exchange our Clinic for a dietetic nursing home. Once there, he telephoned occasionally, complaining of loneliness and asking for visits. Then one day, completely without warning, he committed suicide. Would it not be reasonable to assume that the familiar surroundings of our Clinic and regular talks with his therapist could have prevented this?

We should like to raise the question of how the therapist can stand having spent years doing "futile" work.

To begin with it should be noted that "futile" has been put in quotation marks. Certainly the work of the analyst does not serve to re-establish the patient's "capacity to work and play". But caring for the sick and for invalids is practised everywhere, be it as Christian charity or as some form of social ethos or other. Such an ethos may motivate us for part of the way, but in itself it is not adequate. It is possible to sustain a great effort for any length of time only if one does it for one-self. This observation is not as pessimistic as it may sound, since it refers not so much to the ego as to the self. For even though the ego may enjoy the patient's transference, that is the feeling of being loved and of power, this, too, becomes tedious in time, all due respect to our narcissistic needs notwithstanding.

We believe that our response to the chronic patient has deeper roots. Let us remember the therapist's astonishment when he noticed that the clinical picture of his patient had not changed during four years. Apparently he did not have the impression of doing meaningless work, he did not feel that his work had been wasted although, objectively, this was the real state of affairs. What then gave him the feeling of doing something worthwhile? What is our concern for the chronic patient if it is not the concern for our own chronic illness? It is that which is most distinctly our own, that from which we suffer; although it may have been touched upon during our own analysis, yet it has remained untransformed. It is sick, unproductive, evil, infantile—it is the shadow of our individuality.

This shadow can be realised very little, if at all. Nevertheless, it continues to live and wants to be accepted. Therapy in the spirit of Jung's analytical psychology does not mean, even with chronic patients, "objective treatment"; rather it means engagement and encounter which corresponds symbolically to the alchemical process in as much as both partners are involved. Indeed, the chronic defies transformation but not recognition, and such recognition may become both profound and differentiated. In this way reflection and awareness are brought about.

But why does chronic illness defy transformation? We know that Chronos, the father of Zeus, knew how to prevent all further development by devouring his children. Only Zeus could be rescued by his mother and taken to a safe place until he could outwit his father and defeat him "with guile and strength" (KERENYI [8, p. 29]). Ever since, Chronos, whose reign corresponds to the Golden Age, has lived on the outermost edge of the earth, on the Isles of the Blessed.

The myth reveals that aspect of the resistance which prevents any change in the chronic. He remains where the "honey flows," in paradise where life knows no hardship. Expulsion from paradise is resisted with any and every means; thus a violent attempt to eject him from paradise, to push him into life, may provoke an attempt at suicide. If, however, a genuine rebellion on the part of Zeus takes place—or to put it analytically, if the arousing affect of the therapist is derived from a syntonic countertransference (FORDHAM [4], p. 142 f.), then an unblocking of the chronic condition may yet occur, effecting a transformation to a greater or lesser extent. Even an experienced therapist needs more than just "guile and strength" for the timing and doing of such actions—he also needs luck. In the final analysis, the therapy of the chronic patients consists of waiting for this moment–even if it never comes.

Working with chronic patients suggests, inevitably, the comparison with Sisyphus. Again and again Sisyphus rolls his boulder to the summit of the mountain where it slips out of his hands and disappears into the abyss. Sisyphus follows it into the depths. According to Albert Camus,

It is just during his descent, in the interval that Sisyphus interests me . . . I see this man descending with measured tread, approaching the agony of which he cannot see the end. This hour is like a sigh of relief: it will return as surely as his torment. It is the hour of his conscious-ness. Each time when he leaves the heights and gradually descends into the caverns of the gods he transcends his fate. He is stronger than his boulder (CAMUS [2], p. 155).

The awareness which emerges from our efforts on behalf of the chronic patient includes, in addition to subjective, also objective know-ledge. The increasing differentiation of the analysis reveals psychic micro-structures which do not necessarily become accessible during routine, especially ambulatory, analysis. What we see here is psycholgy in the broadest sense which extends far beyond the individual patient. It seems to have been this aspect which interested Jung above all else during his clinical years. His patient Babette was for him "a pleasant old creature because she had such lovely delusions and said such interesting things" (JUNG [7], p. 128). But he added that he had "seen other cases in which this kind of attentive entering into the personality of the pa-tient produced a lasting therapeutic effect". Meier describes a similar case (MEIER [9], p. 130 f.), and Fierz reports the same of Binswanger who carefully explored cases described in his studies of schizophrenia for months without any therapeutic intention or hope (BINSWANGER [1]). While these investigations were being conducted a significant im-provement was registered in each case.

There is something else which must not be overlooked. It is well-known that a chronic schizophrenic can experience, albeit seldom, a spontaneous remission even after many years. Should this happen, it will make a difference to the patient who has to re-enter life whether the duration of his illness–possibly many years of his life–figures as a great void or whether it was filled in by a stable human relationship and regular meaningful discussions. This, we believe, must be the aim on which to concentrate in our work with chronic patients. For it is by no means certain that severe schizophrenia can be cured by psycho-therapy. Jung was also sceptical in this regard (JUNG [6]). Therefore we do not see our job as technical manipulation but as an empathetic accompanying of the patient. This is far removed from resignation: it is confidence in the regulatory powers of the unconscious which far surpass our conscious potentialities.

It appears that we have arrived once again at hope. It is always there as long as life goes on. But we are not concerned only with hope; we are also concerned with the knowledge that it may not be fulfilled. Hope lives for the future. We believe that work with chronics is to be done in the present, for the sake of the here-and-now person who faces us as well as for ourselves.

Translation from German by A. Plaut.

REFERENCES

(1) Binswanger, L. (1957). *Schizophrenie.* Pfullingen, Neske.
(2) Camus, A. (1942). *Le mythe de Sisyphe.* Paris, Gallimard.
(3) Fierz, H. K. (n. d.) Personal communication.
(4) Fordham, M. (1957). "Notes on the transference," in: *Technique in Jungian analysis.* London, Library of Analytical Psychology, 2 (1974).
(5) Griesinger, W. (1871). *Die Pathologie und Therapie der psychischen Krankheiten.* Braunschweig, Wreden.
(6) Jung, C. G. (1958). "Schizophrenia." Coll. Wks. 3.
(7) Jung, C. G. (1963). *Memories, dreams, reflections.* London, Collins and Routledge & Kegan Paul.
(8) Kerenyi, K. (1951). *Die Mythologie der Griechen.* Zürich, Rheinverlag (Harmondsworth, Pelican Books, 1958).
(9) Meier, C. A. (1975). "Einige Konsequenzen der neueren Psychologie," in: *Experiment and symbol.* Olten, Walter.
(10) Rupp, P. H. (1974). *La disperazione dell'analista.* Venice–Padova, Marsilio.

GORGO

eitschrift für archetypische Psychologie nd bildhaftes Denken

ausgegeben von Wolfgang Giegerich (Stuttgart)- in Verbindung mit: Heino Gehrts (Alt-Mölln), olf Guggenbühl-Craig (Zürich), James Hillman (University of Dallas), Rudolf Ritsema (Eranos-Stiftung, ona).

res-Abonnement (2 Hefte) DM 42.-- zzgl. Versandkosten

Zeitschrift möchte einen Beitrag zur Wiedergewinnung der Seele in der Psychologie - über die naturwissenaftlich-pragmatische Ausrichtung hinaus - und zur Entwicklung einer der Seele entsprechenden Sprache Denkform leisten.

wird sich nicht nur mit den poetischen Produkten der Psyche, mit Traum, Mythos, Phantasie, Bild, Ritual, assen, sondern auch Artikel über den psychologischen Gehalt der konkreten Wirklichkeitserfahrung, die e des Leibes und den metaphorischen Charakter des Erlebens veröffentlichen.

tere Themen werden sein: das Pathologische als eine eigene Sprache der Psyche und sein archetypischer tergrund; die düsteren Seiten der seelischen Wirklichkeit; die strengere und ursprünglichere Durchleutung psychologischen Ideen und Begriffe und die psychologische Kritik der Psychologie selbst; ferner - im Eing mit der Auffassung, daß nicht ausschließlich der menschliche Organismus, sondern die ganze Welt und onders die Kultur der eigentliche Lebensraum der Seele ist - die Verbindung unseres psychologischen kens und Erlebens mit der psychologischen, philosophischen wie religiösen Tradition des Abendlandes umgekehrt die psychologische Dimension dieser Tradition sowie der verschiedenen Gebiete des Wissens der Kunst.

GORGO wird dabei auch die wichtigsten der bisher nur englisch veröffentlichten Artikel aus dem Bereich auf C.G. Jung beruhenden, von JAMES HILLMAN begründeten archetypischen Psychologie in deutscher rsetzung bringen. Damit möchte sie deren ganz neuartige, festgefahrene Denkgewohnheiten auflockernde chtspunkte, die in angelsächsischen und romanischen Ländern starken Anklang gefunden haben, erstmals h einem deutschsprachigen Leserpublikum zugänglich machen.

tenloses Probeheft anfordern)

Verlag
Adolf Bonz
GmbH   D - 7012 Fellbach-Oeffingen   Kaisersbacher Straße 4

Human Development

S. Karger
Basel · München · Paris · London
New York · Sydney

cent and forthcoming
cles are listed on the
erse side

More than two decades of publication

Human Development

An international journal reflecting the directions of developmental psychology.

Unique
Human Development is the only journal publishing on all aspects of development throughout the human life span, from infancy to aging. Both social and cognitive development are covered. Published for more than two decades, **Human Development** has paralleled the emergence of developmental psychology as a major source of research within psychology.

Complete
Content includes theoretical contributions and integrative reviews of the literature concerning research in the behavioral and social sciences, multidisciplinary investigations, and cross-cultural comparisons. The journal also publishes work from areas such as history, philosophy, biology, anthropology, and education which have implications for human development.

Practical
A 'Developmental Issues' section, included in most issues, presents new and unusual ideas in succinct fashion. This section is designed to keep the reader informed on topics of scientific and social significance.

Human Development
appears bimonthly.
One annual volume contains 6 issues of 72 pages each.

S. Karger
Basel · München · Paris · London
New York · Sydney

☐ Please send sample copy
☐ Check enclosed
☐ Please invoice

Please enter _____ subscription(s)
☐ Personal ☐ Student
☐ Member ☐ Institution

Name _____ Address _____ City/Postal code _____ State/Country

e send this order form to your bookstore, to your nearest
r agency or directly to the Publisher: **S. Karger AG,**
nwilerstrasse 10, P.O. Box, CH–4009 Basel (Switzerland)